Disenchanted

Disenchanted

One Woman's Journey for Independence
from the Kingdom of Saudi Arabia

Victoria Kilbury, EdD

LIFESTORIES BOOKS ⁂ LAS VEGAS, NEVADA

Editor: Jami Carpenter
Book Designer: Sue Campbell
Cover Photos: (woman) ©Zurijeta | Dreamstime.com;
(background) ©shirophoto | iStockphoto

First Printing

ISBN: 978-1-935043-69-0 (print)
ISBN: 978-1-935043-85-0 (e-book)

Life Stories

Post Office Box 70
Las Vegas, NV 89125-1600
www.stephenspress.com

Printed in the United States of America

For Nabila and all the women who have been disenchanted with their lives but found strength and courage to make a change.

꙰

My story has been fraught with both promise and pain. As a woman in Saudi Arabia, I was subjected to both laws and ancient practices that have evolved from past cultural or tribal customs. Many people in Islamic countries strictly abide by past practices as if they were laws. The requirement to wear the abaya and the restriction of driving an automobile are two examples of practices, not laws, that govern women.

One of the greatest travesties is the plight of Islamic women when it comes to marriage and divorce in this culture. Women are often not free to select their husbands and must defer to their families' choice for a mate. Most harmful is that if a marriage is dissolved, the woman is not entitled to money, property, cars, or custody of the children. Women are at the mercy of whatever their husbands may choose to give them, even if they have worked and contributed to the family income. Most notable are the procedures that are followed that leads to a sanctioned divorce. If a man wishes to dissolve his marriage, he may initiate the talaq action by saying, 'you are divorced.' The woman is divorced; however, the couple has the opportunity to reconcile during a three-month period called the iddah. The divorce is validated if the couple does not rekindle their relationship during the iddah. The couple lives together during the iddah so that a reunion may occur. Having sexual intercourse will nullify the divorce. This procedure is repeated if the husband chooses to divorce his wife a second time. However, if there is a third occurrence, the husband terminates the union with the talaq pronouncement. At this stage, an iddah exists only to determine that the woman is not pregnant. After a divorce, a younger woman is more likely to remarry than an older woman.

While I can't change the circumstances in my life I'm thankful for the opportunity to share my story with others.

~ Nabila

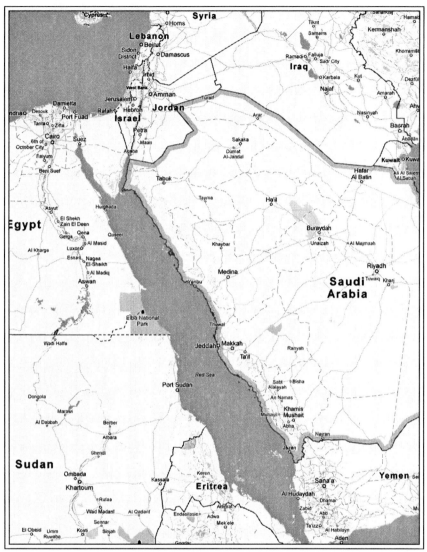

©2012 Google, Mapa GISrael, ORION-ME

Chapter 1

It was Nabila's good fortune to have a chance to begin her life anew in the city of luck. The high temperatures did not deter her, as she was accustomed to extreme heat. She was, however, overwhelmed with the sights of a cosmopolitan city. Nabila stole glimpses at the hoards of people absorbed in the spectacular sites of the wonderland known as The Strip. The crowds moved in waves threatening to overtake all in their path. Tourists seemed to be on a mission to shop, drink, and gamble their way through the city. Nabila cautiously watched the throngs of visitors making little eye contact as their faces were fixed on the sights, her eyes were lowered as she was trained to behave in public long ago. As she moved through the crowd she spotted a woman with a long black dress and a headdress of layered black veils. When the woman turned, her dark brown eyes locked with Nabila's, reflecting the life that Nabila had escaped.

What was I doing here in this place they called the 'home of the brave'? Could I really create a new life independent of my former husband and my estranged daughters? I have lingered at the crossroads of my life for so long, disenchanted with my culture that limits my options and rules my actions. Yet it is hard even now to know if I am running away from my homeland or eagerly returning to a place where I've always felt at home. Either way, it's my choice. And any choice for a female in Saudi Arabia is a rare occurrence.

Like many young girls in her country, Nabila's life had been mapped out for her long before her birth. When her parents, paternal grandmother, paternal uncle—and his wife—discovered that Nabila's mother was pregnant, they formed an agreement. If the baby was a girl, she would eventually marry her cousin, Abdul Rahman, who was nine years older. That type of arrangement was a tradition in the Saudi culture and a duty of the father to secure his daughter's future by finding her a husband even before her birth. The future husband was usually a cousin of either one of the parents.

In mid June of 1957 when Nabila's mother felt her first contraction, all the women in the family began to pray that the child would be a girl so

11

that she would be Abdul Rahman's future bride. After Nabila's birth, her father and Abdul Rahman's father, Uncle Saleh, prayed together reciting the Quran, the Muslims' Holy book. They vowed that the newborn girl, Nabila, and Abdul Rahman would be united as husband and wife and that this promise would not be broken under any circumstances.

Usually a Saudi man prefers sons instead of daughters, but after already having two sons, being the first daughter, she was welcomed. And, because of Nabila's father's arrangement with Uncle Saleh, her birth was part of a master plan that also included her sister, Fatima, who was born about a year and a half later and was promised to Abdul Rahman's brother, Fahad. When the third daughter was born, the family thought it was a blessing from God to give them the bride for Abdul Rahman's youngest brother, Adel. Their families were intertwined like the roots of a willow tree.

Nabila lived in a society where women had no rights. She did not have the choice to meet a man, date, fall in love, and then contemplate marriage. No matter how old she became, or how much education she acquired, as a female, Nabila would forever be considered a dependent. From her birth to her marriage, a female in Nabila's culture is under the control of her father, or a brother if the father is dead. Because of that, women grow up to be completely dependent, unable to function alone. Most Saudi women feel lost and helpless without a man to take care of them. After marriage, a woman is in the custody of the husband who expects complete obedience from her without any consideration for her feelings, desires, or aspirations. A Saudi woman must always have a guardian to take care of her and sign her legal documents.

Nabila lived with her six sisters and four brothers in a single-family dwelling outside of Makkah in Saudi Arabia. Her father, Saad, though he was very good to his children, seemed to have a bad temperament toward his wife. He was the boss who gave orders and she was the obedient worker who acted without asking questions. Marriage for him was simply about securing a woman to cook, wash and iron clothes, bear children, and satisfy his sexual desires without any concern for his wife as a human being.

Nabila's mother, Rahma, was quiet and calm and rarely brought attention to herself. She seemed settled and resolute to her life—as if it were hers to choose. Rahma was barely thirteen years of age when she learned that

Saad, Nabila's father, had sought her hand for marriage. Saad fell in love with Rahma for her tranquil green eyes and fair soft skin.[1] Saad was nearly twenty years her senior, and Rahma was his second wife, though Nabila was never told about her father's first wife; the secret was not revealed until Nabila was a bride of several years.

Like many other girls of her generation in Saudi Arabia, Rahma was married at the age of fourteen, and undeniably devoted to her husband and ten children. Because Nabila was the oldest daughter, Rahma turned to her for help in caring for the other children in the family. She would wake early to look after her younger brothers and sisters while Rahma tackled the endless chores. Having ten children, all less than two years apart from each other, and more than two children in diapers at a time left her no choice but to do laundry every day. Rahma washed all the clothes by hand, as there were no washing machines. An old-fashioned iron, split into two parts and stuffed with hot charcoal, was used to remove the wrinkles in their clothes. Rahma cooked with a *dafoor*, a gas cooker lighted with a pump handle. She dusted and swept with a hand broom, without the luxury of a vacuum cleaner.

While Nabila learned about maintaining a household, she discovered little as a child from her parents' relationship that would serve her in a respectful, collaborative marriage. She never saw her father talking or discussing any matter with her mother. Instead, Saad often yelled and hurled insults at Rahma, particularly objecting to the meals she prepared. Saad was quite particular about the seasoning of his food and at many meals the children sat silently at the table witnessing their father in a fit of rage. He would throw some of the food at Rahma and scream, "Is this food? Do you call yourself a woman, and you can't even cook?"

Once during the fasting month of Ramadan, Nabila's father demanded that Rahma make the customary oat soup. Unfortunately, the amount Rahma prepared was not enough to feed the entire family. In anger, Saad flung the bowl of soup at her. The soup scorched Rahma's face and the rim of the dish cut her lip. Nabila jumped from the table and ran to her mother's side. With a soft cloth she wiped away her mother's bloody tears and tried to keep hers locked away.

A flood of anger built inside Nabila, but somehow through the years she had built a dam that kept them from overflowing. She abhorred her father's heartless actions and ached with her mother's shame, but she was not capable of confronting her father or comforting her mother. Rahma's only recourse was to leave the room to sit and cry. At times, Nabila's father's behavior would escalate beyond the insults and threats. He would beat Rahma if he did not like the way she ironed his *thoub*, the white dress Arabian men wear. Rahma could only sustain the beatings without complaint because a husband was justified to treat his wife as such. At least that is what every Saudi male was taught as his right and many Saudi young girls learned was their fate.

It seemed that the smallest incident would make Saad angry. Once, Rahma went to visit her friend without his permission. When Saad came home and did not find Rahma, he asked every one of his children about her whereabouts. The children told him that she just went next door to visit a neighbor. When Rahma arrived home, Saad confronted her, slapping her face. She tried to run to the bedroom, but Saad followed her, tearing open the closet, and frantically ripping her dresses. The frocks lay in a heap in shreds, as must have been Rahma's heart after so much abuse.

Music was Rahma's only escape. A giant, battery-operated radio hummed in the background most days as she tackled her daily chores. Rahma's most prized possession was the ancient Motorola that she manually wound to play her favorite tune, "If Only." She played the melody repeatedly, and Nabila often wondered if Rahma was thinking about her own life and wishing *if only* ...

CHAPTER NOTES:

1 Many Saudis prefer women with whiter skin and are prejudiced against those with darker skin.

Chapter 2

It is He Who created you from a single self and made from him his spouse so that he might find rest in her/dwell with her.

~ Al Rom 30

Women are not the only hostages of the Saudi way of life. Men are also expected to behave in certain ways. They are taught from an early age that they are superior and must grow up to take care of their helpless sisters and mothers. They are expected to act as 'the man of the house' and give orders that demand obedience from women.

From birth children are completely the responsibility of the mother. The father has little to do with raising the children. As Nabila became older, she learned that her father's treatment of her mother was part of that society's expectations and that her father was living with the same expectations as his father and his father's father.

Saad may have treated Nabila's mother poorly, but he was her father and she loved him dearly. Unlike many average Saudi fathers, he did not discriminate between his daughters and his sons. He loved all his children and treated them the same. Well informed in many matters, Saad was self-taught. He was an avid reader and discussed what he had read with his children. Nabila loved to sit with him, hanging on every word as he spoke of the events in the city. He was very persuasive and could have convinced Nabila that the moon was made of cheese. She never tired of listening to him tell stories of World War II and his visits to Egypt.

Saad loved to play his prized violin. He studied with Mohammed Abdel Wahab and other fine musicians during his frequent trips to Egypt. Because music was prohibited in the kingdom, he only performed for his closest friends within someone's home. Many a night Saad would gather his friends who also played instruments to practice in his home. Crouching silently behind her bedroom door, Nabila would marvel at the melodic feast as the group practiced their repertoire of instrumentals. Eventually, the group improved, becoming well-known, and were requested frequently to perform concerts for men's parties. At night when Nabila would sometimes hear the plucking of a few strings and the soft notes that followed, she knew her father was relaxing, unwinding from the tensions of his day.

In the Saudi culture, it was common for a father to build a massive house where all his sons would live with their families. The house was not a permanent home for the daughters, as they would marry and live in their husband's homes. Traditionally, the young wives of the sons looked after the elderly in the house. They usually rotated or divided the housework and cooking chores. Of course, with all the relatives in the same place day and night, there were arguments and occasional fights. Nabila's family was no exception.

Nabila's family lived in a home owned by Jada, Saad's mother, at the top of a mountain in Makkah, overlooking the immense Holy Mosque. Uncle Saleh and his family, a wife and three sons, lived in the same dwelling. They occupied the first floor of the house, while Nabila's family claimed the second floor. The three meals of the day brought the two families together. But it was the evening that held excitement for the children. Uncle Saleh and Jada held the children spellbound with stories, fairy tales, and historical events until the children's eyes glazed over and their bodies gave in to slumber.

Nabila's family quarters had one tiny living room and a large bedroom where the whole family slept. An artificial, oriental rug partially covered the living room floor. While balancing on her knees Rahma used a hand broom to sweep the dust on the surface of the rug every morning and afternoon. Long, thin mattresses were tossed about the room with petite pillows for lounging. Air conditioning did not exist. The only way to beat the desert heat in Makkah was to soak a piece of cloth and affix it to the window to catch a rare night breeze to cool the air.

Furniture in the house was scarce. The family slept on small cotton mattresses piled in one corner of the room during the day and spread across the floor at night. Every evening, Rahma lined up the mattresses like tin soldiers and fastened all the box-shaped nets to protect the family from being devoured by the thirsty mosquitoes. A string attached to nails around the room held the corners of the nets upright and the remaining netting was tucked snuggly under the mattresses. Nabila's father and mother slept in the same room with the children but under a different net. Kerosene lamps illuminated the nights, as there was no electricity in the house. Nabila was frightened by the lanterns' shadows that lurked like ghosts in the desert night while the family slept.

Nabila could not wait for the summer months when the family moved the mattresses to the roof. In spite of the summer heat in Makkah during the day, the nights were cool enough to sleep in the open air. It was common for most of the families in Makkah to sleep on the roof to get away from the oppressive heat engulfing the house. Nabila loved to lie on her mattress and watch the flickering stars in the night sky. She imagined that a princess roamed the universe searching for an enchanted kingdom. She would watch the princess skip from star to star until she fell asleep.

Chapter 3

We made from water every living thing.

~ Al Anbiyaa

Water was a precious commodity in the household. A waterman, called *sagga*, supplied the liquid for Nabila's family. He carried two ten-gallon water tins on a pole draped across his shoulders, the water splashed over the sides of the containers as the sagga traveled over the mountainous roads. As soon as he arrived at a house, he called '*Tareeg*' (make a way for me), to alert the women of his presence. In the residence the water was stored in a large earthenware barrel with a tap about twenty inches from the bottom. There were no sinks only a floor drain under the barrel.

Other saggas delivered water in animal skins, called *gerrbas*. They carried the gerrbas across their backs as they transported the water. As a child Nabila followed the saggas and created pictures from the water lines that formed in the sand as water leaked from tiny holes in the containers.

At bath time, which was once a week or on a special occasion, the children would line up one by one waiting for a turn. Rahma—or occasionally, Jada—would fill a tin barrel of water, place it on the dafoor, and pump the fuel to get the fire started. She would continue to pump until the stove burst into a yellowish red flame. Then she filled half of another tin barrel with tap water. Rahma took the *mograph*, a tin cup, and filled the rest of the barrel with the hot water. With every cup Rahma poured into the cold barrel, she tested the temperature of the mograph to be certain it was not too hot for the children.

Preparing meals for the family was no small task. Every morning, before Nabila's father went to his photography shop, he would ask Rahma what groceries she needed to prepare lunch. That ritual seemed to frustrate

Nabila's mother. She would turn to Nabila, seeking help in making her daily decision as to what to feed the family. After struggling with her decision, Rahma dictated a list of the food that she needed for the meal. Saad recorded the requested goods and pocketed the list before he left for work each day. Rasil, the young boy who helped Saad in his shop, delivered the vegetables and meat to the family's house. Rahma took the bounty to the kitchen where there were few shelves for storage. Nabila's grandmother, Jada, frequently peeled the vegetables with a small carved knife while perched on the floor in the corner of the kitchen.

Flies were members of the family. They helped themselves to the food and annoyed Nabila's mother when she tried to rest in the afternoon. Jada did not attempt to evict the flies but merely kept a hand fan nearby to shoo them away as she did with her grandchildren when they became too rowdy.

Fruits and sweets were rarely a part of the meal, as Nabila's father could not afford them. More common was rice, vegetables, salad, and few pieces of meat. As children, whenever they craved sweets, they either ate dates or made a sugar sandwich. Nabila looked forward to visits from her affluent Aunt Meriam, who often brought candies and chocolates. She traveled from Jeddah[1] to Makkah to visit Nabila's family and to perform religious duties at the Holy Mosque accompanied by her driver, two trunks, and of course, the delectable confections.

Grandmother Jada was in her sixties, hunchbacked, but otherwise healthy and very active. She always wore the traditional loose pants and full sleeve white top with a high collar fastened with a vertical chain of gold studs. Her long snow-white hair was combed into two thick braids and wrapped in sheer cotton cloth. She gathered the braids and tied them in a knot at the top of her head like ropes securing a prized bundle. Another light, sheer headscarf, decorated with tiny golden tassels and laces covered her head and hung loosely to her shoulders.

Nabila's grandmother was the only one who had her own room, although it was quite small and bordered by the kitchen. An antique sewing machine occupied one corner of her room, as she was the dressmaker for the family. She was constantly asking Saad to buy fabric to make dresses for the girls.

"They are growing so fast," she would say.

The door to her room was always open. Nabila was often at Jada's side while she hovered over a half-made dress, her rickety body moving in time with the spindle.

Curious, Nabila asked Jada about her hunched back. Jada paused, remembering an earlier time after her husband died in World War I, when Nabila's father was just a baby. Jada had to support herself and her child by doing needlework. Years of long hours bending over the fabric to perform the tedious work caused her back to bow.

Being the first granddaughter, Nabila was treated as a favorite. Like a shadow, she followed Jada everywhere. On one outing, Jada took her to watch African girls dancing in the streets to attract people to buy slaves.[2] Nabila was immediately attracted to the rhythmic drumming filling the open air. She had to resist her body's natural movement to the sounds, as dancing by Saudis was prohibited.

Nabila's neighborhood had no surfaced streets, only narrow, unpaved roads and alleys where the children played during the day. They shared the streets with donkeys, cats, dogs, and goats. Leftover food dumped on the roads provided dinner for homeless and wild animals. What the animals did not eat rotted on the cool days or dried to a crisp in the searing summer sun, yet the stench of garbage and the swarm of flies and animals surrounding did not interrupt the children's play. Outside, the children eagerly awaited the black, African woman toting her baby on her back, who often came to sell them roasted peanuts. She charged one *garsh*, which was equivalent to a nickel, for a handful of peanuts. She used an empty tomato paste can to measure the amount of peanuts for each sale.

There was not an adequate sewage system anywhere in the country.[3] Each house had a floor drain that emptied into the rutted street. The water draining from the houses formed a stream, creating what seemed to be an endless river farther down the road. Nabila and the neighbor children competed to see who could find the end of the river, not knowing that the water would evaporate in the molten sun. Because toys did not exist for Nabila, she amused herself playing in the street with endless guessing games and hide and seek.

Not content to let his daughter play all day, Nabila's father was adamant that she receive an education. This was not the typical sentiment, as most

Saudi fathers thought it unnecessary for their daughters to attend school. Since public schools for girls did not exist, he enrolled Nabila in the *Kutab*, a religious school that taught young girls to recite the Quran. With a date sandwich in hand, she and her brother walked along the rocks, rough roads, and sand to reach the school. The teacher positioned himself in the only chair while the children sat cross-legged on the floor in the classroom. The teacher, an older man, would recite a verse of the Quran, and Nabila repeated after him, moving her body in rhythm with the verse. In the afternoon, her brother would escort her home. One day he did not show up and after a lengthy wait, the teacher asked Nabila if she knew her way home. Although Nabila was dependent upon her brother, she knew the route and thought that she could make it alone. She was well on her way when she came to a narrow road where the neighbor's donkey blocked the path to her house. Nabila was frightened by the hefty animal and unable to risk coming near it to reach the lane. Her nervousness was compounded by the fact that she had to use the bathroom. She sat by the side of the road and sobbed. No one was around to help her, and she could not hold her bladder any longer. Her water broke, soaking her clothes and causing her to cry even more. She was upset about the accident but just as troubled that she could not complete the journey on her own. An elderly man passing by merely swatted the donkey, freeing the passageway. Even at this young age, Nabila was disturbed because she was stymied by a docile animal, while a man with a flick of his wrist was able to clear the path. This was the first of many difficult obstacles Nabila would encounter where she would flounder, but a man could so easily succeed.

CHAPTER NOTES:

1 The city of Jeddah, which means 'grandmother' gained its name as religious stories purport that Eve is buried in this locale. According to Islam, Eve is considered the grandmother to all human beings.

2 Slavery was abolished in Saudi Arabia by King Faisal in 1962. Some of those freed slaves chose to continue working for their former slave-owners, particularly those whose former owners were members of the royal family.

3 As reported in 2009, Jeddah—a city of 4 million people—still lacked a sewage system and treatment facility. Sadly, in 2009 unusual heavy rainfall caused massive flooding, destruction, and the deaths of more than 500 people. Another 11,000 were considered

missing, as reported in the Saudi newspaper al-Yaum. Without proper drainage the streets and neighborhoods flooded, creating one of the most deadly nature-related tragedies in Saudi Arabia.

CHAPTER 4

'Can those who have knowledge and those who do not be alike?'
So only the wise do receive the admonition.

~ AL ZUMAR 39:9

From the beginning, Nabila was enthralled with her cousin and future husband, Abdul Rahman. Because they lived in the same residence, they spent most of their time together, talking, playing, laughing, crying, and growing up side by side. Nabila missed him when he went to school and waited for him at the entrance of the house each day to glimpse him rounding the corner on his way back to her. After lunch, she listened to him describe his day's study of reading, mathematics, and history. She wanted to be like him, to go to school, and learn what he was learning. However, he frequently reminded her that there were no schools for girls and that girls needed only to learn how to cook, clean the house, and take care of a husband and children. Nabila was sure that he spoke the truth, but she was mesmerized by the thought of going to a real school and thought it quite unfair for being left out.

Summer dry heat was unbearable in Makkah; however, Nabila's family spent most of the summer in Taief, in a breezy mountain climate, where electricity was available. They all enjoyed going to Taief, not only because it was cooler, but also because her father was able to rent Egyptian movies from the black market. Saad's frequent trips to Egypt made him aware of modern things, including movies. Nabila considered any day that her father brought a movie to the house to be a day of celebration. Her mother cooked a special meal before they watched the motion picture. Nabila was amazed as the film rolled around a wheel and the people came alive moving across the white wall of the living room. Since movies were banned in

Saudi Arabia, the windows were covered with thick blankets to prevent anyone from seeing the novel gift Saad had bought for the family.

Viewing the movies introduced Nabila to a city quite different from Makkah, one that held promise for her family. During the late fifties and the sixties, Egypt was still under the influence of the British and offered the best education programs in the Middle East. Wealthy families sent their children to study in Egypt while some of them moved there permanently. Travelling at that time was rare unless you were wealthy, and not very many people were able to travel outside their country. Nabila knew little about Egypt, only what she had gleaned from the movies that she watched during the summer months in Taief and through the radio that her mother played throughout the day. As a child, she idolized actors, actresses, and Egyptian singers.

However, it was the promise of education for his children that made Saad hold Egypt in high esteem. Once, Nabila overheard Saad talking to her oldest brother, acknowledging that he was happy to see his two older boys excelling in school.[1] On the other hand, Saad felt sorry that his daughters were school age, and he was unable to give them an education. Therefore, he decided to move the family to Egypt where education was available for girls. Like any average wife in the country, Rahma had no opinion or voice in the matter. She merely listened, as Nabila did, to the conversation between her husband and her oldest son.

When Saad announced that he was planning to move to Egypt where his girls could have an equal opportunity for an education, not everyone in the family was pleased. Nabila's brother, Samir who was almost eight-years-old, did not like the idea. He was thinking of his friends at school and the change of his environment. He would rather stay in the country and finish his education. However, Nabila's oldest brother, Aneese, was delighted with the idea of getting an education outside Saudi Arabia. He was willing to go at any time. Soon it was summer and the boys' schools closed for vacation. The family continually talked and daydreamed about what they expected to see in Egypt.

Nabila was so anxious to attend school that she never considered that this newfound opportunity would come with a sacrifice. She had lived with Abdul Rahman since birth. He was her past, her present, and her future. She assumed her cousins were going with her family to Egypt.

When she broached the subject with her father he replied, "Your cousins are all boys. They can have their education in Saudi Arabia. If it was not for you and your sister," Saad explained, "I would never think of leaving Saudi Arabia."

Nabila was overwhelmed with emotion knowing that obtaining an education would separate her from her companion, Abdul Rahman. She ran to her cousin hoping that he would say her father was wrong and that he would accompany them to Egypt. However, Abdul Rahman confirmed what Saad said but promised he would join her when he finished school and was ready for college.

Nabila had conflicted feelings about the move, one minute fueled with excitement, another aching with the impending separation from Abdul Rahman. She longed to experience the Egypt that she had heard so much about from her father and from listening to the radio and watching the movies. Egypt was a place of freedom, entertainment, and education. Nabila had heard that women in that country were free not to wear the *abaya*, the black cloak Saudi Arabian women wore to cover their faces and bodies whenever they left the house. She heard a rumor that women even drove cars in Egypt! Nabila felt she was destined for an incredible adventure, but her joy was tainted with sadness about leaving her home and being separated from Abdul Rahman.

In preparation for the move, Saad took his two sons shopping for western clothes. When they returned, his son Samir did not appear pleased. He was adamant that he would not wear the new clothes or conform to the style of cropped pants. While Samir lamented over his change in wardrobe forfeiting long pants for shorts, Nabila was about to lose her best friend.

CHAPTER NOTES:

1 In some local schools for male students all bars of soap were removed from the schools' restrooms. Officials cited the reason for the action was that boys were using the soap for masturbation.

CHAPTER 5

The acquisition of knowledge is a duty incumbent on every
Muslim, male and female.
~ PROPHET MUHAMMAD (PBUH) – AL SAHIH[1]

In the summer of 1963 Nabila's family boarded the plane to Egypt. A sophisticated lady wearing a red beret spoke to the passengers about the airline procedures. Her long hair cascaded down her back from under her cap. She wore a red top, short black skirt, and high-heeled black pumps. Passengers were served turkey sandwiches on French bread and soda pop. She attracted Nabila's attention not only because she looked lovely in her uniform, but also because she was the first woman Nabila had ever seen without the abaya and in a short skirt that showed her knees! As Nabila nibbled the sandwich, she kept one eye on the flight attendant. She had no idea that a woman could look so beautiful in public.

Nabila's extended family dominated the passenger section. Saad, dressed in his western suit, moved about the plane checking on his children. Jada sat in the corner at the back of the plane trying to chew her food with the few teeth she had left. On the other side of the plane, her two brothers were amusing themselves with games while Rahma sat quietly in the front of the plane.

Cairo was an unfamiliar world. Peering through the taxicab window that took them to their hotel, Nabila marveled at the wide paved streets with sidewalks where pedestrians escaped the oncoming traffic. The streets were lined with soaring buildings and people hustled past them in the cool summer air. She was astonished to see men and women walking hand in hand, and children running and playing in the open city while cars sped past. To her amazement, the rumor was true: some of the autos were driven by women!

While Saad was checking the family into the hotel, Nabila was standing in the lobby by a "little room" watching it go up and down eagerly hoping that her father would allow her to have a ride. A polished man came to assist Saad with the luggage and to Nabila's delight directed the group into the "little room." Nabila enjoyed the rapid ride so much that she begged her father for a second turn. Saad laughed and explained that the ride Nabila had enjoyed so much was merely an elevator that transported hotel guests to their rooms.

The food at the hotel was also very different from the food Nabila was accustomed to in her country. Toasts and biscuits were served which she mistook for cookies. She was used to a rice meal covered with vegetables. The children disliked the western style food.

Nabila and her family lived comfortably in Egypt. There were two maids to serve the family as well as a cook. The apartment in Egypt was more spacious than the family house in Makkah. Nabila shared a room with her sisters while each of her two brothers had a room of his own. The apartment had a guest room for Jada and an extra room for the new baby who would be born in a few months.

Saad entertained his family, treating them to the movies and theaters almost every night, and to the zoo or to the parks on weekends. He loved classic comedies, Laurel and Hardy, Abbot and Costello, and Charlie Chaplin. The family would spend hours in the evenings laughing and commenting on the movies.

Nabila's family, especially Rahma, was elated with their new lifestyle. Nabila had never seen her mother so happy. Rahma was able to go shopping alone, go for coffee, dinner, or to a movie with some of the new neighbors and friends. Unlike her life in Saudi Arabia, Rahma had a full life in Cairo. But as much as Nabila loved her new home, she wished she could reach Abdul Rahman to share the wonders of Egypt and have him join her family.

The summer scurried past and Nabila's dream of attending school soon became a reality. Since Saad was not worried about his sons' education, he enrolled them in public schools; however, Nabila and her sister attended a private school for protection and what was assumed a higher quality education. Even purchasing the schoolbooks and being fitted for the required school uniforms set Nabila's heart racing.

A few months later, Saad had to return to Makkah to work. He put his oldest son, Aneese, in charge of the house and advised the family to treat him with respect and to be obedient to him. Although Aneese was only fifteen-years-old, he was already a person with responsibilities whereas Rahma, who was in her early thirties, was denied authority simply because she was a woman. Aneese was rude and abusive and would not listen to the family's concerns or help them when they needed him. He insisted that the girls must follow his every command.

Nabila escaped her brother's rules at the private school in Cairo. The school followed the British system of education and curriculum with classes in music, sports, and dancing. During the lunch hour, teachers would instruct the students as to the proper way to eat, to sit, and to speak politely. Exhibiting good manners was an expectation at the school. Teachers were like older sisters treating the girls with respect and under-standing, yet they were firm with discipline and study skills.

Rahma became involved in the girls' education as well. She attended many school plays, graduation ceremonies, and a Mother's Day celebration complete with presents and all the attention she deserved. She joined her daughters on the school excursions to historical locations and a camping trip.

Together each morning Nabila and her sister Fatima walked to school. Fatima depended on Nabila for almost everything. Fatima would follow her to school blindly and certainly would have gotten lost without her. Fatima was so innocent and good-natured, but powerless to take care of herself. Like her brothers, Nabila shouldered some responsibility for her sister. But despite her father's absence and her sister's dependency, Nabila prospered in school.

Saad faithfully sent money for the family's living expenses and Aneese took care of the family budget. Every morning before Aneese went to school, he handed his mother enough money to take care of the family meals. Even though her needs were met, Nabila still missed her father and wondered when he would return. She was even more confused when she overheard her two older brothers whispering that their father had gone to Makkah to be with his new wife. Troubled by this news, Nabila could not comprehend how Saad could do such a thing to Rahma. As a child, she could not fully understand what it meant for her father to have another wife. *What about my poor mother, sisters, and brothers? And what about me?*

Saad had been gone for a few months when the family received a new addition. The nanny met Nabila and Fatima on the path as they were returning from school. She took the girls to the local park because their mother was having the baby and it was not advisable to have the children in the house at that time. When permitted, the sisters hurried home anxious to see their new baby sister, Shaza, and their tired but healthy mother.

The months quickly passed as Nabila settled into her routines and family life without her father. Soon it was time for Saad to return to his family in Cairo. This time Saad stayed for six months to everyone's liking except Nabila's mother. Rahma truly seemed happier when Saad was gone, even as she bore another daughter shortly after Saad left again for Makkah. They became a family of nine children, a mother, an absent father, and his mystery wife.

CHAPTER NOTES

1 Practicing Muslims add (peace be upon him) whenever hearing or speaking Prophet Muhammad's name or use (PBUH).

CHAPTER 6

Seek knowledge from the cradle to the grave.
~ PROPHET MUHAMMAD (PBUH) – AL SAHIH

N abila's love affair with school came to a halt when her father decided that it was time for her to leave the sheltered private school and venture into public education. As a seventh grader forced into a crowded classroom with over forty students, she suffered. The teachers intimidated her, as they were quite strict. The punishment for any small mistake was severe as the students were struck with two long rulers that the teachers carried from class to class. If the students behaved improperly, they received five hard strikes on the palm of each hand. If the pupils were not able to keep their hands open to endure all the raps, the teacher would then hit the child on another part of her body, usually the shoulder. Some teachers would even slap the child across the face. Others would humiliate the students in front of the class or force them to leave the class.

Being weak in math resulted in Nabila being punished many times. It was common for the teacher to ask her to come to the chalkboard to solve a problem. As soon as Nabila heard her name, her whole body shook uncontrollably. Nabila was so frightened of being disciplined that she was not able to concentrate. *Think Nabila, think!* When it became obvious that she could not solve the equation, the teacher's response was to pull Nabila's hair and slam her head on the chalkboard. The teachers were never successful at knocking the numbers into Nabila's head. She made every excuse she could think of not to attend the math class. When Nabila ran out of excuses and had to go to class, she would sneak into the back of the room and hide behind one of the tall, heavy girls praying that she was out of the teacher's sight.

Nabila's sisters experienced similar episodes of pain and humiliation at the hands of the teachers in that school system. However, the girls were to have no reprieve because as their family continued to grow Saad could not afford to provide them with an education he valued. It must have weighed heavily upon Saad because in the next year when Rahma become pregnant and in the following year as well, Saad insisted Rahma terminate both pregnancies. After the procedures, Rahma was listless and weak. However, for the first time, Nabila noticed that her father took good care of her mother. After each abortion, he fed Rahma well and kept in touch with the doctor, and even postponed his return to Makkah for a few months, probably out of guilt. Who knew that the absence of a child would evoke his tenderness?

During the upheaval at home and school, Nabila was surprised to receive a telegram from Abdul Rahman revealing his decision to come to Cairo. This was unexpected, as Nabila had lost touch with him since she left Saudi Arabia, seven years earlier. Abdul Rahman intended to finish his senior year in high school in Cairo and then stay to attend college. Nabila could barely remember what he looked like. Nevertheless, she was excited about the reunion with her beloved cousin.

Nabila's two brothers fetched Abdul Rahman from the airport, and she waited anxiously to see him. When Nabila opened the door and saw a tall, handsome man with broad shoulders, dark eyes, and tanned skin from the sun in Saudi Arabia, she was pleased. Although Nabila was only thirteen-years-old and Abdul Rahman was twenty-three, she knew that she wished to marry him. The two cousins easily reconnected and talked late that night. Nabila was curious as to why Abdul Rahman had not finished high school. He divulged that his father had become ill with a heart ailment, so Abdul Rahman quit school to work and support his father and his two younger brothers. Abdul Rahman's immediate plan was to finish high school and apply for a scholarship from the Saudi government to study engineering in the United States.

Abdul Rahman joined Nabila's two brothers at their high school as well as their room at the family's residence. Since the apartment could not accommodate everyone, Aneese decided to rent another apartment below the one the family occupied.

Nabila's school was about six miles from her home, which necessitated her taking an early public bus to get to school on time. Abdul Rahman faithfully escorted Nabila to the bus station every morning, before he went to his school, and he was there waiting for her each afternoon. Soon Abdul Rahman and Nabila spent more time together than they did with anyone else in the family. Their conversations sparked Nabila's intellect and enthusiasm for their future together. Even schoolwork could not separate them. At night, Abdul Rahman would study in the lower apartment, but soon she would hear his footsteps on the stairs and look up to find him laden with books and his numerous suggestions about how they could study together. Unfortunately, a scandal erupted at Nabila's school about her supposedly improper relationship with a young man. Many of her friends began to desert her because some teachers had warned them against any association with Nabila. Abdul Rahman did not give it any thought, as long as Nabila's family approved of their relationship, but Nabila was humiliated and disgraced at school by the teachers who were supposed to protect her, and friends who should have defended her.

During Saad's annual summer visit, he brought the approved scholarship for Abdul Rahman and Aneese to study engineering in the United States, beginning in the fall. Nabila offered "congratulations" and waited anxiously for Abdul Rahman's response. One month before his departure, Abdul Rahman walked to her father's bedroom and sat on a chair near the balcony. Saad was sitting on his bed, reading the newspaper. Nabila was perched next to her father discussing an article in the newspaper. Abdul Rahman asked Saad if Nabila could accompany him on his journey to the United States. Saad explained that she was too young to go that far away from home. He advised Abdul Rahman to go alone and get adjusted, and in two years, Nabila would be old enough to marry. Abdul Rahman covered his face with his hands and sobbed. Saad tried to comfort him by promising that Nabila would be waiting for him. Abdul Rahman had no choice but to accept Saad's judgment. Saying goodbye again to Abdul Rahman was gut-wrenching for Nabila. Abdul Rahman promised her that he would wait to marry and be very faithful and loyal to her. Nabila also pledged to wait for his return and to write at least once a week.

Abdul Rahman kept his promises. During his absence, Nabila received his detailed letters regularly describing his activities. He even numbered his letters to be sure that she would answer every one of them. Occasionally, when Nabila missed answering a letter, Abdul Rahman would send a telegram asking her to explain the reasons for not writing. Those two years passed quickly with Abdul Rahman and Nabila maintaining a strong connection despite the distance. It was as if they were never apart as they shared every facet of their thoughts, actions, and dreams in the volumes of letters.

Fahad, Abdul Rahman's younger brother, came to spend his summer vacation in Cairo. At nineteen, he was athletic and muscular from lifting weights and wrestling. Nabila's family welcomed Fahad, especially Fatima who considered him her fiancée. Fahad had a pleasant personality, always teasing Nabila, calling her "sister-in-law." When the summer was over, Fahad sadly returned to Saudi Arabia. He insisted that the entire family write him as many letters as possible so that he could stay connected. He did not have many friends so he especially valued Nabila's family. Fahad vowed that he would be back the following summer and would attend the wedding of his brother and Nabila.

Surprisingly, months passed and no one in the family had written to Fahad. Nabila decided to write him and apologize for not having written earlier. Nabila asked her mother if she wanted to tell Fahad anything, and Rahma shocked her by prohibiting her from writing to Fahad. Rahma was adamant against Nabila corresponding with Fahad but offered no explanation why. She persisted in trying to convince her mother that they should write Fahad as they had agreed, but despite her logic, Nabila could not convince Rahma. She eventually gave up, focusing on her studies and did not broach the subject again until months later.

Summer was approaching, and Abdul Rahman was due back in about three weeks. Nabila reminded Rahma that Fahad had remarked that he might come back during the summer to Cairo. She knew Fahad wanted to attend her wedding, and she wanted to write to inquire if he was still coming. This time Rahma revealed the truth. While exercising in the smoldering sun, Fahad had suffered sunstroke, and the doctors could not save him. Rahma had been afraid to tell Nabila the horrible news, because she thought Nabila would tell Abdul Rahman, and that might affect his studies. Rahma knew that Abdul Rahman would be hurt because he didn't have the money to return to Jeddah for his brother's funeral. Shocked by Fahad's passing, Nabila agreed to keep the news of Fahad's death from Abdul Rahman. Her heart ached for her younger sister, Fatima, who had lost her fiancée, thinking *I could never live without my true love, Abdul Rahman.*

Uncle Saleh, Abdul Rahman's father, came to Cairo one week before his son's arrival from the USA. Abdul Rahman arrived late in the night exhausted from the sixteen-hour trip. Adding to sleep deprivation, his body was temporarily sickened by required vaccinations designed to protect him against common diseases in Cairo. The family barely greeted him before showing him to his room so he could sleep. The next morning Abdul Rahman confessed how much he missed Nabila and wished that she had been with him every moment he spent in America. They eagerly discussed their wedding that was to take place in ten days. They hoped to spend one honeymoon week in a fine hotel by the pyramids and then travel to Jeddah, staying a week with relatives. Then the couple would fly to the United States. Of course, the rest of the family had approved all their plans.

As elated as Nabila was about her upcoming nuptials, she knew that her happiness was marred by Fahad's tragic death. Abdul Rahman had yet to learn of his brother's fate. Unable to keep his grief hidden any longer, Uncle Saleh called for Abdul Rahman to join him on the balcony. He requested that Abdul Rahman sit close to him so he could somehow convey the heartbreaking news. With uncontrollable emotion, Uncle Saleh spoke in a shaky voice with tears running down his cheeks. "Your brother, Abdul Rahman ... your brother, Fahad, died of sunstroke."

Abdul Rahman buried his grief, showing little emotion. Instead, he recited a verse of the Quran: "Every soul shall have a taste of death" (185, Al-Imran).

CHAPTER 7

Our Lord, let our spouses and children be a source of joy for us,
and keep us in the forefront of the righteous.

~ AL FURQAN 73

It is customary in the Arab world that two ceremonies symbolize a marriage. One is the celebration of signing the contract which, according to Saudi culture and the Muslim faith, the bride does not need to attend, as long as she has previously given her father her consent to marry. Nabila legally became Abdul Rahman's wife on July 19, 1972, when Saad, Abdul Rahman, Aneese, and Rajab, a family friend, signed Nabila's marriage contract, which included reciting part of the Quran and determining the dowry. The other ceremony—the *farah*—is the festivity where the bride dons her white wedding dress. After the farah, the bride and groom live together and start their married life.

Nabila's Aunt Meriam took care of all the arrangements for the wedding. She purchased the wedding dress, the food, and engaged the orchestra and the belly dancer. Rahma was merely a member of the audience, doing little to help with the wedding. Rahma trusted her sister and counted on her to organize the entire event. The home wedding started at nine o'clock in the evening. The party started at the ground floor when Nabila arrived from the bridal beauty shop with Aunt Meriam. She met Abdul Rahman, who looked very handsome in his black suit, at the entrance of the building. Abdul Rahman and Nabila slowly climbed the seven floors led by the belly dancer, followed by the orchestra and the young girls in white dresses carrying ivory roses. Behind them strolled relatives and friends. Nabila waved to curious neighbors in the building opening their doors as the music and the dance continued to the seventh floor. As the couple moved to sit on the special chairs designated for the bride and groom, Nabila overheard the belly dancer whisper to a member of the orchestra, "The bride is so young ... she is a child."

At fifteen, Nabila *was* just a child, but she was old enough to know that this was the destiny she would have selected had she been given the choice.

Ten days later, Rahma prepared Nabila's abaya and *tarha* for travel. Nabila was not used to wearing the abaya, having grown up in Egypt. She looked and felt like a shadow of a woman. The garb obstructed her senses—sight, smell, taste—and she struggled to keep the layers of veils from slipping off her slight shoulders and the tarha from falling in her face. Nabila had to peek through the cloth to see her way and stumbled about as if she had been drinking. She thought how lucky she was not to belong to the tribes in the Nej'd region of Saudi Arabia where women were never permitted to remove their veils. This long-time custom commences when a woman begins menstruation. At that time she dons the veil, and it remains on her face until her death. In fact, a tribal couple can be married for decades and the husband will never have seen his wife's face (only her eyes)!

Before Nabila left, her father told her that she was about to get the chance of her life and that she should take advantage of being in America and try to finish her education. Saad surprised Nabila by saying that he believed education for a woman was more important than for a man, especially in a society like theirs. He said, "Man can always find a job anywhere, but a woman, unless she is educated, will be lost."

Jobs for women in Saudi Arabia were confined to teaching or practicing medicine in certain fields.

Saad said, "Remember, no one will take of you unless you take care of yourself."

Nabila had no premonition that this would ultimately be the case.

◆ ◆ ◆

As soon as the plane landed on Saudi Arabian soil, Abdul Rahman ordered Nabila to wear her veil and abaya. It was almost August and the temperature in Jeddah was over 120 degrees with 90 percent humidity. Just walking from the plane to the airport, Nabila was soaked with sweat as if she had been baking in an oven. The abaya was heavy and the black georgette veil was made with four layers of fabric. Nabila tried her best to keep the veil centered on her head but tripped over it several times before she was able to get inside the airport. Her arm ached from clutching the veil below her chin to keep it in place until she could get out of public and into the relative's house.

The newlyweds were met at the airport by two male relatives unknown to Nabila. She was not even certain Abdul Rahman remembered them. The car had no air conditioning and felt like a traveling sauna. Eventually, they arrived at a high-gated house where Abdul Rahman was led to a room filled only with men. Nabila was greeted by six elderly women clad in long, ivory dresses with elbow-length sleeves over loose, soft white pants. The dresses had high collars decorated with white lace and fastened by golden studs on chains. The women's heads were covered with sheer cotton cloth that wrapped around their two braids—another light, sheer white, scarf decorated with tiny tassels, and lace was layered across the top. All the women seemed to wear the same hairstyle, parted in the middle and pulled to the back. Their kohl-lined eyes were fixed on Nabila. The women sat on long, thin floor cushions where they tucked their bare feet under their dresses. They took turns quizzing her about her mother and the rest of the family. Nabila had to repeat the same answer to each of the women. Shortly, three men joined them and introduced themselves as Nabila's uncles: Uncle Hamza, Uncle Hassan, and Uncle Aban.

Abdul Rahman and Nabila were treated quite special. Saudi people are known to be generous and hospitable, so the newlyweds were given the best room in the house. The relatives wanted to be sure that the guests were as comfortable as possible. As lunch is the main meal in the Arab world, the young couple attended daily lunch parties hosted by family and friends. The food was always the same: a roasted whole lamb over rice, bowls of tomato sauce, a salad, and some pickled vegetables. Fruit was the only dessert.

Nabila enjoyed the festivities, except she could not understand all Saudi customs and traditions. She had left Jeddah as a small child and was not reared in their ways. She made many mistakes and felt embarrassed and ashamed at her lack of understanding. Nabila was raised in Egypt, not in Saudi Arabia; nevertheless, she was chastised for being Saudi by nationality and not knowledgeable about the customs. One of the traditions unknown to her was that men never mixed with women. At mealtime, a long piece of cloth was spread across the floor in both the men's and women's rooms. The food was served in one giant dish, and everyone gathered around the bowl and ate from that dish using their hands. All heads swiveled in her direction when Nabila politely asked for a spoon. She did not understand her offense. Feeling self-conscious, she excused herself from the meal. To her surprise, everyone else exited the room with her before the hostess began to beg everyone to return to the table and finish eating. Nabila later learned it was a custom that all the guests must leave the meal at the same time, whether they are finished eating or not. Nabila's blunders continued.

After the meal, one of the women graciously showed Nabila her wedding picture. She looked so beautiful that Nabila complimented her.

The woman appeared upset and replied, "You must say *Mashaa* Allah."[1]

Many believe if you do not say Mashaa Allah, which means "God willing," that person will incur the 'evil eye' and may get sick or lose whatever you admired. Nabila continued in error by asking if she could show the picture to her husband.

The woman's temper flared once more. "Do you not know that men are prohibited from looking at women's pictures? It is in Islam. Aren't you a Muslim?"

The custom that seared Nabila's heart and has been forever etched in her memory were the gatherings held in Deera Square, the justice square to view executions. Saudi Arabia's criminal justice system, based on ancient sharia religious Islamic law, uses beheading with a sword as an official method of execution for severe crimes such as murder. The practice of beheading stemmed from the original Islamic law from 1300 years ago that was used for most executions. The violent crime rate in Saudi Arabia was relatively low but had risen with the presence of foreigners in the workplace. Many believed that severe punishments like beheadings, stoning, and floggings deterred the people from committing crimes.

Murder, apostasy from Islam, adultery, drug smuggling, and sabotage are subject to death by beheading, firing squad, or stoning of the offender. Even offenses such as stealing can have severe consequences. Multiple instances of theft can result in amputation of the right hand. In cases of aggravated theft the culprit can be punished by cross-amputation of a hand and a foot. Flogging with a cane is a punishment used for infractions against religion, drunkenness, gambling, and the neglect of prayer. Floggings can also accompany prison sentences, depending on the crime. The victim's pardon and opinion, as well as the thief's willingness to repent and make restitution, can impact the judgment.[2]

Nabila's unfortunate ignorance and displeasure of Saudi customs continued until she left her hosts' home. She was relieved when they finally departed for Beirut to begin their honeymoon. Summer in Beirut was as hot and humid as Jeddah, so the couple headed to the mountains where it was cooler. The girls in Beirut attracted Nabila's attention with their trendy fashions. After three days in Beirut, they flew to the beautiful city of Rome. Nabila loved the spicy Italian food and dining at the outside trattorias. Each evening was filled with romance listening to the violinist as red roses were offered to the guests. The young couple marveled at the city's many attractions. At a museum, the guide led them to a room displaying the largest book ever written with the smallest book in the world on top of it. The guide shared with a chuckle that the smallest book contained a man's question, and the largest one offered the woman's answer.

From Rome, they flew to Berlin to visit Nabila's brother, Samir. While the city was amazing, filled with artifacts detailed in Nabila's earlier school history lessons, they were deterred by the language. It was frustrating when they could not find anyone who could speak English; even attempts at sign language were to no avail. Eventually, the couple located Samir who told them that Saad and Uncle Saleh were coming to tour Germany in two weeks. While Nabila was eager to travel to America, it was difficult to say goodbye to her brother. She left Germany feeling depressed and weepy, with a husband who did not know what to do to comfort his emotional bride.

CHAPTER NOTES:

1 Mash' Allah or Mashaa Allah is translated "as God has willed it." It's used by Saudis and Arabs whenever someone or something is being praised or admired as a reminder that all good things come from God and are blessings from Him.

2 The convicted are given large amounts of drugs in preparation for the beheading to reduce pain and to immobilize the criminal. Lesser offenses are met with whippings, floggings, stonings, amputation of limbs without anesthetics, and crucifixions as punishments in Saudi Arabia.

Chapter 8

*What is the essence of America? Finding and maintaining that
perfect, delicate balance between freedom 'to' and freedom 'from.'*
~ Marilyn vos Sava

America, the land of the free! Alexandria, Virginia had captured Nabila's heart the moment she entered the city. Women moved about the streets, some in pairs or groups, others with their children, and most amazingly, alone. They were fashioned a variety of clothing; dresses, pants, shorts of such vibrant hues that Nabila was mesmerized at the sight. She felt like she was walking out of a black-and-white movie scene and into the wonderland of Oz. She had never seen fair-haired people before and thought the children looked like talking dolls. Even the weather was a novel experience as heavy rain and thunder storms both delighted and frightened her. The simplest landscape of green grass and tall oak trees was a portrait worthy of the finest museum. The lush green plants bordered with wide clean streets were surroundings Nabila used to read about in books. She did not expect ever to live in such beauty.

The United States was unlike any land Nabila had lived. Although Egypt is a free country, it is still controlled by Islamic law, customs, and traditions. Boys and girls are separated in schools and are only mixed socially with a family member present. Both religion and law prohibit dating. Conservative clothing is mandatory for all girls. To introduce a young man as a boy friend to immediate family members is shocking. In Saudi Arabia, a woman cannot be alone with a man who is not a relative.[1] If a woman has a relationship with a man, she could lose her life. A woman's relationship with a man is only sanctioned through legal marriage arranged by a male family member. Therefore, to see men and women together in public, demonstrative in their actions, was quite unexpected.

Abdul Rahman's host family, Mr. and Mrs. Johnson, and their two teenage boys helped Nabila adjust to life in America. With her pleasing demeanor and classic beauty, Mrs. Johnson became a role model for Nabila. She wanted to become the ideal homemaker, and loved Mrs. Johnson's family, cooking, and the way she took care of herself and her home. Mrs. Johnson treated Nabila like her daughter, taking her everywhere, introducing her to people and helping her to make friends. Through Mrs. Johnson, Nabila learned the importance of manners in saying "please," "thank you," and "excuse me." In Nabila's culture, well-mannered people were rare—quite stingy with niceties. To be punctual is highly valued in America but was not considered a virtue in Saudi Arabia. Nabila mastered the fundamentals of being a gracious guest, as she and Abdul Rahman were invited to spend holidays, Christmas and Thanksgiving, in the Johnson home. These holidays were unknown to her, as practicing any religion other than being a Muslim is prohibited in Saudi Arabia.[2]

Nabila dreamed of being a good wife and mother to her future children. She had a plan to attend home economics school, because she heard that it taught girls how to be successful homemakers by cooking, sewing, and decorating. Nabila loved beautiful, stylish clothes and was very particular about her appearance. Unfortunately, she never had a suitable role model in Egypt, as her teachers, who should have been mentors, were rude, unmannered, and never dressed well.

Becoming a good cook was an early interest of Nabila's. As a young girl, she used to save her allowance to buy cookbooks. However, the Egyptian books were disappointing as many of the recipes were not accurate. Nabila was discouraged when her prepared dishes looked nothing like the pictures featured in the book. Nabila tried sewing as well but had difficulty, as readymade patterns were not available in Egypt. The teachers taught students how to draw a pattern, but the process appeared much too complicated. Failing to make a delicious meal from the recipe and unable to draw sewing patterns was disheartening. Nevertheless, young Nabila was diligent and whenever her father was invited for an outside meal, she would prepare the supper for thirteen people in the household. In those days Abdul Rahman was Nabila's biggest fan as he was enthusiastic about everything she cooked. Many times, he asked her to prepare his favorite meal of meat and rice stew, and she obliged with pride.

When Mrs. Johnson discovered Nabila's sincere interest in cooking, she bought Nabila her first English cookbook. Nabila scoured the dictionary to decipher the unknown terms and began attempting the recipes while her husband was at school. Abdul Rahman, of course, only sampled Nabila's successful dishes.

Abdul Rahman was not without friends in America. Issa, who was also on scholarship from the Saudi government was Abdul Rahman's best friend and lived nearby. Issa was lonely, and Nabila and Abdul Rahman were his only refuge in America. Issa spent most of his time at their house, a peaceful retreat that curtailed his homesickness. Nabila did not mind Issa's extended visits at first, but soon longed for the privacy that newlyweds crave. Their campus apartment was tiny, not even the size of one of the rooms in Nabila's residence in Egypt. After a few months, Issa disappeared from their lives as quickly as he had appeared. Because Issa's visits were rare, Nabila assumed that his studies were consuming his time. Eventually, Abdul Rahman and Nabila discovered that Issa had a nineteen-year-old fiancée, Margaret, who was also a student. The young women talked many times on the telephone before they actually met months later. Margaret and Nabila became fast friends, visiting each other often.

While Issa's homesickness was subdued by his relationship with Margaret, Nabila's had mushroomed. She received the first family letter from her younger sister, Fatima, since she had left home. Fatima described her sadness in leaving Egypt and returning to the harsh life in Saudi Arabia. She was distraught that her father had moved the family to the disheveled, primitive house on the mountain of Makkah, which had no supply of clean water, electricity, or sewage network. Rahma, too, was greatly depressed since her return from Cairo. She was overwhelmed with the housework and the cooking with no assistance, as Jada had aged and was unable to help. There was no place to go and nothing to do. Theaters and movies did not exist in the country, nor was there TV. Their only entertainment was visiting girlfriends and gossiping.

Nabila knew what life was like for her female family members in Saudi Arabia and was dismayed that they had to endure those conditions.

Distressed, she became sick and had several episodes of vomiting every day. Abdul Rahman was extremely worried about her and insisted she see a doctor. If the doctor determined everything was physically all right with Nabila, Abdul Rahman thought he might have to send her to visit her family to combat her homesickness. Nabila could not help comparing her life to those in her family. She was in a country where women had the most freedom while her sisters and her poor mother were living in a society where women were treated like property. A woman in Saudi Arabia was in the custody of her father as long as he is alive, and after that, in the custody of her husband. If she is unmarried after her father's death, she was in the governance of her brother and was never free to have an opinion or choice in what she wished to do. She was always under the control of a man no matter her age and could even be in the custody of her son if he was old enough. Nabila wanted to help her mother and sisters leave the country, but she did not know how. She felt helpless and guilty for having a husband who cared for her and did not mistreat her. While she was having a great time, her sisters were living miserably, lonely, and homesick for their past life in Egypt. They were, like other Saudi women, prisoners in their own homes. They could not even look out a window in their home for fear of exposing themselves to men.

The doctor did not believe that Nabila's homesickness was making her ill; instead he told her that she was pregnant. At fifteen and only married for two months, she could not accept the idea of having a baby. When Nabila was not crying, she was suffering from morning sickness and fainting spells. Abdul Rahman suffered along with her, as he was not pleased with the news. He repeatedly declared that he was not ready to have a baby and complained that he was not able to concentrate on his studying.

In 1972 Abdul Rahman and Nabila were the only Arab couple in the small university town, which contributed to her feelings of isolation. Her shyness prevented her from making friends with Americans, and the language was an obstacle that kept her away from people and escalated her homesickness. Corresponding with her parents, grandmother, sisters, and brothers was the only relief from her bitter feelings. Writing and receiving letters was Nabila's focus. She cherished the one from her father congratulating her on her pregnancy, expressing his great concern, and asking her again not to neglect her education.

Nabila was weak from bouts of vomiting and weighed only ninety-eight pounds. She did not feel better until her seventh month of pregnancy. Abdul Rahman patiently listened to all her concerns and did his best to keep her comfortable. He handled household problems with gentleness and understanding. To make Nabila happier, he found a larger apartment complete with a view of a lake and a park.

Mrs. Johnson was the only person Nabila was able to talk to freely. She called Mrs. Johnson to tell her she was pregnant, hoping to receive sympathy about her plight. Mrs. Johnson voiced a convincing lecture about the beauty of motherhood and the happiness Nabila would experience when the baby arrived. She was able to provide a completely different outlook, and Nabila began to look forward to having a child. Weeks later, Nabila received an invitation from Mrs. Johnson to a baby shower. Nabila had no idea what a baby shower was but was elated when it turned out to be a festive party with many presents for the baby. The gifts eliminated Nabila's financial worries about buying a crib, bath top, and clothing for the infant.

Being pregnant and without family made Nabila realize how much she missed having a close confidant. Therefore, when Abdul Rahman met Saber Kamal who just arrived at the university to prepare for his PhD in chemistry, she welcomed meeting his family. Saber and his wife Faten were from Egypt and upon meeting them, Nabila knew they'd become close friends. Faten was only a few years older than Nabila with two small children, a three-year-old boy, and a month-old little girl. Faten was like a big sister to her, which she sorely needed at that time in her life. Nabila consulted Faten on all issues, especially those concerning children.

During the first two years at the university, Abdul Rahman was not able to afford a car, but Faten and Nabila managed to spend hours together, Faten in the role of Dr. Spock and Nabila as the eager expectant mother. It was inevitable that the Kamals moved downstairs in the same apartment building. The couples were together most of the time, just like a true family.

Nabila discovered the greatness of America through its people. One particularly kind woman, a next-door neighbor, Laura, was a nurse. Knowing Nabila was expecting her first child, Laura checked on her regularly. She explained what to expect when the baby was ready to be born and brought Nabila a book about taking care of the expectant mother as well as a baby. When Nabila apologized for her broken English, Laura rebuffed the apology saying, "Your English is good. I don't speak a word of your language."

Whenever Nabila was with Americans and tried to speak English, they cheered her on, building her confidence. Television was a great English teacher, especially the commercials. The repetition taught Nabila the correct pronunciation and the spelling. Her English improved, and she felt confident enough to communicate with others. Mr. Johnson was so proud that Nabila had learned English. Whenever he had a chance, he told everyone how smart she was to learn to speak English by watching TV.

Abdul Rahman finally reconciled himself to the fact that he was going to be a father and began to plan for the infant's arrival in late May of 1973. As seems to be fodder in conversations about babies, Abdul Rahman was often asked if he would prefer to have a boy or a girl. His answer was always the same: a girl. Preferring girls to boys was an unusual response for an Arabic man. Abdul Rahman explained he wanted a girl as he had never had a sister, and he also wanted to prove to everyone he knew in Saudi Arabia that girls were as good as boys. Nabila was flabbergasted. Her Saudi husband was really becoming Americanized!

When the anticipated labor pains began, Abdul Rahman called the doctor and they rushed to the hospital. Nabila was more annoyed than afraid as the hospital staff kept asking questions about her age. She was not quite sixteen, but hated people telling her that she was too young to have a baby.

One of the nurses passed by Nabila's room, looked at her and said, "Imagine, a baby having a baby!"

Nabila's irritation was soon overcome by waves of agony. During the nine hours of labor, a nurse kept watch and finally delivered the painkiller that mercifully put Nabila to sleep. She vaguely remembered being wheeled to the delivery room and groggily looking up to see Laura assuring her that she would be okay. Laura's presence in the delivery room allowed nature to take its course and Nabila to relax. Later, coming out of the drugged darkness, Nabila heard her husband's gentle voice confirming what her body had given up. Their beautiful daughter had arrived.

Faten and Laura were the greatest help to Nabila with the new baby, Leila. They visited daily, assisting with chores and teaching her how to care for an infant. Mrs. Parker, an elderly lady from the nearby Methodist church, visited every Sunday after the last service. Nabila looked forward to her visits as she offered advice and gave Nabila a chance to practice her English.

One fateful day, Mrs. Parker broached the subject of age saying, "Honey, you look very young. In fact, you look too young to have a baby."

Nabila was quite defensive and loudly snipped that she was not too young. Mrs. Parker was startled at Nabila's rudeness and assured her that she meant it as a compliment. But Nabila had suffered enough references to her young age and the connotation that she was not prepared to be a mother, so the conversation abruptly ended. Regretfully, that was their last encounter, as well-meaning Mrs. Parker did not visit her again.

Having a child changed everything! Leila made Nabila incredibly happy, helping her forget her homesickness and putting aside her sisters' and mother's troubles in Saudi Arabia. Like most newborns, Leila had her mother's devoted attention both day and night. Nabila treated Leila like a doll, dressing her up, styling her thick, black hair and playing with her whenever she was awake.

Leila was a healthy baby until nine months of age when she became very sick with diarrhea and vomiting. She had lost one third of her weight and was severely dehydrated. Leila had black circles around her eyes and her temperature was 106 degrees. She was hospitalized for a week, and Nabila never left her bedside. Leila was subjected to ice baths designed to lower her temperature. Abdul Rahman was worried, too, missing many of his classes that week. Nabila did not sleep much, as she was afraid to close her eyes for fear Allah would take Leila from her. The Kamals and Mrs. Johnson were supportive, keeping vigil along with Nabila and Abdul Rahman. Nabila prayed as much as she cried, and soon Leila began to improve.

Out of kindness, Mrs. Johnson brought Leila a stuffed toy, Zippy the monkey, which Nabila placed in the crib. Abdul Rahman objected to the toy and instructed Nabila to take it away because he believed it would frighten the baby. Nabila disagreed with him, and an argument ensued.

Abdul Rahman yelled, "If you give that toy to Leila, you are divorced," and stormed out of the room.

Nabila was shocked at his threat, as it was inconceivable to her that Abdul Rahman would even think of divorce.

In Islam, it is law that a man can divorce his wife if he says, "you are divorced" on three different occasions in their marriage. Because of Abdul Rahman's emotional outburst, Nabila would be considered divorced once legally. They could still live together and he would have to verbally divorce her twice more before they would not be able to live together as husband and wife. As unbelievable as it sounds Abdul Rahman and Nabila would be legally divorced if that was to happen.

Nabila was exhausted and Abdul Rahman was tense, so to avoid further conflict, she did not give the toy back to the baby. Nabila stepped outside of the hospital room to talk to a mother of another patient, and when she returned she noticed Leila was happily playing with the toy again. A nurse must have found it and returned it to the crib. Before Nabila could act, she saw that Abdul Rahman was staring grimly at the toy in the baby's crib. He did not utter another word, and she thought the matter was forgotten. Besides, the doctor had announced that Leila was well enough to go home, and Nabila felt the stress of the week instantly evaporate. Nabila adored her baby and her husband, and she was certain that nothing bad could permeate the web of love that she had weaved.

CHAPTER NOTES:

1 In 2008 an arrest case shocked those around the world. Yara, 37, a married mother of three and a businesswoman, sat together with a male colleague in the family section of a public coffee house. The business associates' offices had lost power and they were temporarily using the free internet at the coffee shop to complete their work. The religious police arrested Yara for immoral behavior, seized her cell phone, stripsearched her, kept her from calling her husband, prevented her from seeing a lawyer, and forced her to sign documents admitting guilt. The police and judges may interpret the Quran at their own discretion, which results in inconsistent arrests and convictions.

In order to resolve difficulties associated with sex segregation, some clerics issued a *fatwa* in 2010 encouraging women to provide breast milk to any man with whom she comes into regular contact. Breast milk kinship is perceived to be the same as a blood relationship in Islam. If a child under two receives breast milk from a woman other than his birth mother he becomes part of her family, a sibling to her other children. In the 2010 fatwa a man drinking the milk (five fulfilling breast milk meals) is deemed a relative of the family, permitting him to come in contact with the women without breaking Islam's rules. Abdel Mohsen Obeikan, an Islamic scholar and adviser to the royal family and the Ministry of Justice, promoted this fatwa but noted the milk should not come directly from the woman's breast. However, other clerics asserted that the milk should come directly from the woman's breast. Breast milk kinship is perceived to be the same as a blood relationship in Islam. This would enable foreign drivers to mix freely with females in their host family without violating the Islamic rule. Right-to-drive activists have capitalized on this absurdity by threatening to start breastfeeding professional drivers, so that they can be freed of Saudi's segregation laws: "We either be allowed to drive or breastfeed foreigners."

2 In 2010 the U.S. State Department reported that proselytizing by non-Muslims is punishable by death under Islamic law. In addition, Muslims converting to another religion (apostasy) is punishable by death; however, there had been no confirmed reports of executions for either crime in recent years.

CHAPTER 9

Narrated Aisha: (The Prophet Muhammad, PBUH) never beat anyone, neither a woman nor a servant.

~ AL SAHIH AND MUSLIM

A new family moved into the neighborhood. The father was a professor at the university; the mother a housewife. They had two children: an eight-year-old boy and a girl, Kathy, two years younger than Nabila. The girls became close, with Kathy at Nabila's house more than her own. She spent considerable time helping Nabila improve her English. The two families also became friends, and they often went out for dinner or on short trips together.

While Nabila loved being with Leila during the day, she was beginning to think more and more about her father's urging that she complete her education. Working with Kathy, Nabila's English had improved and the time seemed right for her to finish high school. Abdul Rahman was concerned because they could not afford a babysitter, but Nabila was determined. She went to the Adult Education Center and requested all the books that were required to secure a diploma. Nabila learned that she was still young enough to attend the local high school so that became her goal. She studied the material in the texts during the day and spent the evenings trying to convince Abdul Rahman to allow her to enroll in high school to earn a diploma. It took several discussions and shifting of plans, but Abdul Rahman eventually relented and registered her for afternoon classes in order to take care of Leila while Nabila went to school.

Leila was well into the terrible twos and their family was thriving. But Nabila's joy was shattered when she received a letter from her sister Fatima in Jeddah. Fatima revealed that their mother, who was almost forty, had given birth to a baby boy. As with every delivery of his children, Saad was not with Rahma when she gave him his tenth child. At the same time, Saad married an Egyptian woman who was the same age as Nabila's oldest brother. Fatima's letter recounted the pitiful way Saad told Rahma about his marriage. As expected, Rahma was anxiously waiting for Saad to arrive from Egypt to show him his newborn baby boy. Rahma clutched the infant in her arms and hurried to meet Saad at the front door. However, Saad entered the house with his own agenda. He repeatedly asked Rahma to listen to him; he needed to talk to her, but Rahma was so focused on showing Saad his baby that she was not listening. Saad finally screamed at Rahma to get her attention and told her that he was married and had brought his new wife to Jeddah. At the shocking news, Fatima rushed to catch their newborn brother just as their mother slumped to the floor in shock.

Nabila internalized her mother's pain, causing sleep to elude her for days. She had admired and loved her father unconditionally, but she disliked him for what he had done to her mother. She began to distrust Saudi men, characterizing them as cheaters, deceivers, and beasts with no feelings for anybody in this life except themselves. *Didn't my father have any concern for my mother? After twenty-five years of marriage, didn't he think that his second marriage would hurt my mother?* Nabila came to realize that the way many Saudi men think is different from many other men in the world. They strongly believe that as long as Islamic religion permits men to take more than one wife, they are not doing anything wrong and that their wives should welcome the new brides. They are completely unaware of the torture the first wife may go through when she knows she is facing another woman who will be sharing everything in her life, including her husband.

My poor Mama. Nabila could not imagine how she would cope, as she was unable or unwilling to express her feelings and emotions. As a child, Nabila knew the kind of life Rahma experienced with Saad, though she had never heard her mother complain. Rahma kept her feelings submerged, her confidence dwindling with each of Saad's hurtful acts.

Nabila had often asked her mother, "Why aren't you upset and worried?"

The only answer Rahma gave was, "Leave it to Allah. He will take care of me."

Women of Rahma's generation had to accept their husbands'

indiscretions and stay in the marriage because they had no education, no way to support themselves, and no place to go. Marriage was "until death do us part."

Feeling depressed and angry, Nabila went to bed early hoping that her ill thoughts would dissolve in slumber. Unfortunately, Abdul Rahman was wide-awake and feeling amorous. When she declined his sexual advances, telling him she was too tired, he became angry. He insulted Nabila and told her that she was a horrible wife. He reminded Nabila that a good wife must never reject her husband when he asks for sex. He called her a bad Muslim and said she would be cursed by God if she did not obey him. Abdul Rahman shouted so loudly that he woke Leila. Nabila fetched Leila, rocking her to ease her tears, while she desperately tried to talk to Abdul Rahman explaining her preoccupation with her mother's situation. But Abdul Rahman would not listen and slapped Nabila across the face to quiet her. Stunned, Nabila dropped the child to the floor and Abdul Rahman repeatedly pummeled her. Leila was frightened and screaming as she ran between her parents. Abdul Rahman continued beating and kicking Nabila before shoving her out the front door and into the cold November night.

Nabila was hurt both physically and emotionally and unable to think clearly. It was 11 p.m., and she did not know where to go at that time of the night. Her friend Kathy was the first person she thought of, and luckily, found her home. Nabila was sure Kathy wondered why she would visit her at that late hour, but when she saw Nabila's battered face stained with tears, she hurried her inside. Nabila explained that her husband beat her and she had no place to go. Kathy assured Nabila that she could spend the night. Kathy phoned her parents who advised Nabila to call the police, but she would not do that to her husband and chance him being sent to jail. Nabila believed that everything would be fine when Abdul Rahman calmed down in the morning.

The next day, Kathy's father brought the advisor of the Foreign Students at the university to see Abdul Rahman. The advisor warned Abdul Rahman that beating a wife was against the law in the United States and that he could go to jail for his actions. Nabila returned home but her trust in Abdul Rahman was as bruised as her body.

Three years had passed since Nabila moved to the United States, and her life had changed completely. She was not the same innocent fifteen-year-old girl from Cairo. She had blossomed in America. While her faith and culture were untouched, America had educated her, taught her how to have an open mind and how to live a free life, no matter her beliefs. Nabila learned that freedom is precious, yet Islam is even more precious. She believed that the combination could be heaven on earth.

In America, Nabila discovered that her future held promise but it was up to her to seek what she wanted in her life. Education became paramount to her. Sadly, Nabila received no encouragement from Abdul Rahman. He summoned all the excuses as to why she would not succeed. He told her that she could not compete with the native speakers, that they could not afford the tuition, and finally that they might have another child. Determined to go to college, Nabila sent a request to the Saudi Representative of Ministry of Education in the United States, asking them to include her in her husband's scholarship. Nabila received a letter from the ministry stating the rules and regulations for a spousal scholarship and was concerned that she had to finish twenty credit hours with a B average in order to receive a scholarship.

To find the money for the tuition was not easy. Nabila plotted to go to school and look for a job at the university to finish the required hours before she discussed it with Abdul Rahman. As for her daughter, Nabila would find a suitable preschool near the university. Nabila was fortunate to find a job at the university library as well as the university preschool for the married students' children. When she broached the subject with Abdul Rahman, she was surprised to gain his consent. In fact, he suggested that they schedule their classes on opposite days of the week to save money on the preschool, at least for that semester. Nabila was not certain what prompted Abdul Rahman's change of heart but she moved ahead with her plan and finished the required hours with success and received her scholarship. Nabila was only able to use the scholarship for three semesters, though, because Abdul Rahman had finished his engineering degree and they had to leave the United States.

Nabila never wanted to return to Saudi Arabia. Her life in America was so full of rewards. She longed to remain to finish her education. However, if she had to return, Nabila believed that her education would be the catalyst to help make a difference in Saudi society. She knew most Saudi children and adults lacked manners and respect. Arabs are known for their respect for the elderly and for their parents, but the respect for others is not practiced. Nabila had often observed children playing selfishly, using foul language, or hitting and kicking each other to snatch a toy while the mothers stood by unconcerned. Some mothers would use a stick to hit a child to correct his behavior, but they neglected to explain how the child should behave. The words "please," "thank you," or "sorry" did not exist in most of the natives' vocabulary. She wanted to educate children to foster a different generation, in academics as well as social manners.

CHAPTER 10

To those weak of understanding
Make not over your property,
Which God hath made
A means of support for you,
But feed and clothe them
Therewith, and speak to them
Words of kindness and justice.

~ AL NESSA

Issa and Margaret had decided to get married in a beautiful home wedding. It was the first wedding Nabila attended in the United States. Margaret's mother was concerned that her daughter would be away in a strange country and asked that Nabila look after Margaret in Saudi Arabia.

The four friends decided to leave together for Saudi Arabia. They planned to take a cruise from New York to Paris and visit London before flying to Jeddah. While it seemed an adventure to Margaret, living in Saudi Arabia frightened Nabila. Although she was born there, Nabila left when she was only five. She could only remember the week she spent there with her husband at the beginning of their marriage.

In spite of Nabila's worries, she was excited to see her parents, brothers, and sisters. They would be meeting four-year-old Leila for the first time. Days before leaving the U.S., Nabila talked to Leila about going to Jeddah. She tried to make Leila understand that America was not their country and that they must go to Jeddah, which was their home. Nabila told Leila about her relatives and explained that she should not expect to have the same life she had in the U.S.

When the plane exited the runway, Nabila could not hold back her tears. Despite her explanation to Leila, the United States had become her country and home over the past five years. After experiencing freedom's sweet embrace, Nabila knew she would miss those open arms. Sadly, she realized it would be almost impossible for them to come back to the states, because traveling was only for the wealthy.

The group spent two days in New York before they boarded the ship to France. The vessel was a floating city. It was fourteen floors high with three elevators, two theaters, a dancing floor, a library, shopping centers, swimming pool, and many sports activities. In the beginning, they could barely believe their glorious surroundings, but as soon as the ship reached the open sea, Margaret and Nabila were green with seasickness. The women became hysterical and irrational, screaming at their husbands to get them off the ship. Luckily, Abdul Rahman, Issa, and Leila were not affected by the sea. The two husbands hustled to find the ship doctor who offered tablets that would induce sleep. Unfortunately, the pills did not help because the women could not keep them in their stomachs long enough. The constant vomiting with an empty stomach warranted another trip to the ship doctor who gave them suppositories that finally suppressed their symptoms.

After the seasickness passed, they relished the lifestyle the voyage provided. Nabila felt energetic, running up the stairs, eating all the food offered, shopping, dancing at night, and watching movies. All too soon, the ship anchored in London for a few hours before continuing to Paris. The group stayed in Paris for two days, but Nabila already missed America. To Nabila, after living in the United States, no other country could compare.

The group was met with hot and humid temperatures as they arrived in Beirut, Lebanon in August. Nabila could not believe that the five years away from the Arab world could change her so much. Arabic words and letters appeared strange, the culture and the behavior of the Arabs were unusual. Everything was new, as if she had never been to Arabic countries. In Beirut, they laid awake most of the night while Om Kathum (a famous singer) blared from a radio competing with the other noisy street sounds.

During the two-hour flight to Jeddah, Nabila tried to focus on reuniting with her family, avoiding all other thoughts of missing her wonderful life in the United States. When they arrived at three o'clock in the afternoon, the temperature had reached 115 degrees and the humidity was 100 percent. Nabila's oldest brother, Aneese, met them with the required abaya and a veil for her. A member of their family took in Issa and Margaret. Nabila and Abdul Rahman would be staying with Abdul Rahman's cousin, Yasser. Abdul Rahman and his brothers had grown up with Yasser after their mother died from tuberculosis when Abdul Rahman was about ten-years-old and his youngest brother was less than two-years-old. Aunt Jameela took care of the children as if they were her own.

During the car ride, Nabila quizzed her brother, asking if their father's Egyptian wife had come to Jeddah from Makkah with the rest of the family. He informed Nabila that the relationship was in peril, and the family disapproved of the marriage.

Nabila gazed through the car window at the road full of garbage and rotten food as street cats, goats, and donkeys searched for their lunch. The countryside looked exactly as it had five years before; Nabila's family did not. She was surprised to see how much her sisters and brothers had changed; her mother looked beautiful, but not happy.

They were joined by Abdul Rahman's father, his uncle Sidi Hassan and his son, cousin Yasser, with his wife, Zain, and their five teenage daughters, two second cousins with their wives, and spinster aunt, Jameela. Sixty-year-old Aunt Jameela had never been married, because her brother Sidi Hassan, the eldest uncle, selfishly refused all her suitors for marriage. He feared that if his only sister got married, he would not have anyone to take care of his brothers and him.

Later, Saad called Nabila to another room to tell her that he was worried about her because she looked much thinner and not very healthy. She denied any problems and explained that when she left the country she was only fifteen, a teenager with no responsibilities. He advised her to take care of herself, to be happy, and if she had any problems to consult him. With tears in his eyes, an uncharacteristically emotional Saad kissed Nabila goodbye and headed with the rest of the family back to Makkah.

Abdul Rahman and Nabila spent the night in a small room at the roof of the house. It was empty, except for two rigid sponge mattresses and a small fan. The night was hot and sticky from the humidity. The pillows were hard and uncomfortable. Despite being quite tired, she could not sleep. She checked on Leila who was sound asleep while Abdul Rahman was tossing and turning uncomfortably. Luckily, the extreme heat during the summer deterred the mosquitoes. As soon as the sun was up, Nabila walked around the house. She noticed that the house was still the same as it was five years ago; nothing had improved, and a few things were worse. The air-conditioned room offered to them as newlyweds no longer existed. In fact, there were no air conditioners in any of the rooms. There was only one fan, carried from space to space. A single light bulb dangled from each of the high ceilings. The main square room had thick white cement walls and two tiny windows closed at night and opened in the morning to the hot, Jeddah air that soon overcame the trapped cool mist.

The living room had a large old artificial Persian rug and thin sponges arranged on the perimeter of the floor. Thick cushions used as back supporters lay near the thin mats; other smaller cushions were used for armrests. Prayer rugs and *shurshuf* were rolled up and scattered in different places in the room. One corner of the floor was always reserved for the tea serving, which consisted of a tray with the teapot, the *fingans*, the small teacups, small spoons, the sugar container, and a towel that was used to cover the teapot to keep it warm. The tiny kitchen had two dafors used for cooking. Breakfast was usually goat cheese, olives, homemade jam, and flat bread. Occasionally, Aunt Jameela would fry or boil a few eggs.

The people who occupied that house were very kind and hospitable as before. Seventy-year-old Hassan controlled the whole house. He was addressed as Sidi Hassan out of respect for being the elder. Every member in the house, young and old, obeyed his orders. In addition, he considered himself the house doctor. Whenever anyone became ill, he would dole out the medicine. He had a chest filled with left over medicine from other relatives or friends he knew. Expiration dates were meaningless to him. Unfortunately, Sidi Hassan had also decided to reduce water usage by removing the flush from the only toilet in the residence.

The water supply was still provided by the sagga. With little improvement from the past, the pole balanced on the back of a donkey, instead of the man's shoulders. The water bounced and splashed as it traveled through the narrow streets, exposed to the flies, dust, and dirt in the air. By the time it arrived to the customer's house, the containers were usually half-full.

Each house had a large water tank with an electric pump used to force the water into another larger water tank on the top of the house to enable the residents to use the water through the taps in the bathroom and in the kitchen. Bottled water and water filters did not exist in the country. Boiling the water was the only alternative to have germ-free water.

Since Abdul Rahman and Nabila were not able to rent an accommodation of their own, they became additional members to the already crowded household. Sidi Hassan allotted them the lower floor of the house, reached through a hole in a wood panel that was cut open to connect that part of the house with the upper floor. The lower floor apartment was filthy and full of dead roaches, spiders, and lizards. It depressed Nabila to think of living there, but there was no other choice. The apartment had no furniture or kitchen cabinets, stove, refrigerator, or sink. A water tap hung on the wall about five feet high above a drain hole on the floor. The kitchen had one large window without a screen. Flies and dust were daily visitors, while mosquitoes and other insects buzzed at night. The bathroom had no windows or any kind of ventilation and no bathtub. The toilet was only a small, round opening on the floor. There were two steps for the person to step on or to rest on his knees. There was no water tank to flush the toilet.

The bedroom had two small windows that Abdul Rahman sealed with wood panels to deter incoming insects. Abdul Rahman's father furnished the couple with two floor sleeping mattresses, a small dafoor cooker, a miniature refrigerator, and a few aluminum pots and pans. Saad offered an air conditioner for the bedroom. The other two rooms were completely barren.

For entertainment, they occasionally borrowed the television from their cousins upstairs so Leila could watch cartoons. That was her only entertainment. Abdul Rahman promised Nabila a better life when he found a job. Nabila had to cope with incessant dust, dirt, and insects of all kinds: roaches, mosquitoes, lizards, and flies. Cleaning, laundry, daily cooking, and taking care of Leila were almost impossible for one person. Nabila lived day after day within the confines of those walls. There was no place to go. The only window offered the view of garbage and the smell of rotten leftover food that people dumped in the streets. She could not accept that her life was misery in a prison masquerading as her home. Nabila ached every day for the freedom she had in America. From the time she awoke each morning until she laid her head on the hard uncomfortable pillow, she wished for a reprieve from her current existence. Her only release was when she asked Abdul Rahman to take her to Makkah to be with her parents. Abdul Rahman never refused the idea of going to Makkah; however, because of limited funds they were not able to go as often as they liked. Nabila's parents lived a much better life in Makkah than did her in-laws. Her parents, sisters, and brother now resided in a well-furnished and clean three-bedroom apartment. An Ethiopian woman came every day to help Rahma clean the house.

After one month of living with relatives, Abdul Rahman's father insisted that Nabila take care of his meals and his laundry. Saudi people believe that it is the duty of the wife of the oldest son to take care of her in-laws, especially a single father or mother. Uncle Saleh's decision put a lot of pressure on Nabila. She had to prepare a meal for nine people, three of her family and six for the people in her uncle's shop. Arabic food takes hours to prepare and cook as everything is made from scratch. Moreover, Arabs do not like one-dish meals. The average lunch consisted of rice, two or three kinds of vegetables prepared Arabic style, some fried meat, salads, and appetizers like homemade pickles with sauces. Ovens were not available. Everything had to be cooked on the two small gas ranges, dafoors. Nabila had to begin cooking as early as eight o'clock in the morning to have the meal ready at two p.m. She spent most of the day in the kitchen to try to please her father-in-law.

Abdul Rahman tried to comfort Nabila and assure her that everything was only temporary. Although Nabila prepared the meal, Uncle Saleh did not eat with his son's family. Instead, a twelve-year-old boy, Mansour, from Yemen, delivered his meal to him. Mansour helped Uncle Saleh in his small photo shop, as child labor was very common in the country. Many Yemen sent their sons to Saudi Arabia to work and sent the money back to their fathers. Nabila's father-in-law considered Mansour to be the substitute son that Allah sent him after he lost his son Fahad. Mansour became the focus in Uncle Saleh's life. He was treated special, even better than Adel, Abdul Rahman's youngest brother. Mansour attended the best school that Uncle

Saleh could afford. Since adoption was forbidden in Islam, Mansour was not able to carry the family's name and could never be a legal son.

In Nabila's lonely and tedious lifestyle in Saudi Arabia, she lost all ambition. She wanted to be someone special, not an uneducated housewife. She felt that she was only a maid, consumed with chores of cooking, cleaning, washing, and ironing. They had no car to go anywhere, and even if they did, there was no time or special place to visit. Life became as boring as it was difficult. To make matters worse, Uncle Saleh complained that the food was not ample for the five people with him in the shop and that Nabila should cook more. Nabila then spent all morning cooking, unable to do anything else for half of every day. The remainder of the day was spent washing dishes, cleaning the kitchen, and dusting. Nabila had to neglect Abdul Rahman and Leila for things that were never important, but forced upon her. She rarely had a moment's nap during the day and often did not go to bed until the early morning hours, and while her responsibilities were not so different from many other young women in her land, Nabila was not content with this lifestyle and openly resented it.

As was the custom, the family asked Abdul Rahman to relinquish their apartment for a few days for male guests. Nabila asked politely if it was possible to find another space for the guests. The family thought Nabila was too outspoken and unreasonable because she refused to give them the apartment. They would not speak to Nabila or associate with her. Every time they saw her, they commented about the incident to hurt her and make her feel guilty. The men in the family complained to Abdul Rahman about Nabila, but her husband defended her. Nabila was forever embattled in an unspoken war with her relatives, rejecting the customs and way of life she had interited.

Several months passed, and Abdul Rahman was still searching for a job. Every day from eight o'clock to two in the afternoon he looked for employment. He finally came home with jubilant news that he had been accepted as an engineer in one of the most important ministries in the kingdom. Nabila thanked Allah for his blessing. Abdul Rahman promised that they would move away from the relatives and into their own place. Nabila felt fortunate to have Abdul Rahman, a kind family man who loved his daughter and her very much.

Nabila passed time by writing letters to Kathy. She was Nabila's confidant as Nabila told Kathy about every event and incident she had suffered. She shared her displeasure about Abdul Rahman's father and the terrible quarters where she lived. Kathy was understanding and sympathetic. Kathy, too, was open describing her life through letters, pictures, and cards that reached Nabila at least twice a month. The women were each other's pulse, sharing more than sisters would.

One year passed, yet Abdul Rahman and Nabila were still not able to move to another apartment. The money that Abdul Rahman was making was hardly enough for daily living expenses. Nabila's relationship with her in-laws was worsening, as they disagreed on almost everything. Abdul Rahman's father interfered with every argument she had with any member of the family. He would shout and blame Abdul Rahman for not dispelling his wife. Poor Abdul Rahman; he tried to balance calming his father and not hurting his wife. And while Nabila was having difficulty adjusting to life with her extended family, the freedoms and liberties for all females in Saudi Arabia were about to drastically be curtailed.

● ● ●

In 1979 in a surprise invasion, a group of 400 terrorists led by Juhayman Al 'Utabi seized the Holy Mosque and clashed with authorities for two weeks. With armed forces the police finally recovered the holy grounds and beheaded the extremists. The backlash of this turmoil was the creation of severe restrictions and the latitude of the religious police to enforce them at will to prevent another uprising. Because of society's response to the seizure of Makkah, women's freedoms quickly disintegrated. All pictures of women in magazines and on television were removed, music was banned, and women's jobs in the workplace were reduced.

● ● ●

The 1980s were known as the *sahwa* time for women. Nabila was not allowed to leave the house, not even to walk in her gated yard, without being completely covered with the abaya. If a woman was only partially covered, men would immediately think of her as a cheap woman, and they would probably approach her. Talking to a strange man was considered a sign of something immoral. If a woman had to talk to a stranger for any matter, she had to act seriously, otherwise, men would interpret the message differently. Nabila feared such an exchange when one day the sagga brought the water as usual in the two tin containers on the back of the donkey. He was supposed to empty the water into the large container outside the house, but that bin was already full of water. Usually a man from the house would go out and turn the motor on to pump the water to a bigger container on the top of the house in order for the sagga to refill the container. Unfortunately, Nabila was alone in the house that day. The sagga asked her to turn the motor on. As a Saudi woman, Nabila was not supposed to leave the house exposing herself to a man. She was afraid to do so thinking that a man might take advantage of her when he found out that she was home alone. Nabila peeked from behind the door to tell the sagga to come back later when one of the men would be available to help him. Later in the evening, Uncle Saleh yelled at Nabila for asking the sagga to leave without delivering the water. Uncle Saleh's anger seemed unjustified. *Hadn't she done what everyone expected her to do, according to the custom?* Not knowing what to do, she had only told the sagga to come back later when one of the men would be available to help him. Uncle Saleh would not accept her excuse.

He turned to Abdul Rahman, shouting at him, "Divorce her now. Divorce her right now, and I will provide you with a much better wife. Tell her she is divorced at this minute, or I will deny you as my son until the judgment day."

Abdul Rahman was very worried about his father's outburst because of his heart condition. He ran to get his father's medicine and begged him to calm down.

Later, Uncle Saleh explained to Abdul Rahman, "Your wife should ask the sagga to turn his face to the other side, and then she could turn on the pump."

The incident made Abdul Rahman think seriously about leaving the house, but he did not know how to manage the rent and how to tell his father he wanted to leave. Finding a place that he could afford was very difficult. Nabila cut all communication with the family members upstairs except for cooking and taking care of her father-in-law's laundry. She was too hurt and depressed from the constant turmoil to defend herself. Abdul

Rahman comforted her and assured her that within a month they would be able to move to a new apartment away from the family. Thankfully, Abdul Rahman received a promotion at the ministry and the pay increase was enough for them to rent an apartment.

Nabila wanted to talk to her parents about her difficulties, but telephones were not available. Her parents still lived in Makkah, which was about 75 kilometers from Jeddah. Nabila had no car to visit them. Letters from Jeddah to Makkah often took two weeks but sometimes did not get there at all. Nabila missed the visits with her family chatting with her sisters and the rest of the family about the good days in Egypt when they were younger, looking forward to the future.

Fatima was still bitter about their housing situation after returning from Egypt. During that time Fatima had become severely depressed, unable to cope with life in Makkah. When Saad learned of Fatima's mental state, he wrote to Aunt Meriam in Cairo and asked if he could send Fatima to a boarding school in Egypt under her care. Aunt Meriam refused, not wanting the responsibility. The rejection devastated Fatima. Fatima believed Saad moved the family to a new apartment after he got married only to impress his new Egyptian wife.

Fatima was still angry with Saad over money matters as well. It started when she was thirteen-years-old and had just finished elementary school. The Saudi government opened the first girls' school and needed schoolteachers. Any girls who were able to read and write and were at least sixteen could have a job as a teacher in the public schools. The idea of his daughters teaching appealed to Saad. At that time, Saad had difficulty supporting two families. He was able to forge Fatima's and Najat's ages to make them eligible for teaching. Fatima was listed as eighteen-years-old and Najat as sixteen. Soon they became schoolteachers, teaching in the morning and studying at night to complete middle school. At the end of their first month of work, the two young teachers returned home proud and happy with their salaries. When Saad saw the money, he asked them to give it to him. Najat refused to give him her money. He cursed and shouted at her for not helping him when he needed it.

He asked her, "What do you need this money for? You're getting three meals and shelter over your head."

Najat was very strong, unshaken by her father's actions. Saad finally agreed to let Najat keep her first salary; however, the next month's salary must be surrendered to him. On the other hand, Fatima was very kind and naïve and immediately handed him the money. Najat celebrated the event with a good meal for the family without informing her father. According to Fatima, the Egyptian wife, Soso, was always spying on them as to what they ate and how they spent their money. Soso discovered the girls had a delicious meal without inviting their father. She reported everything the girls did with some evil embellishment that turned Saad against his own daughters and resulted in him angrily beating them. Najat complained that Saad even refused to give them a few pennies for an afternoon snack. They often licked sugar to satisfy their craving for sweets. Nabila listened in disbelief and finally asked her mother if it was the truth.

Rahma replied, "What can I tell you? Your sisters have told you everything."

The relationship between Nabila's grandmother, Jada, and Nabila's stepmother was also strained. Jada had repeatedly asked Saad to put her house in her will for his first family, not for Soso or her children. Saad never gave Jada's wishes any credence on the matter of the house or the will.

No matter how just the cause or how valid the reasoning, the voices of most Saudi women are silenced.

CHAPTER 11

... and He ordained between you love and mercy.
~ AL ROM 20-21

Because Nabila had little opportunity for life outside her home she welcomed the idea of having another child. She approached her husband about having a second child and he admitted that he had been considering it for a long time, though he was worried about their financial situation. Nabila reminded him that Allah would always give them children and provide them with the food they needed. That same month, Nabila conceived. Abdul Rahman was ecstatic about the pregnancy. He decided that the new baby should not live in an unhealthy atmosphere. Nabila was thrilled knowing Abdul Rahman wanted the move. A colleague was awarded a scholarship abroad that made his residence available. Abdul Rahman suggested they move there. Nabila did not know how Abdul Rahman broke the news to his father, but she was content as long as she had her family and no interference from anyone.

The landlord of an apartment or a house in Saudi Arabia is not responsible for any repairs or cleaning for a new tenant. Paint, repairs, and any restorations are the responsibility of the new renter. It is not unusual to find the property in poor condition after a tenant moves out. The new rental was really too large; the living space covered three floors so it took a great deal of effort to clean and repair. The worn furniture that they purchased from Abdul Rahman's colleague included one small wardrobe closet, two single, rock-hard beds that pushed together to create a larger bed, a tattered sofa, and two uncomfortable arm chairs. They managed to buy one badly used air conditioner for the bedroom and a refrigerator that kept their drinking water tepid at best. Because they could not afford a second air conditioner, Leila had to sleep in the same room with her parents.

Washing machines were a luxury and quite rare. Nabila had to wash all the laundry by hand and hang the clothes on the third floor roof to dry. The floors of the house were barren except for the desert dust. She mopped the entire house every day to keep the dust away from their food, clothes, bodies, and belongings. Saudi society was a class society where people judged each other on the kind of clothes they wore, the car they drove, and the house they lived in. The more people showed off the better they were in the eyes of others. Classes in society were never mixed. Wealthy people associated with the rich only, never with the middle class, and certainly not with the poor. In Saudi's society servants such as housekeepers and drivers were considered the lowest class and were always treated as such.

Nabila was mostly isolated from society events and entertaining. She was too poor to afford any clothes. To meet women and to associate with them was very costly. It was very important for a Saudi woman to wear luxurious clothes and expensive jewelry. Most of these clothes were worn only once, as women did not wish to be seen twice in the same garment. Posh dressing became a competition between wealthy women. They policed each other as to not repeat the wearing of an ensemble, and gossiped and ridiculed the unfortunate woman who made the fashion faux pax.

Nabila did eventually meet pleasant couples, mostly foreigners working in Saudi Arabia or Saudis with American or British wives. These friends were co-workers with her husband or friends of Margaret and Issa. Away from her in-laws, Nabila was able to entertain and visit Saudis with non-Saudi wives. She began to cultivate friendships with people who were not regulated to the Saudi caste system and did not care about her house or the amount of money she had. Unfortunately, her foreign friends left Jeddah when they finished their work contracts. Only two couples remained that Nabila was close to, her old friends, Issa and Margaret, and Majed and Suzan. Interestingly, both were Saudi men married to Americans. Majed and his wife, Suzan, visited quite often. Majed would drop his wife at Nabila's house and pick her up later in the evening. Many times the couples would come for dinner. Nabila thrived, visiting and entertaining her friends despite the strict anti-social mores of her country.

As Nabila's pregnancy advanced, house cleaning became more difficult. Her feet mushroomed several sizes from standing all day with no time to rest. At Nabila's regular pre-natal check up, the doctor concluded the swelling was due to water retention and a slight increase in blood pressure. Moreover, Nabila's urine test showed an elevation in albumin. The doctor suggested medication for one week to lower Nabila's blood pressure and advised her to rest as much as possible. With no improvement after a week, and since the baby was due soon, the doctor gave Nabila medication to induce labor and told her to return to the hospital when she was ready. He also advised Nabila not to get pregnant again for at least five years. Abdul Rahman was worried and second-guessed the doctor. He did not sleep all night thinking they should have gotten another opinion. Abdul Rahman feared that the medicine Nabila was taking would harm the baby. Nabila tried her best to calm Abdul Rahman and encourage him to sleep.

At five a.m., Nabila was awakened by her first contraction. Since this was her second child, she knew she needed to make haste to the local hospital. When they arrived, they were dismayed at the dirty, dust-ridden hospital and lack of personnel. There was no nurse to greet them, only swarms of mosquitoes. Abdul Rahman searched for someone to help, but could find no one. Nabila's contractions were rapidly getting closer, and she was beginning to panic. A nurse finally appeared to take her to the labor room at about seven o'clock. The room was stark, housing a bed, small table, and void of any machines. Abdul Rahman stayed with Nabila holding her hand, offering encouragement. The doctor arrived sans gloves and a mask and gave instructions to the nurse. For the first time since entering the hospital, Nabila was relieved to think she would get some help and drugs to temper the unbearable pain. The nurse returned with a white sheet to cover the table, a large pot of hot water, but no drugs! The baby came quickly and the doctor placed the crying infant on the table and turned his attention back to Nabila. A few minutes later, the doctor swung his foot around the small table and dragged it toward him to cut the baby's umbilical cord.

The nurse promptly dressed their daughter in clothes Nabila had brought with her, because the hospital did not supply gowns for the infant or the mother. Nabila knew Abdul Rahman had wished for a boy, but he was most relieved that the baby was healthy. He thanked Allah, and went to pray for the health of their daughter who they named Lamia.

Nabila moved to a room on the ward where Lamia stayed with her full time. Abdul Rahman had to buy a net to protect the baby from the uncontrollable mosquitoes. Two days later, the couple thanked Allah again that Nabila and the baby could leave the hospital in good health.

One of the Saudi customs is to celebrate the child's seventh day, called *saboo*, when all the relatives bring presents to the baby and gather for a special dinner. After the meal, the baby's father or any older male member of the family holds the baby and turns to the *qibla*, the direction of the holy Makkah, to recite some verses of the Quran. Then the rest of the family prays for the child. On this day, according to religion, the parents must also sacrifice a sheep to feed the poor.

On Lamia's saboo in April of 1976, after Abdul Rahman went to the neighborhood store to buy the drinks for the party, Majed came by to offer congratulations for the new baby. Innocently, Nabila asked Majed to come in and wait for Abdul Rahman, who would be back soon. Nabila was holding Lamia and Leila was at her side as she greeted Majed. Within minutes, the doorbell rang again. It was Uncle Saleh with his son Adel. He saw the stranger in the house and noticed that Abdul Rahman was not home. Uncle Saleh gave Nabila a dirty look and turned his glare to Majed, who was very embarrassed, and without speaking immediately left. As soon as Abdul Rahman returned home, Nabila pointed out in front of her father-in-law that Majed stopped to congratulate them but did not stay when he discovered Abdul Rahman was not home. It seemed Nabila's father-in-law was forever piling ammunition to use against her. Sadly, Majed and Suzan never socialized with Nabila again. Because of Uncle Saleh's objections, Nabila had lost two close friends.

Later that evening the rest of the relatives came for the celebration, but Uncle Saleh did not stay for the dinner. The men went to the mosque for the last prayer of the day. The women stayed at the house gossiping and soon began to criticize Nabila's life with her husband.

One of her sisters snipped, "You have been married to a Saudi, well-educated man for over five years, and you still live in poverty."

Cousin Mona continued, "You are suffering and tortured between the house work and the kids and you have no life for yourself."

"Look at all of Abdul Rahman's classmates who graduated at the same time," Aunt Amna added. "They all have homes of their own, cars, maids, and good positions in the government."

An elderly cousin advised Nabila, "You ought to talk to Abdul Rahman to find a better job, or do something about this poverty you are living in."

The criticism and comparisons to Abdul Rahman's other colleagues went on until the men returned from their prayers. Nabila had tried to defend Abdul Rahman and their life. Nabila wished to say that her life was no one's business; instead she recounted Abdul Rahman's strong work ethic and how he was doing his best. She tried to make her family understand that all she really wanted was a good man who cared about the girls and her.

Even though Nabila defended Abdul Rahman, she was overwhelmed with two small children, a three-story house to keep clean in a very dusty city, as well as the daily cooking and laundry. Because they had very little, Nabila waded through others' trash cans to claim household items such as dishes, pots, and pans that they had abandoned. Friends sometimes gave Nabila their old clothes to replace her tattered ones. Readymade diapers were not available, so Nabila had made cloth diapers for the baby during her pregnancy. Not only was washing diapers in the old-fashioned wringer washer hard work, but also hanging them to dry was even more difficult with the baby. Nabila had to put Lamia in her crib, then take her seat to the roof, take the baby and fasten her in her seat, climb down the three floors to pick up the laundry, and return to the third floor. The same procedure was repeated to collect the laundry from the clothes' line. Lamia and Nabila were subjected to Jeddah's scorching heat every couple of days just to keep the family in clean clothes.

CHAPTER 12

*O ye who believe! Ye are forbidden to inherit Women against their
will. Nor should ye treat them With harshness.*

~ AL NESSA 19

On their next visit, Issa and Margaret announced that they had
received a scholarship to England for two years. Nabila was thrilled
for Margaret because she knew Margaret needed to leave the Saudi lifestyle
at least for a while. Nabila could not help wishing that Abdul Rahman
could secure the same scholarship and they could go as well. Issa suggested
Abdul Rahman apply for another scholarship if he was interested. Issa
encouraged Abdul Rahman, telling him that he had all the qualifications
to be accepted. However, Abdul Rahman declined and indicated that if
a scholarship were sought, it would be for Nabila. Her devoted husband
knew how tired she was and how much she needed a break from her present routine.

A year had passed since baby Lamia's birthday, and the couple's money
situation was getting worse. They still could not afford a car. Leila, their
older daughter, turned six that summer and was to begin school. There
was not a school close enough to their apartment where Leila could walk.
Abdul Rahman had to buy a bicycle to take his daughter to school every
day. Nabila received even more disapproval from the relatives.

"No Saudi man uses a bicycle in this country," a sister said.

"Abdul Rahman is giving himself a bad reputation among his relatives
and his colleagues," commented one of the cousins.

"Doesn't he know anything about life in Saudi Arabia?" asked Salem,
another cousin.

Nabila's younger brother suggested that Abdul Rahman should
apply for one of the assignments that the government was offering to all

employees who wanted to make extra money. Abdul Rahman could work in Riyadh or another part of the country for a week or so, and he would earn a month's salary for that short time period. He could also go abroad to Europe or America, and he could make twice his monthly salary plus compensation for accommodations and living expenses. The idea sounded fantastic. Nabila was perplexed as to why her husband did not know about this. Surely, Abdul Rahman would rejoice to learn of such a terrific opportunity. She eagerly approached Abdul Rahman about the job prospects. To her surprise, Abdul Rahman knew about the work. In fact, he had refused an offer to work in Vienna for two weeks. Nabila was upset and disappointed but most of all confused. Why had he not accepted?

"I didn't accept because they won't give you and the girls tickets to go with me," Abdul Rahman said with disappointment.

Nabila did not understand why they had to go with him.

"Do you think I will go anywhere in this world without you and the girls?" he reasoned. "If they want to send me anywhere in the country or outside the country, I will go on one condition: that you and the girls go with me."

Abdul Rahman angrily added, "I will not go alone. That is final."

Nabila could not say another word. She wanted to try to convince Abdul Rahman that he should go to earn more money, but she knew he would not accept any discussion from his wife. The subject was closed, sealed as tight as a coffin.

Nabila had few pleasant distractions so when her next-door neighbor, Isha, appeared at the door, Nabila was surprised but genuinely eager to welcome her. Isha explained that she was having the neighbors over for dinner and wished that Nabila would join them. Isha earnestly tried to persuade Nabila to forgo her isolation and to socialize with Saudi women. She insisted that Nabila attend her party at eight o'clock that evening and dinner at nine. Nabila thought of refusing the invitation, as she had only one dowdy flowered dress with scuffed shoes that her sister had given her when Lamia was born. Nabila was self-conscious, wondering if her outfit would appear out of style to the other guests.

Nabila arrived promptly at the party at 8 p.m., eager to make a good impression. It was her first visit to any Saudi house outside of her relatives.

The hostess met Nabila at the door, took her abaya and tarha, and hung it on the guest hanger by the entrance. The apartment looked luxurious with expensive furnishings. The smell of bakhor (exotic burning incense) permeated the air. Like any other guest, Nabila stopped by the mirror in the foyer to fix her hair before she met the rest of the ladies. On the mirror was a comb and a wood-carved hairbrush for the guests' use. As Nabila entered the main room, all the women stood in respect for the incoming guest. Following the custom, Nabila moved from right to left greeting each guest with a kiss on both cheeks. Then she settled in to the nearest chair.

The room was unnervingly quiet as each of the guests stared at each other without benefit of introductions. Other women arrived at about eleven o'clock and the ladies in the room stood for each woman to greet them with a kiss and greet them. Then they all were seated again and stared silently. Each one of these women was clad in a fancy and undoubtedly expensive evening dress with matching shoes and bag. They accessorized their beautiful dresses with sparkling gold and diamond jewelry.

The hostess finally came in carrying cardamom Arabic coffee and delicate coffee cups. Two young girls were following behind her carrying two enormous, beautifully decorated trays. One of the trays was full of dates stuffed with nuts, and the other contained chocolates and candies. The hostess used her right hand to hold the cups and the left hand to pour the coffee, because it was impolite to serve anything with the left hand. Isha served the coffee to the ladies one by one, starting at the right side of the room and continuing left until all were served. After serving the coffee, she sat next to Nabila. Isha asked Nabila if she knew any of the women. When Nabila answered no, she started pointing at each of them reciting their names, their husbands' names, their positions in their jobs, if they were poor or rich, the houses they lived in, and other pertinent information. Shyly, Nabila asked if she arrived too early for the party because the rest of the guests did not come until about ten o'clock. Isha indicated that people are never on time in Saudi Arabia and are usually two or three hours late. Meanwhile, other guests arrived, filling the chairs, leaving others no recourse but to sit on the floor.

As if a silent chime had sounded, everyone started talking and laughing with high-pitched voices. The women all chattered at once and it was difficult to discern who could possibly be listening. One of the guests requested a cassette player. She turned the music on, tightened a scarf around her waist, and started to belly dance. The other ladies were cheering and clapping their hands with the beat. Suddenly, one of the guests stormed to the cassette player, abruptly stopping the music.

"Harram, harram," she said disapprovingly. "Music is a sin." She expounded on the virtues of the Islamic religion, explaining that music can lead people to commit sins; therefore, they should never listen to music.

A minute later, the hostess came in and called the disgruntled guest to the other room.

"If she doesn't like to join us, she shouldn't be here," said the belly dancer.

"Yes, she should be with a group of her type," quipped another guest.

The room was completely silent when the religious woman came back to excuse herself to leave. Soon after she exited, the belly dancer reaffixed the scarf on her waist and returned to her festive dance. Other women joined her, forming a rumbling circle. The rhythmic dancing continued until after midnight when the hostess called for dinner.

The meal was served in the traditional way. A long piece of cloth was spread across the floor and served as a table for the serving dishes and spoons. There were two large dishes of whole roasted lambs served on a bed of rice, several kinds of stuffed dough, small plates of salads, and some fruit for dessert. The women gathered around the meal on the floor. Most of the guests used their hands, eating from the main serving bowl. As soon as the meal was over the women asked for their abayas and returned to their homes.

Nabila had just experienced the most typical social event for most women in Saudi Arabia. Men and women almost never mixed in the culture, dividing society into two groups. Men had their own jobs and social life and women had theirs. Schools were separated by gender from the first grade up to the university. In addition, the rich almost never associated with poor and native Saudis almost never associated with foreigners. Even some Saudis from the western region of the country were prejudiced socially against Saudis from the eastern region.

CHAPTER 13

*Allah enjoins you to treat women well, for they are your mothers,
daughters, your wife, aunts.*

~ AL SAHIH

Abdul Rahman surprised Nabila one afternoon saying the ministry
was offering a post-graduate scholarship for engineers and he was
considering applying for it.

"I know how much you wish to go back to America," he said. Then he
added, "I am doing this for you because I want you to be happy."

Nabila was elated and the possible move consumed her thoughts. All
their discussions centered on going to America, how long they would stay,
and the girls and their education.

Abdul Rahman applied for the scholarship, and he waited anxiously
for acceptance. Months dragged by and there was still no word. Abdul
Rahman ceased to believe that there was any hope of him securing the
grant. He strongly believed that his request for the scholarship had been
rejected, and he was sorely disappointed. But unlike her husband, Nabila
did not give up hope. She understood that government routines could
be agonizingly lengthy. While waiting for the pending papers, Nabila
spent most of her time daydreaming about leaving Jeddah and returning
to America. Nabila was positive that this scholarship would be just what
Abdul Rahman needed to gain his doctorate degree and land a better job.
If only he could be selected for the award, they could live a much better life.

Months multiplied into years and there was still no news about the
scholarship. Nabila's once vivid dream of returning to America dimmed
with each season. Her disappointment faded to thankful contentment for
their family. Leila was in the second grade doing well in school and content
with her friendships and baby Lamia had grown to a toddler of three years.

An unscheduled visit from Nabila's brother-in-law brought more than just the joyfulness of connecting with family. He carried a newspaper detailing the surprising news that Abdul Rahman was one of several employees chosen for a scholarship to the United States for the coming fall. Nabila was overwhelmed with happiness, as well as doubts. They had waited for the scholarship for years, but the timing was not ideal. It would be very difficult to remove Leila from her beloved Arabic school and enroll her in a school that required her to learn a different language and culture. Nabila did not want to adversely affect Leila's future in any way. Leila would receive a good education in the United States once she adapted, but presently she was excelling. It took weeks of deliberation but Nabila was optimistic about the final decision to go to America.

Leila was not happy about the idea of leaving her friends and her school. It became a daily topic of discussion as Nabila tried to explain the advantages of life in the United States. She wanted Leila to understand that she could always make new friends. Nabila longed to return to the small college town that had been the first home for her and Abdul Rahman as a couple. It was the place of so many cheerful events for them—their first home as a married couple, the city of their first child's birth, and the home of their long time friends, Issa and Margaret.

Even the scuffles between the girls could not dampen Nabila's good humor. Leila had always been a well-behaved child with a good sense of responsibility for her schoolwork and chores at home. In spite of her young age, she was a great help to her mother. Nabila was able to depend on her to look after her sister, and Leila eagerly helped cook and clean the large apartment. She excelled in school, often earning rewards for being an outstanding student. Leila was reserved, calm, and smart, taking her schooling seriously. She knew how to set her daily schedule to study as well as have fun.

Lamia, on the other hand, was always annoying Leila and was jealous of her. Although they were almost three years apart, Lamia tried to emulate her sister, doing whatever Leila did. Sometimes she went as far as destroying Leila's schoolwork because she could not compete with her older sister. When Leila received a school reward certificate with a beautiful purple ribbon, three-year-old Lamia grabbed it from her sister and ripped off the ribbon.

After six years of weathering the inflexible, harsh life in Saudi Arabia, Nabila was going back to America. She had more than rosy dreams to cling to; she had a promising future, a chance to reclaim her sense of purpose.

Saad and his Egyptian wife, Soso, came from Makkah to say good-bye to Nabila and Abdul Rahman. Soso actually came to claim any items Nabila might leave behind in the move. Since Soso's children were a couple of years younger than Nabila's, Soso intended to help herself to clothing that might fit her children. Even though Nabila did not have anything of great value in her house, Soso continued to search for items that she might desire. Nabila was annoyed but she did not let Soso dampen her high spirits for the move.

The children barely slept the night before in anticipation of the trip. Leila could not make up her mind as to what to wear on the plane and what to take. She spent the night packing and repacking her tiny carrying case with almost all her belongings. Nabila could not convince her to take out a few things and put the rest in the larger suitcase. She guessed Leila was trying to keep everything dear to her close in her own little bag. Nabila was restless as well, excited and optimistic about the trip, yet very worried about the girls and the cultural shock that they'd face. She prayed that night to Allah for an easy transition and for support and help for her dear husband to accomplish his assignment in the United States. Nabila had fantasized about this move for so long; she could not fathom that her dream could be any less than she had envisioned.

CHAPTER 14

Abu Hurairah (May Allah be pleased with him) reported: The
Messenger of Allah (peace be upon him) said, "Allah makes the
way to Jannah (Paradise) easy for him who treads the path in
search of knowledge."

~ MUSLIM

As Nabila had changed in those six years, so had the town. She was no longer the only Saudi in Alexandria. Many Arabs had now come to study at the university. Nabila need not have worried about the transition to the American way of life. The girls readily embraced the culture rich in limitless opportunities for youngsters. Nabila admitted to being ambitious especially for her two daughters. Like most parents, she wanted to give them the chance to have everything that she was not able to have as child. She enrolled them in as many after school activities that they could afford. In spite of the initial language difficulty, Leila was not averse to participating in the abundant activities. The two girls enjoyed baton twirling; cheerleading, tap dancing, and ballet.

Boys have the privilege of learning and practicing sports in Saudi schools. Sports were believed to be too strenuous for girls to participate so they were unavailable for females. Many Saudis forbid both boys and girls from listening to music or playing an instrument. So these two subjects were not taught to girls in Saudi schools. Leila began to show interest in activities that were previously restricted, and music and gymnastics became her favorite hobbies.

Nabila and Abdul Rahman lived on campus close to the football stadium. During football season, the marching band practiced in the late afternoon. As soon as Leila would hear their first chords, she would scramble to the sidelines to imitate the baton twirlers. Once one of the baton twirlers stopped to admire Leila and encourage her to continue practicing. Leila reveled in the recognition and soon began to practice at least an hour a day. Abdul Rahman often argued with Nabila because he believed the activities were useless, since they would not help the girls in their culture. Nabila could not convince Abdul Rahman that the girls should participate in all kinds of activities, and that what they learned now might not be immediately useful but could be quite valuable in the future. Nabila had no inkling then that this would be true for her as well.

Leila shared her grandfather's love for the violin and learning to play became her favorite hobby. They rented a violin and coped with her shrill and off key practices. However, by fifth grade, Leila had improved and joined the children's concert in her school. Nabila beamed with pride sitting in the theater listening to her daughter playing the violin, a chance that she would never have had in Saudi Arabia.

Lamia joined the four-year-olds at the university-operated nursery school. She argued vehemently against missing a day of pre-school, as she considered herself a student as well. With the other family members content in school, Nabila contemplated having a baby before she left the states. Abdul Rahman, though, was against the idea. Nabila tried to convince him, but there was no way to change his mind. She could not understand why he disapproved; perhaps he was still worried about the doctor's warning when Lamia was born. Without telling Abdul Rahman, Nabila made an appointment with a gynecologist. To her relief, the doctor told her she was healthy and young enough to have as many children as she wished. But Abdul Rahman did not want to have children while he was still in school. He promised Nabila that when they returned to Jeddah, he would consider the idea of more children.

That month, Nabila's period was late. Since she had always had a regular cycle, she hoped that she was pregnant, but she did not know if she should tell Abdul Rahman what she suspected. After ten days, Nabila was bubbling over with anticipation of being pregnant and told her husband the news. To her surprise, he was excited, often calling her in between his classes to be sure she was all right. It appeared that Abdul Rahman would not plan to have a child but if it happened by Allah's will, he was pleased.

Plan or no plan, they were both disappointed when Nabila got her period a couple of days later.

Since having a child was not to be before they returned to their country, Nabila decided to pursue her educational aspirations. She applied as a teacher aide at the university nursery school. Nabila was not sure if Abdul Rahman would support her plan but he liked the idea that she would be with Lamia in the same school. Nabila worked hard and overtime whenever possible. She also found another job in a nearby school taking care of children while their parents were on service Sunday mornings. She saved every penny to better their lifestyle when they returned to Jeddah.

Part of Nabila's plan was to finish her education while she worked. She received approval to continue her education on her husband's scholarship. Abdul Rahman thought Nabila would quit her jobs in order to have time for the family and school; however, she was able to convince him she could do both. Abdul Rahman was cooperative, scheduling his classes so that he would be home when the girls returned from school. Nabila made it home by five to prepare dinner and then hurried to her classes from six to ten each evening. Studying, taking care of the family, and working two jobs was impossible to handle, so reluctantly she dropped the Sunday job to have time to study.

Abdul Rahman and Nabila received letters regularly from both families. Uncle Saleh sent a letter to Abdul Rahman telling him that he had sent Mansour to Egypt to prepare for his education. Uncle Saleh wanted Abdul Rahman to help Mansour financially because Mansour, who was in high school, intended to attend medical school in Cairo. *How could they help Mansour with money when they needed the help?* But Abdul Rahman, like any other Saudi, would not refuse any of his father's requests. He began to send money to Mansour on a monthly basis. The money Abdul Rahman sent to Mansour adversely affected their budget, and Nabila had to use her savings to help keep them afloat.

For two years Abdul Rahman faithfully continued to send Mansour an allowance from their meager bank account. Nabila could not discourage her husband from sending money to Mansour when their family really needed it.

Abdul Rahman was about to finish his master's degree and complete his graduate project. Sadly, Nabila would be leaving the United States and everything she loved. Many Saudis, who were on the same scholarship as Abdul Rahman, chose not to leave to give their children a better education and they were never asked to return to their country nor had to face any kind of penalty. Abdul Rahman, however, was a stickler about rules. He would not take a chance that might put him in any trouble. Since the Saudi government had sent him on a scholarship, he felt obligated to go back to work for them, even though the Saudi government did not specify such a rule for scholarships.

Nabila tried to explain to the girls about going back to Saudi Arabia. It was hard for them to understand that America was not their country and that eventually they would have to leave. The girls often voiced their desire to stay in school with their friends and continue with all the activities they loved. Even though they were children, they loved the U.S. and were adamant about not wanting to leave. Their talk broke Nabila's heart as she, too, felt the pain of leaving. She realized the hard time they would face readjusting to a completely different and strict culture. Even though she tried to convince the girls that they were going to be fine, and pointed out the positive points of living in Saudi Arabia, Nabila felt she needed someone to convince her. She was determined to make the best of what they had to make her family prosper. Nabila wished she had enough time to get a degree to be able to teach in Jeddah. Teaching was not her ideal career choice, but it was one of the few jobs for women, besides being a doctor or a nurse.

With only one semester left to graduate, Abdul Rahman was spending more hours on his studies to finish his engineering project, though he kept his schedule to come home for dinner with his family. A few weeks before his graduation, Abdul Rahman informed Nabila that his professor rejected his project; therefore, he would not be able to graduate for another year. Nabila felt sorry for her husband, but secretly thrilled that she could stay for another year to take a few courses and earn more money. Nabila worked hard attending two summer schools and completed her degree in 1984.

All too soon, the day of departure arrived, and leaving friends was difficult. Lamia was crushed having to leave her pet parakeet that she had received from one of her friends on her sixth birthday. It was a well-trained bird that would sit on the dining table and eat from her plate. Lamia would throw a penny on the floor and he would pick it up and bring it to her. Lamia was very attached to the bird.

Lamia could not be consoled. A woman who adopted the bird for her son gave Lamia a hug and said she'd keep the bird safe. Lamia ran to her room and locked the door. Nabila could hear her sobbing.

When Nabila called to her to open the door, she screamed, "Go away; I do not want to go back to Saudi Arabia. You are forcing us. Why does it always have to be your choice?"

In an attempt to console them, Abdul Rahman and Nabila sat with the girls and discussed their return to their homeland. Abdul Rahman assured them that as soon as he could afford it, they would come for summer vacation and maybe again for college. Just like the girls, Nabila desperately clung to the promise of returning to the U.S.

CHAPTER 15

Prophet Muhammad (PBUH) advised Muslims to go forth and marry bearing children, and they will be praised come judgment day.

Leila would not part with her violin during the flight to Jeddah. She slouched in the airplane seat resting her head on the instrument. Both girls looked forlorn, occasionally whispering to each other. Nabila was devastated at their sadness and lack of enthusiasm for returning to their home. She wondered if she did them more harm than good by bringing them to the U.S. for a short time. If the girls had never been outside their country, they probably would have been much happier, but Nabila rationalized that traveling was an educational experience, especially for children, and hoped that it would not take the girls long to adjust.

The family arrived in Jeddah in January to pleasant temperatures. Nabila's youngest brother met them at the airport. During the car ride, Nabila noticed that construction had rendered the city in disarray with grooved and unpaved streets. Tall buildings appeared as skeletons, not yet finished. There were barren plots of scraped earth readied for future building while emerald trees lined the few new streets.

They had returned to Saudi Arabia at one of its most unsettled periods in history. The booming oil interest had summoned many investors from around the world to Jeddah. The rapid growth made renting any type of accommodation impossible to find or competitive to secure. Houses and landowners were primarily renting to foreign and international companies working in Saudi Arabia. Since telephones were still a luxury they could not afford, Abdul Rahman had to look for an apartment on foot. He spent several hours every day going from one street to another, building to building, asking for availability of any sort of family space to rent. There were many unoccupied buildings, but the property owners refused to rent to individuals, as they wanted to rent their properties to international companies for far more money. With no other choice, the family moved to one room in Rahma's three-bedroom apartment. The other two rooms were divided between Nabila's sisters and brothers. Rahma occupied a small space in her daughters' room and Jada went to stay with Saad in Makkah.

Besides the difficulty of finding an apartment, Nabila had to consider schooling for her children. Saudi schools would not accept student registration at the beginning of the second semester; therefore, it was not possible to find a school for the girls. A director of one of the girls' schools advised them to skip that year and to start at the beginning of the new school year. Neither Abdul Rahman nor Nabila wanted the girls to sacrifice the remainder of the school year. Nabila's sister, who was at the time a schoolteacher, was able to get Leila into one of the public schools in a primitive part of the city.

The school was not a good match for Leila who, once an enthusiastic star student, became depressed and distraught. She came home every day with tales about her classmates' disruptive behavior. In addition, the students made fun of her Arabic and tried to disgrace her for being of a higher class. Even the teacher did not understand that Leila's education was in English and that she should give her time to learn Arabic. The teacher continued to punish Leila for every mistake she made by striking her hand with a ruler or two. One day Leila came home covered with dust. She explained that the home economics teacher asked her to clean a long deserted room in the school as part of her curriculum. Leila couldn't even find solace in her music. In spite of Nabila's sisters' fascination with Leila's talents, the violin was soon stored away and became only a memory. Leila never tried to play again.

Nabila believed that her daughter had lost interest in all the things she once loved. Her violin was buried in the closet and her baton abandoned. Life in Jeddah appeared meaningless to her.

Leila repeatedly said, "One day I will return to America; you will see." She became obsessed with the idea of going back to the U.S.

Lamia was spared the humiliation that Leila suffered, as she did not go to school that semester. Instead, she stayed at home and worked to improve her Arabic.

They had intended to stay only a few days at Rahma's place but it was five months before Abdul Rahman finally secured a rental in the southern part of the city. The building was still under construction, but because it was not in a desirable area, the landlord decided to rent it to families. When they moved to the new apartment, it did not have kitchen cabinets, a kitchen sink, or any closets. The rental had four-square walls with a light bulb dangling from the center of the ceiling of each of the five rooms. They were only able to buy the very basics—a stove and small table for the kitchen. For the living room, they purchased a sofa, a piece of rug and sponge mattresses to sleep on the floor. The amount of money Nabila had saved in the past three years barely covered necessities, but Nabila was content to have privacy and just be with her husband and daughters.

Summer arrived and Leila transitioned from the torture of school to the boredom of home. As young girls, there was nothing for them to do outside the home except visit family. Television was the only entertainment in Saudi Arabia. It only broadcast for four hours a day, mostly local programming of city news and some cartoons. At first, no women were permitted to be shown on Saudi TV, not even on shows. Eventually, Egyptian women, conservative in actions and dress, appeared in the daily soap opera series. The show broadcast only thirty minutes a day. Old American shows and movies were rarely shown on Saudi TV, as all the love scenes and women with short dresses were censored. Often Nabila watched an entire movie, speculating as to the movie plot because the story was built on a love scene that was cut out at the beginning of the movie.

After some time, eight-track tapes were available; however, it was too expensive for their budget, and the tapes were very limited and censored. Even pictures of women on the tapes' covers were marred with black ink. It was hard to believe that some men were actually hired to search the newspapers, magazines, books, videos tapes, and even cassettes to ink out pictures of women to uphold the religious society's convictions.

Since they had returned to Jeddah, Nabila's time had been absorbed caring for the house and family. She truly wanted another child and often tried to broach the subject with Abdul Rahman. Nabila was almost twenty-seven and her youngest daughter was seven-years-old. The time seemed right and besides Abdul Rahman had promised that they could expand their family once they returned to Jeddah. Nabila was determined to have another child and did her best to convince Abdul Rahman that they should make this their plan. He was busy with his new job and had to work hard to get a promotion; he had no time for the responsibility of another child. He explained that since the girls were older, life was calm and quiet and having a baby could be a hardship for both of them. Nabila still wished to have a son. Because life in Saudi Arabia is not easy for a woman, having a son provides future protection for the family.

Nabila reasoned, "Not only for us, but think of yourself, Abdul Rahman, and think of the girls. Wouldn't you like to have a son to carry your name and to look after you in your later life? We are three women and life can be very cruel to us. May Allah give you good health and long life, but we should plan for our future and the only security in this country is to have a son."

Abdul Rahman was unmoved. He stared at Nabila. "Well, can you guarantee me a son?"

Stunned, Nabila did not expect this from a man who was educated and too religious to utter such a question. Nabila stared at him, her husband, this stranger. She finally appealed to his religious heart.

"Don't you believe in Allah and the Quran?" she asked. "Allah said that He gives couples girls, He gives others boys, and some couples may have no children."

Abdul Rahman's eyes never left the floor. "Well, I am one of those whom Allah wanted to give only girls."

His voice reeked with disappointment as he added, "I have tried two times so far, and I'm not going to try for a third daughter."

Nabila was crushed that Abdul Rahman did not really want any more children. Through a torrent of tears, she pleaded with him to reconsider.

Abdul Rahman sternly cut her off. "I want you to stop this discussion right now!" He stormed toward the door.

Abdul Rahman's final reproach terminated any hope Nabila had of having another child.

"I want no more talk about this subject ever again. Do you understand?" With that edict, Abdul Rahman exited the room.

Nabila was heartbroken and Abdul Rahman was so angry that they did not speak for days. The silence was broken when Abdul Rahman returned from work to inquire if Nabila would like to have a job as an interpreter in one of the best government hospitals. He explained that there was a new government hospital with American and British doctors, and they were looking for interpreters to work as part of their team. Depressed for days because of their past conversation, Nabila was delighted for a new focus. She felt as if someone were freeing her from a locked cage. To get out of the house, to see people, and to have a social life, especially with Americans, would be such a treat.

Nabila had thought of going back to school, but with no transportation and the university about fifty kilometers from their house, she did not have much hope of continuing her studies. Money was tight and the girls soon would be in school, so having a job was a good solution. Traditionally, teaching, practicing medicine (which was limited to gynecology and pediatrics), and nursing were the only jobs approved by the government and accepted by society. Even nursing jobs were rejected by most of the Saudi families because of contact with male patients. New jobs were available during this time as hospitals recruited women who were bilingual to work as interpreters to help American and non-Arabic speaking doctors.

An American middle-aged head nurse who seemed very friendly interviewed Nabila for the hospital job. She asked Nabila a few questions, testing her English-speaking ability as well as her writing and comprehension. The head nurse was impressed with Nabila's responses, and Nabila knew she had clinched the position when the nurse smiled and remarked, "Welcome to trying to read the doctors' handwriting."

Nabila worked from eight o'clock in the morning to five in the afternoon. Because she did not have transportation, she had to take the hospital bus at 6:30 a.m. and did not make it home until about seven in the evening. Since she lived in the southern part of the city, and the hospital was located at the northern part, Nabila was the first on board and the last to be dropped off the bus.

With only certain jobs approved for women, the female interpreters were categorized as nursing aids. The title was hardly appropriate, as the interpreters had nothing to do with nursing duties. Their job was only to interpret what the patients said to the doctors and explain what the patients did not understand. Nabila could not quibble over a job title, as she desperately needed the money to help pay for her daughters' private school tuition.

At that time, there was only one private school in Jeddah. The school was too crowded, and they rejected the application for Nabila's daughters to attend. Abdul Rahman was determined that the girls would attend the school no matter who he needed to contact or what favors he had to procure. Somehow, he managed to get the children in the private school, but the director of the school wanted Lamia in second grade because the first grade was too full to add an extra student. Her parents were against the idea, because Lamia had just turned six-years-old and did not speak much Arabic, which might make her feel inferior to the other girls in her class. Abdul Rahman and Nabila dug their heels in and the director finally relented, placing Lamia at the correct grade level.

Working in the hospital changed many of Nabila's negative thoughts about living in Saudi Arabia. The people she worked with were American and British doctors, British nurses, and most of the other staff were non-Saudis as well. Only the interpreters were Saudi who were educated abroad and came from high-middle class families. Nabila was relieved that a veil and abaya were not part of the hospital dress code, and her hair need not be covered.

The best perk was the hospital recreation facility for all the employees and their families. Nabila was able to watch uncensored movies and American TV shows, enjoy swimming and picnicking with western people. Each interpreter was assigned to a certain doctor or area. Often, they had to rotate to get to know the numerous doctors and tasks. During free time, they would volunteer at the reception desk, setting appointments and directing the patients to different departments.

At the hospital, she met people from different walks of life. She met a few Bedouin patients (Arabs who live in the desert areas from the Western Sahara to the Arabian Peninsula). Long ago Bedouins were tribes of nomads, continually moving to find water and food.[1] The Bedouins are simple people, preferring the floor to a bed and using their hands to eat instead of silverware. Nabila thought they must never be lonely as they had large families and one or two family members were with them day and night. Late in the evening after prayers, the Bedouins could be found huddled around a sheet of food spread across the floor. Nurses would squabble with them to wash their hands at the hospital, but the tribe members were conservative with water, using it mostly for prayer rituals. They presented no real problems for the hospital.

In spite of the freedom Nabila had within the hospital as a Saudi woman, she had to face two different forces of people, those who encouraged her for daring to take a job not accepted by society and those who attacked her for working with members not of her gender. The latter did not afford her any respect. Each day many cursed, insulted, and scorned her. Nabila often had patients who refused her help and would rudely demand a male interpreter. Once when the doctor and Nabila were on their way to the ward a Saudi patient asked the doctor for some information concerning his medication. He started talking to the doctor in Arabic and Nabila turned to the doctor prepared to translate.

The patient shouted, "Shut up! I do not need your help. I can get the best male interpreter in this country to help me."

The doctor nodded at Nabila to leave. Nabila never became desensitized to the disrespect to women, and it usually reduced her to tears.

Some of the patients did not trust her interpretation, as they did not think she was interpreting their messages faithfully. One of her toughest critics was a middle-aged patient with a heart condition. He explained his symptoms, and Nabila interpreted them to the doctor. The patient hounded her to tell the doctor word for word what he had said. Nabila eventually asked the doctor to assure the patient that he was receiving the complete summary of his symptoms.

Countless women came to the hospital with injuries because of their husbands abusing them. Many had broken bones, black eyes, or body bruises. One evening Nabila met a young woman in the lobby balancing one child on her hip and holding another child's hand. The young mother had many bruises on her face that could not hide her misery. Her husband walked nearby showing no interest in helping with the children. In the doctor's office, the woman broke down with a river of tears. She pulled the shoulder of her dress down to reveal more bruises on her upper arm and shoulder. She said the beating was the outcome of an argument with her husband. He worked for the airlines and was frequently traveling outside the country. In spite of the fact that the airline provided her with free tickets, her husband refused to take her with him. She added he had not spent a single weekend with her and the children. Nabila surmised that traveling with small children was not easy, and perhaps that was why her husband was reluctant to travel together. But the woman replied that the children were not the reason, because she could leave the children with her mother for a weekend or more. The present fight erupted because she desperately stole his passport and hid it to prevent him from traveling. Dressed in western clothes, her husband looked very gentle. He did not look like a religious fanatic or seemed particularly prejudiced against women. He was easy to approach, and Nabila politely inquired if traveling was part of his job. He shook his head in denial and instead explained that he loved to travel to have fun. Nabila hoped to make him feel some sympathy for his wife, so she suggested that since he had free tickets, he could take his wife with him on a short trip. Certainly, she deserved to have a good time, too.

He silenced Nabila with his response, "Would you go in to the best restaurant carrying a sandwich in your hand?"

His wife reacted to the insult clutching her baby and leaving the office without a word. "La ellah ila Allah," sighed the husband. He grabbed his older child and they left the hospital without seeing the doctor.

Another incident, which Nabila could not clear from her mind, involved a middle-aged woman who was following up with her doctor. The doctor inquired if the couple had any children. They had eight children, *Alhamd llah, thanks to God*. The doctor told the husband that his wife had a disease that prevented her from having any more children. Surprisingly, the husband did not ask what was wrong with his wife.

Instead, his only response was, "No problem; I'll just get another wife."

The woman's deep hurt bubbled from every pore, and she retreated as if her sorrow was the disease.

Personal relationships between hospital workers were understandable since male and females working together was a new concept for Saudi society. One of the notorious love stories in the hospital was between Alia, a doctor's assistant, and an older doctor. Alia was always in the doctor's room with the door closed, whether they had patients or not. The western doctor was thirty years her senior, married with children who were older than Alia. Alia carried cakes and desserts to the office with her every morning. When Nabila looked for Alia to help her with a patient she discovered Alia and the doctor in his office dining by candle light. The scandal spread throughout the hospital.

One day, Nabila heard screaming and crying coming from the doctor's office. She found Alia with a man in his late twenties who was shouting, cursing, and insulting Alia. He was slapping and kicking her. The angry young man would not listen to Alia's pleas. The male workers in the hospital tried unsuccessfully to intervene, to stop him from hitting Alia. The hospital authorities called to restrain him and escorted the man to the administration office. Nabila tried to calm Alia who was bleeding from the corner of her mouth. Nabila asked about the identity of the young man, but Alia refused to say anything. Alia continued crying, burying her face in her arms. Nabila went back to work, knowing nothing about the man or his reason for attacking Alia. About an hour later, the angry young man came back and pulled Alia from the hospital. Eventually, Nabila learned that the assailant was Alia's brother. She did not return to work that day; in fact, Nabila never saw Alia again.

Even Nabila was not immune from Cupid's misguided arrow. She received an anonymous telephone call where the caller expressed his admiration and professed his love. He said he was so much in love with Nabila that he could not sleep at night. He thought the only solution for his problem was to marry her. He wanted to meet Nabila's parents to propose. When Nabila told him she was already married, he dismissed her response believing all the girls say that when they want to reject a man politely. He told Nabila that he was a very good man and that she should try to give him a chance by accepting him as a future husband. He ended the phone conversation by telling Nabila that he was going to find out if she was married. Thankfully, Nabila did not hear from him again.

Another incident occurred with a young man who always accompanied his mother to the hospital. She was an elderly woman with a thyroid condition. She was always happy to see Nabila but she talked so much that Nabila dubbed her, "the lady with oral diarrhea." Because of her excessive talk, Nabila learned everything about the woman's family life. While the three of them were waiting for the doctor, she started her usual talk about her life and her children and then pointed to her son. "See this son of mine; he is so much in love with you."

The son tried hard to stop his mother's ramblings.

Mercilessly, she went on and on expressing her son's feelings toward Nabila. "All he talks about at home is you. I am telling you this man is deeply in love with you."

Nabila tried to squelch the conversation saying she was already married and a mother of two daughters.

The son continued to try to silence his mother. "Mother, she is telling you she is married. Mother, please."

The mother still would not stop.

He had to shout, "Mother, stop it now."

Nabila escaped, telling them she would be back with the doctor. As she walked out of the office, he followed her, asking for the truth about her marital status. He asked Nabila's age, because she looked too young to be married with two children. Saudi men choose to believe what they want, not trusting a woman's response.

Each day, Nabila returned home exhausted, wishing to go directly to bed, but there was so much to do at home. She had to vacuum daily and cook dinner and prepare the next day's lunch for Abdul Rahman and the girls. Abdul Rahman was like any average Saudi man; he had nothing to do with housework or cooking. Laundry, ironing, cleaning, and storing groceries filled Nabila's weekends. At the end of every month, Nabila handed over her salary to her husband to help with living expenses.

When Uncle Saleh visited unexpectedly, Nabila sensed that he was not coming only for a visit but for a reason of his own. During lunch, Abdul Rahman asked about the family in Makkah and about Mansour's progress at school in Cairo. At the mention of Mansour, Uncle Saleh launched into an argument that Mansour should have a condominium, so he would not have to worry about paying the monthly rent and could concentrate on his studying. Nabila had suspected he was coming to ask for more money for Mansour. They were barely able to pay their own rent, and now Uncle Saleh wanted them to buy a condominium for Mansour. Nabila waited to hear Abdul Rahman's reply to such an outrageous request.

"Well, I will discuss the matter with my brother Adel. In Shaa Allah, it will be okay," answered Abdul Rahman.

Nabila was angry, but kept quiet. Later that day, she asked Abdul Rahman if he was going to buy the condominium for Mansour in Cairo.

"What else can I do? Adel will help, too," he answered.

Nabila looked at him with frustration. "But where would we get that amount of money? I know your brother has the same financial situation as we do."

Nabila could not stop Abdul Rahman from securing a five-year mortgage and supporting Mansour from their combined savings.

At least Nabila was successful in her job at the hospital; she received a promotion as the head of the interpreters. Her salary doubled with her appointment to work with the internal medicine and cardiac departments. The morning rounds with the doctors had taught her a lot about medicine. She became involved professionally as well as emotionally with seriously ill and terminal patients. A favorite of Nabila's was a burn victim, three-year-old Zainab. She badly burned her arms and hands playing with matches in bed. Changing the dressing was torture for her as the cloth stuck to both of her tightly wrapped arms. Zainab hated the doctors, as they were responsible for changing her bandages. Any person in a white coat would make her scream and run to Nabila for protection. Zainab would beg Nabila to spare her from the doctors, not understanding they were trying to restore her health.

A forty-year-old man admitted to the hospital for heart failure required much of Nabila's attention. During the rounds, he would beg Nabila to translate his complaints to the doctors word by word. Because the doctors continued their discussions, they did not give him enough attention. Nabila made certain to give his message to the doctors. She met his daughter who spent many hours with him every day and she visited the patient on a daily basis during the weeks of his hospitalization. The last time Nabila saw him, he was excited to be leaving the hospital the following day, but when she stopped in to say farewell before he left the hospital, he was not in his room. Nabila was glad he was able to go home, even though she missed saying good-bye, and was distressed to learn that he hadn't gone home but had died earlier that morning.

Nabila enjoyed her job at the hospital; however, watching people suffering was not easy. She witnessed many deaths and families' agony at the loss of their loved ones. On too many nights, the rerun of those moments played in her head, thwarting sleep.

The sad situations at work made Nabila thankful for her relationship with her daughter, Leila. Being only sixteen years apart, they were more like sisters or friends. They talked about everything. Leila had never kept a secret from Nabila and asked her opinion on very delicate matters. Nabila was very proud of Leila, and all their relatives and friends loved her. Many mothers wished to have a daughter like Leila, as they considered her a role model for young girls because of her responsible attitude toward her schooling and studying.

Lamia, on the other hand, was the baby in the family. She was her father's pet. She would not study or do her homework unless her father was with her. Lamia wasted many study hours distracted and procrastinating while waiting for her father to return. Abdul Rahman was adamant that the girls excel in their studies and Leila and Lamia were eager to garner his approval.

CHAPTER NOTES:

1 The Bedouins are divided into tribes, of which the largest ones are Al-Shammari, Al-Harbi (Makkah area), and Al-Mutairi, Al-Qahtani, Al-Subaie, Al-Dossary, all originally from the Najd valley. Most Bedouins have very common surnames.

CHAPTER 16

... and all men and women who are patient in adversity, and all
men and women who humble themselves before God, and all men
and women who give in charity, and all self-denying men and
self-denying women, and all men and women who are mindful
of their chastity, and all men and women who remember God
unceasingly: for all of them has God readied forgiveness of sins and
a mighty reward.

~ AL AHZAB 35

Nabila was working eleven hour days standing on her feet and still taking care of her family, unlike almost every other woman in her class in Saudi Arabia who had at least one housekeeper, often two. Even homemakers who had responsibilities with visiting relatives and friends to entertain in their homes had hired help.

Weekends were the worst time for Nabila. At times, she felt that Abdul Rahman had no consideration for her. He knew how hard she worked during the week and that she had laundry and ironing to do during the weekend. In addition, Abdul Rahman insisted on purchasing the week's groceries, but this was not a help to Nabila as his shopping was excessive. Every week, after Friday prayer, Abdul Rahman traveled to the Alhalaga, the wholesale market, and came home with hordes of boxes of all kinds of fruits and vegetables. He also patronized the butcher to buy kilos of meat and chickens, enough to feed the entire block! Nabila had to clean, cut, and store all the food in their small refrigerator that bulged with their daily supplies. The freezer was at capacity as every other week he would cart home a whole lamb for Nabila to cut, clean, and wrap for storage. Each Friday, Abdul Rahman and Nabila would quarrel over his extreme shopping. She could not convince him that it was too much, and it was a waste of money and food; by the end of the week she had to dump out the past week's groceries in order to store the new produce and meat.

"But it is cheap in Alhalaga," Abdul Rahman would say without any consideration for Nabila's labor to prepare the food for storage.

Nabila wished Abdul Rahman would ask her to leave everything to relax and join him with the girls, but he never did. Occasionally, during her work in the kitchen, she would peek at the girls and Abdul Rahman to see what they were doing in the living room. They were relaxing watching cartoons and laughing while Nabila was buried with the household chores like Cinderella. She wished he would at least ask the girls to come and help her and not take her hard work for granted. With her work both inside and outside of her home she was missing valuable family time. Eventually, Nabila decided not to bicker about the huge amount of shopping that Abdul Rahman enjoyed purchasing each week. Instead, she stored only what she thought was enough for the four of them and distributed the rest to the poor Africans and the needy who gathered in the streets waiting for someone to offer food and clothing.

Before his regular summer departure for Egypt, Uncle Saleh came to their house again to collect their contribution to Mansour's annual allowance. Uncle Saleh asked for extra money, because Mansour needed a car, and, of course, that came out of the meager funds they were trying to save. Nabila knew it was useless to broach the volatile subject with Abdul Rahman time after time.

One month after Uncle Saleh left Jeddah, he telephoned requesting more money, because Mansour was getting married and needed cash for the wedding. The latest request from Uncle Saleh took Nabila over the edge.

"Does he think we own a bank or something?" Nabila seethed.

Abdul Rahman hung his head and muttered, "What can I do? Any suggestions?"

Nabila glared at him and collapsed in the nearest chair. "You mean you will give it to him?"

"Yes, what else can I do?" Abdul Rahman replied in a barely audible voice.

"Well, where are you going to get the money from now? Do we even have any left in the savings?" Nabila wondered aloud.

"We have some and my brother, Adel, will help," conceded Abdul Rahman.

Mansour and Uncle Saleh once again pilfered their purse.

When the summer was over, Uncle Saleh returned from Egypt to reside with Amena, Yasser's married daughter. Hers was a traditional Saudi residence with two floors and gated with a garden and some palm trees. When Nabila and her family visited, Amena's four children, ranging in ages from four to ten, were playing in the warm September sun. Nabila kissed the sweaty children and walked to the house. Amena greeted her, *Ahlan was sahlan*, and removed Nabila's abaya and hung it on a nail on the wall. She directed Nabila and Abdul Rahman to an ample area by the entrance confirming the space Uncle Saleh claimed as his room. The typical Arabic style room had ordinary white walls and ceilings, an artificial red Persian rug with ruby floral cushions, matching pillows for arm resting, and bigger cushions, misnads, for back support.

Uncle Saleh was lounging in a corner underneath a high window and in front of the oversized circulating fan. He was wearing his usual fota, the tube-shaped piece of cloth that men wear wrapped around their waist, with a plain white t-shirt. Leila and Lamia kissed their grandfather and sat next to him. He was delighted to see the girls, noting how much he had missed them, and how he wished he could see them more often. He inquired about Nabila's parents and how the "old man" (her father) was doing with his Egyptian wife.

While Amena made tea, Abdul Rahman asked about the Egyptian trip and Mansour and his wife, Abeer. Uncle Saleh tucked his crossed legs under his fota before proceeding. He grumbled about Mansour's Egyptian wife, because she complained that the money they were getting every month was not enough, and that Mansour's allowance should be increased because of his marriage, and soon they would have children. Uncle Saleh admitted that a great deal of money had been spent on Mansour's education, his condominium, his car, and his marriage, plus his monthly allowance for the past seven years. Now Mansour's wife wanted them to increase the allowance in case they may have children. Even Uncle Saleh doubted

Abeer, believing she was only interested in gaining more wealth. Uncle Saleh lamented that he wished Mansour would finish his schooling and take care of himself and his family.

Then to Nabila's disbelief, he turned to Abdul Rahman and asked, "Can you increase Mansour's allowance to help out and keep his wife from annoying me?"

Just then, Amena brought the tea on a shiny silver tray with fragile tea glasses, called fingans. She poured the hot liquid in the fingans and served it on the tray. As they were sipping the tea, Amena began to tell them about her father, Yasser. She revealed how her father had greatly changed, unfortunately for the worst. Yasser's neighbor, Mr. Hamid, who was a close friend to Yasser, had died a year before. He left a wife with three children, a seventeen-year-old daughter, another fifteen-year-old daughter, and a ten-year-old son. Yasser began to help them with groceries and maintained a few minor things at their apartment, which Amena's mother accepted for a while. However, later, Yasser's wife began to complain about the shortage of money and that Yasser was not taking care of his family as he used to. Amena finally heard that Yasser had married the seventeen-year-old neighbor girl and was expecting a child. Yet another story of a Saudi man taking an additional wife who was still a child.

Uncle Saleh was unmoved by the story. "Ya lateef ya lateef."

Abdul Rahman, on the other hand, looked away and did not give comment. Nabila smiled at the girls and politely offered Amena "Maskena zena maskena," an expression of giving sympathy to Zana. Nabila was not focused on Amena's family tale; instead, her mind was working overtime planning how to stop Abdul Rahman from increasing Mansour's allowance. Nabila hated arguing with Abdul Rahman over Mansour. She resented Mansour taking advantage of both Abdul Rahman and Uncle Saleh. Mansour's Egyptian wife appeared to be cut from the same cloth.

Mansour had been in medical school for over seven years. Originally, his application to medical school was denied for not being qualified. Uncle Saleh, however, managed to get him in through a special contact in the Saudi Embassy in Egypt. Mansour seemed in no hurry to finish school as long as the money was coming regularly every month.

They returned home in the nine o'clock hour, and the girls went to their rooms to prepare for school the following day. Abdul Rahman changed into his pajamas and turned on the TV. Nabila asked him if he was going to increase Mansour's monthly allowance.

Abdul Rahman growled, "Are you going to put me down in front of my father and my relatives?"

"Then give him your money, not mine," Nabila said angrily. "You know how hard I work to help save some money. I have deprived myself of many things that I wished I could have, only to help you save some for the future."

Abdul Rahman tried to minimize the matter by saying, "I'm only going to increase his allowance by 200 Saudi *riyals*."

Abdul Rahman seemed to believe that they should continue giving Mansour money, simply because Uncle Saleh asked them to do so. They were not supposed to refuse any of his requests, engage in discussions or negotiations, or point out the downside of giving Mansour money any time he asked for it. The financial situation with Mansour caused continued dissention between Abdul Rahman and Nabila, eroding their relationship.

Visits from Issa and Margaret helped take Nabila's mind off the problems they had with Mansour. On one of their visits, Issa told Abdul Rahman that Prince Sawaz was building a housing project for all government employees for a very reasonable price. He said that these houses were going to be on an appealing compound with many facilities, such as schools, supermarkets, and stores. Issa captured Nabila's attention when he said that the project would be located in the middle of the desert close to Makkah. She hypothesized that having a house in the middle of the desert was a poor idea, because any slight wind would probably bury the house with sand. Abdul Rahman thought such a great project must have some sort of protection against sand. Besides, he said, they should be thankful for such a project. Otherwise, they would not be able to build or buy a house with the little money they were making. Both families decided to put down the first payment from savings, hoping in two years, they would both have their own homes. With limited funds Abdul Rahman was able to pay for the girls' school, the new house, the rent, and Mansour's monthly allowance. The idea of having a house of her own gave Nabila a sense of well being. She had seen many women have difficulty trying to rent in their later years after retirement, death of a spouse, or after divorce. Having a house represented a social and future security, and she was thankful that Abdul Rahman was protecting her. At least that is what Nabila believed until she received the mail the following week.

When Nabila found an official letter from the housing project explaining that their house payment was a few months overdue, turmoil ensued. Nabila knew that her husband was usually punctual with the payment, so she was perplexed. When Nabila confronted Abdul Rahman, he explained that he had to put the idea of having a house aside for a new restaurant business that he and his brother had formed. Nabila tried to convince Abdul Rahman that it would only take one more year to own the house. After they had a secure home, Abdul Rahman could use all the rent money in any business he liked. As usual, Abdul Rahman rarely considered Nabila's thoughts and ideas concerning financial matters.

Adel, Abdul Rahman's brother, worked in an office that was close to where they lived. He often stopped by to see the girls and to say hello. Nabila broached the subject of Abdul Rahman preferring a trial business to owning a home with Adel. Nabila was disappointed when Adel agreed with his brother's idea of opening the restaurant before paying off the house. He said even if he did not concur, he was not supposed to question his older brother. Abdul Rahman's speculative restaurant business, which was only open four months, closed, depleting all their savings.

Weeks later, Issa and Margaret visited them celebrating Issa's promotion to a high position in the government. Issa became the general manager of the entire region in one of the government's ministries. He encouraged Abdul Rahman to change jobs and work with him. He said that Abdul Rahman would have a better position with higher pay and a brighter future. Issa promised he would use his connections and give his recommendation to the minster to transfer Abdul Rahman's years of service from one ministry to another. Abdul Rahman's job prospect was terrific news, and they were both excited about the upcoming change. However, the process for the transfer dragged on, and Nabila was afraid that Issa had changed his mind or forgotten about it. Nabila was Abdul Rahman's best advocate. She called Issa every week or sometimes twice a week to encourage him to do his best to transfer Abdul Rahman as soon as possible. She reminded Issa that Abdul Rahman was a very diligent worker and aimed to prove himself in the ministry, but no one seemed to appreciate him. Abdul Rahman really deserved a better position. Nabila pleaded with Issa for help, and he assured her that Abdul Rahman would get the job but to be patient as the transfer was a tedious process. Abdul Rahman did not know Nabila had been hounding Issa, trying to rush the progression. When Nabila again quizzed Issa about the new job, he said that the only complication came from the person who Abdul Rahman thought was his friend and schoolmate, Mr. Hani. Abdul Rahman's boss was complicating the matter and delaying the process of the paperwork for no reason other than jealousy that Abdul Rahman would be in a better position.

Week after week passed, and the boss held the transfer request hostage. Nabila's calls to Issa accelerated, hoping he could he could do something to release the necessary papers. Issa finally concluded that as long as Abdul Rahman's boss did not approve the transfer, no one could do anything about it. Issa suggested that Abdul Rahman should talk to his boss and convince him to sign the release soon, or he might lose the chance for the job. Nabila did not believe Abdul Rahman would be proactive so she braced herself to take action. She prayed to all mighty Allah that her call would not create an unexpected or unwanted result. *Besm Allah Al Rhamn Al Raheem*; Nabila dialed the boss's number.

The operator answered the call indicating that Mr. Hani was not in his office. Nabila waited patiently for about thirty minutes and dialed the number again. Mr. Hani was still absent, having gone to prayer. The operator suggested Nabila call immediately after prayer to catch the manager before he went home for lunch. She waited for prayer to be over and dialed the number again. The operator told her to hold for a minute. Nabila waited, willing her mind to formulate the speech that would sway the administrator. She did not want to destroy the only hope for Abdul Rahman to get the job. Mr. Hani came on the line and Nabila introduced herself as Abdul Rahman's wife. Mr. Hani asked the nature of her call.

"Well, Abdul Rahman told me you were his roommate and classmate in the States. He talked about you a lot, and he was very happy when he knew you were his boss," Nabila said.

"But he wants to leave this ministry; didn't he tell you?" he quizzed.

"Yes, he did, and that is the reason I am calling you now. You are his

friend, and I am sure you want the best for him. I'm also sure you would
help him when he needs you," she explained.

Nabila hurried on knowing that it was the hour for her finest sale's job.

"From what Issa and Abdul Rahman said, the job offer is promising,
and it is more in his field. It would probably give him a better chance for
the future. I really want him to have it," Nabila said.

"But he is also a very good worker here; we don't want to give him up.
We need him in this job," he pointed out.

"I appreciate what you are saying, but I don't think you would prevent
him from getting a better job with more pay and opportunities," Nabila
continued.

"*In shaa Allah*, only the best will happen. Call me next week. I can't
promise you anything, but we'll see," he said.

We'll see was what Nabila's mother said when she did not want to be
bothered with Nabila's childish pleas. Nabila wanted to get him to commit.
She inquired about the best time to call and he suggested the following
week at the same time.

"Thank you very much. May Allah bless you and your children," Nabila
prayed aloud for him. Somehow, she felt confident that Mr. Hani would
release her husband.

Nabila feared Abdul Rahman's reaction to her attempts to help him
advance his career, so she thought it best not to tell him of her actions.
She was quite frightened and hoped she would not regret what she did.
Nabila only wanted to help her husband succeed, but Abdul Rahman
would not see it that way. He would not like his wife talking to his boss
on his behalf. Nabila was relieved when the day after the call passed in
peace. As time elapsed, Nabila began to believe that Abdul Rahman would
not discover her deed. Then one day, Nabila arrived home finding Abdul
Rahman there earlier than usual. As soon as she entered the house, he
called to her. Terrified, she expected the worst. Abdul Rahman met her
at the entrance of the house and studied Nabila quietly for a few seconds.
Nabila's mind was a rolodex of all the excuses and explanations that she
had prepared. Abdul Rahman asked Nabila if she felt okay, because her
face was grave. To Nabila's relief, Abdul Rahman shared that Issa had
called to congratulate him on his new job. His boss signed the request, and

Abdul Rahman was the new superintendant of the region for the ministry beginning the following month.

"*Al Hamdllah*, thanks God," Nabila uttered in appreciation. Neither of them mentioned Mr. Hani.

Abdul Rahman had been on the job for a week, when he came home carrying a hefty envelope. He handed it to Nabila to open; she was aghast as she emptied the contents. She had never seen that much money. Nabila carefully extracted the bills wondering where the money came from and to whom it belonged.

"It is eighty-five thousand Saudi riyals for our first new car!" Abdul Rahman rejoiced.

Everyone in the family was excited about the prospect of a new car. Lamia wanted a convertible sports car, thinking it would be fun to drive. Leila wanted a Jeep to maneuver Jeddah's bumpy roads. Nabila coveted a Cadillac for luxury, and Abdul Rahman envisioned a practical family car. They laughed at each other's choices and consulted many dealers before settling on a luxury American Impala.

While everyone was excited about the new car, Nabila still was not permitted to drive. Ironically, that same year, women did attempt to fight the driving restriction. In 1990, during Operation Desert Storm, forty-seven Saudi women drove cars through Riyadh protesting against women being denied the right to drive. The fundamentalists demanded strict punishment for the women who had driven the cars, resulting in their arrests. Some called the women "whores" for their protests and their male guardians had to sign to take responsibility for the women. The participants were banned from receiving any future government jobs or government education.[1]

Abdul Rahman began his new job, the girls were excelling in school, and Nabila received a promotion as secretary and translator of the internal medicine department at the hospital. Best of all, the ministry offered Issa and Abdul Rahman free villas in a compound by the sea. The area had many facilities including a swimming pool, a playground, and a recreation area. Maintenance, electricity, and gasoline were included free of charge. Issa and Abdul Rahman selected two villas across from each other by the pool. The house was a one-floor plan with two medium size bedrooms, an ample living room, a sizable kitchen, and two bathrooms. Attached to the house was a maid's quarter with an outside entrance. The back yard was game worthy and a garage was available to protect the car. The style of the house was European and quite suitable for the family. Because the furniture was not to their liking, they ordered new furniture from Germany.

There were no moving companies so Abdul Rahman and Nabila had to gradually move everything in their small car. Since both were working full time, they had no time to pack except on the weekend, taking weeks to move. Everyone readily adjusted; the girls were having fun with the new neighbors at the swimming pool. Nabila was delighted to decorate her new home in her taste, although the girls picked the color for their rooms. Lamia wanted purple carpet and matching curtains, where as Leila chose her favorite—blue. With the right shade of carpet, curtains, and accessories, Nabila transformed the bland living space into a beautiful room. The bleeding heart plant that they had for many years thrived, threatening to overtake the room.

A few weeks before the girls' school finals, Abdul Rahman asked where they would like to spend the summer. He explained that the ministry was sending him to southern France for two months for a special assignment. They wanted him to depart immediately, but Abdul Rahman told them he would not go without his family. The ministry agreed to wait. The family was jubilant at the thought of vacationing in France.

Abdul Rahman advised the girls if they really wanted to enjoy the summer vacation, they should study hard each evening and make good grades on their final exams. As he was sitting at the dinner table, he quizzed Lamia, "So what are you supposed to do after dinner?"

Being clever, Lamia raised her finger to her forehead, as if she was thinking, and said, "Mmm, digest my food?"

While the girls jabbered to their father about the details of the trip, Nabila reflected on the past years of her marriage. She thought how hard she had to work—days when she was lucky to get four hours of sleep a night. She had frequently worked overtime to make more money, took care of the house, and cooked daily. Finally, she was going to live a grand life!

Nabila was delighted to share their good news with family. Her father came to visit at their new home and verbalized that he was impressed with the vast changes in Nabila's life. She fixed Saad a cup of tea and they settled in the garden.

As Saad sipped his tea, he said, "Abdul Rahman is a good man. You must take care of him. Good men are rare to find now. Give him your best. He deserves it."

Her father's words brought Nabila to tears. "Yes, Father, he is a good man. You know, Father, this is the life I always wanted for Abdul Rahman, and I worked to help him accomplish it. It took us sixteen years to reach it, but we finally did. Thanks to Allah for everything."

Saad reminded Nabila that things in life do not always come easily and that one must work hard and remain patient.

He ended their talk by saying, "You are a good girl. Pray as much as you can to Allah to protect you, your husband, and your children. Be thankful for everything that Allah gives you."

Their prosperity continued as Abdul Rahman became popular in the Saudi community. He was featured on Saudi TV for special interviews, and his name regularly appeared in the newspaper. He also was with his Majesty, the king, on several occasions. Nabila's co-workers and friends at the hospital gave her special treatment for being the wife of an important official in the government. The girls began to associate with the elite girls in their school. They were able to invite them to the house for a meal or a party. At Leila's birthday party, Nabila entertained some of her daughter's high-class friends. Leila was proud to have them over and was excited by the expensive presents she received. One of Leila's guests was a former neighbor, whose mother used to drive Leila to school until she found out that Leila was not of their class. Now that had changed and the two young girls were friends again. During the party, one of the girls accidently broke a glass. To prevent anyone from being cut, Nabila hurried to vacuum the glass.

Leila stopped Nabila. "Not now, Mother; these girls have maids and servants. Their mothers never do anything. You're embarrassing me!"

CHAPTER NOTES:

1 Again, on June 17, 2011, women were encouraged via the Internet to drive to protest the ban. Forty-two women took to the road and arrests were made. In July 2011,

the Saudi Minister of Interior, Prince Nayef Ben Abdul Rahman Aziz announced a decree that any woman driving a vehicle inside Saudi Arabia would be punished by imprisonment for a term of five years. The woman's guardian—a father, a husband, or a brother—would also be imprisoned.

CHAPTER 17

On the contrary live with them (women) On a footing of kindness and equity.

~ AL NESSA 19

Two weeks before the family trip, Abdul Rahman shared some of the final details. He wanted to visit Rome for a few days and then take the train to France. From there, they would take another train to Lyon, believing the girls would enjoy the ride. Mr. Trianfo, head of the work project, was Italian, so he would take care of their accommodations. He offered a car with a driver who was also a tour guide to chauffer them around the city of Rome. As an additional surprise, Mr. Trianfo gave them one week on a yacht in Nice. The vessel included a great cook who would prepare the meals as they traveled the Mediterranean. Nabila was overwhelmed with anticipation, as the trip sounded incredible! Abdul Rahman did not want the girls to know the itinerary of the trip until they finished their exams, fearing they would be too excited to study.

Nabila had to apply for a leave of absence, so she met with Mr. Wilson, the head of the department at the hospital. He was a friendly American, about thirty-five, tall, and blond. Nabila explained that her husband was going on a business trip for two months, and she would like to join him. Mr. Wilson complimented Nabila on her good performance at the hospital and told her he would be happy to grant a leave. He also proposed a new position for Nabila on her return, an assistant director of the hospital nursing school that would open the following month. Besides an increased salary, Nabila would have an office next to the director. She would work five days a week with Thursdays and Fridays off. He wrote Nabila a letter of recommendation in case he had to leave the country for any reason.

When she returned home, Nabila told Abdul Rahman about the

promotion and showed him the letter. She suggested that with her raise, she could take care of their daily expenses and Abdul Rahman could then double the house payment. Nabila's dream of having her own home was coming to fruition. Her father-in-law and Mansour could not stop them now!

School finals began; Leila depended on herself to complete her studies whereas Lamia waited every evening for her father's help. She would sit on the floor with her books piled high on the coffee table waiting for her father to come home. At their study time, Nabila was usually busy in the kitchen, washing dishes, cooking the next day's meal, or baking bread. She was still only able to catch four or five hours of sleep each night.

One morning, Abdul Rahman could not take Nabila to work, so she called the hospital transportation to send a cab. While Nabila was waiting for the cab, the phone rang. It was a long distance call from Cairo, Egypt; Mansour was on the phone. He offered congratulations for Abdul Rahman's new job and mentioned that he had seen Abdul Rahman on Egyptian TV the previous night.

He rushed to continue. "Listen, I had a car accident, but I'm alright. I only need money to fix my car. Tell Abdul Rahman to send me money as soon as possible; bye."

The phone call ruined Nabila's day. Defiantly, she decided not to tell Abdul Rahman about the phone call. She was miserable at work at the thought of being dishonest with her husband and most of her friends noticed her bad mood. Nabila swore that she would not change her mind even if she calmed down and was willing to face the consequences. Of course, Uncle Saleh telephoned Abdul Rahman about Mansour's car accident. After talking to his father for a few minutes, Abdul Rahman asked Nabila if Mansour had phoned. Nabila answered honestly. Frustrated, she asked if Uncle Saleh wanted them to help Mansour once again. Abdul Rahman avoided eye contact but confirmed yes, both he and his brother would help.

Quivering, Nabila said, "But you told me he graduated a year ago after fourteen years of struggling in medical school, and that you and your brother helped him to set up a medical office for his practice, didn't you?"

Abdul Rahman calmly affirmed that he had.

Nabila continued, "Then why are you helping him? Isn't it enough that you helped him all those years with the money that we needed for our daily bread? Why are you helping him now that he has a practice and making money?"

Abdul Rahman walked out of the room without answering.

Nabila erupted like an angry volcano. She decided to take action and wrote a letter to Mansour. She tried to be polite and respectful, explaining that they had helped him throughout his long years of studying, helped him to get married, bought him a condominium and a car, and even set up a practice for him. Nabila told Mansour it was about time that he depended on himself and should not need their help any longer, then signed the letter and mailed it. After a few days, Nabila received a phone call from Yasser, Abdul Rahman's cousin, ridiculing her for sending such a letter to Mansour. When Nabila asked how he knew about it, Yasser said that Mansour had sent him a copy. Even Saad came to Nabila's house unexpectedly to tell her that Mansour had made several copies of the letter and distributed it to all the elderly males in the family complaining about her. Saad thought the letter was respectful and held nothing against Nabila. Unfortunately, that was not the case with the rest of the family. Abdul Rahman was livid. He shouted that Nabila had no right to send the letter, and his father and other relatives were saying he was not man enough to control his wife. Nabila explained that someone had to stop Mansour from pilfering their money. After all, Mansour was a doctor and should be able to support himself.

Nabila could not stop herself from doing battle against every injustice that affected her or her family, even if Abdul Rahman was caught in the crossfire. They were different in that respect; Nabila strong in her beliefs to champion her immediate family and Abdul Rahman never shirking his implied duties of being a good son.

Because of the disagreement, Abdul Rahman and Nabila did not speak until the day of their trip to France. A luxury American car arrived to take them to the airport where an official produced the tickets and passports. He explained to Abdul Rahman that with a diplomatic passport he should not have any difficulty with the customs in any part of the world. It was the first time Nabila knew her husband was carrying a diplomatic passport.

"You are a big shot, Daddy," commented Lamia.

It took five hours to get to the airport in Rome. Their luggage arrived only moments after them. Leila noticed a driver holding a sign with her father's name. Neither Abdul Rahman nor Nabila expected anyone to meet them at the airport. The chauffer carried their luggage to the limousine and drove them across the city. They arrived at a five star hotel where the driver took care of their reservations and luggage. They declined an interpreter during their stay in Rome to maintain privacy.

Two days after arriving in Rome, an Italian colleague, Mr. Bollotti, invited them for dinner and to meet his wife. At the elegant restaurant, Abdul Rahman asked that Mr. Bollotti order their entrees, anything without pork or liquor. The waiter brought each of them a bowl of soup with bread and butter. A salad arrived with bread sticks, and then what Nabila assumed was the main course, a dish of delicious meatless spaghetti. The girls were delighted with the meal choice. Unexpectedly, the waiter returned with large cuts of thick, tender steaks. Being so full of spaghetti, Nabila was not able to eat the meat. Minutes later, the waiter served rice and vegetables followed by potatoes and fish dishes. They were laughing and protesting against more food. Lamia joked that those were only appetizers and the meal had not yet started. Sure enough, more dishes arrived, and they just had to leave some foods untouched. They rolled out of the Roman restaurant like four stuffed meatballs.

Mr. Bollotti had confirmed that his yacht was at their disposal for a week in Nice, so after their stay in Rome, they traveled to Paris by overnight train. They later learned this was not a good idea for anyone who did not speak French or Italian. Abdul Rahman managed to ask for tickets from Rome to Paris, then to Lyon. As they understood, the train was supposed to depart at 10 p.m. from track 8, so they had enough time for dinner before leaving Rome.

The train was on time and they made their way to the first class section. The compartments were comfortable for sitting, but not for sleeping as the seats were small. They did not tilt back, nor were the armrests detachable. The girls slept on the floor, and Abdul Rahman and Nabila tried to sleep sitting down. They were sound asleep when Nabila awoke to the ticket taker's knock on the door. When Abdul Rahman handed him the tickets, the official pointed to something on the stub. Because Abdul Rahman was unable to understand what he was saying, the official pointed to the outside of the train. They finally understood that they should get off at the next station, because they were on the wrong train.

The train station was deserted. It was about 1:30 in the morning, and only one person was at the window. He did not speak English but took the tickets, examined them, tore them up, and threw them in the trash. He issued new tickets after charging Abdul Rahman more money. The official wrote down the track number that was supposed to take them to Paris. Assuming the train would come within an hour, they waited by the track. Two hours passed; there was no sign of a train. Not a single person was in sight; not even a car passed by. There was no telephone to call the company in Paris. The girls were frightened, and Abdul Rahman was worried. He walked up and down the street, trying to find a person to talk to or a telephone to use. There was nothing along the street or around the train station. Nabila feared that such a night would not pass safely. In the cool evening air they huddled together on a bench clinging to each other for warmth and safety.

Nabila spotted an old, inoperable train in the distance. One of the cars was off the track. They walked to the train and found the doors open. They climbed inside and immediately felt warmer. Nabila checked her watch; it was four o'clock in the morning. Each of the girls took a seat, put their head on their folded arms, and promptly fell asleep. Nabila sat next to the girls wearily watching Abdul Rahman pacing back and forth staring at the tickets in his hand. Nabila eventually dozed and awoke suddenly, not knowing how long she had slept. Exhausted, Abdul Rahman had settled into the seat in front of Nabila unable to fight sleep any longer.

"Abdul Rahman, Abdul Rahman; have we missed the train?" she asked.

"I don't care," he answered without looking up. "If we missed it, we will try to take the next train."

It was 7 a.m. when Abdul Rahman left the derailed train and headed toward the station. The girls were still asleep. Nabila waited for Abdul Rahman to return, praying to Allah that everything would be all right. Abdul Rahman had to buy new tickets to Paris for the third time, because the old tickets were for the train that had passed two hours before.

Frustrated, they woke the girls and headed to the train track, which they hoped this time was destined for Paris.

They boarded a train and Abdul Rahman threw himself on the nearest seat and sighed. Nabila was worried that they might be on the wrong train again. She walked around the train looking at the people trying to guess who may speak English. She spotted a woman who was reading a book and sat in the empty seat next to her waiting for her attention.

"Paris?" Nabila quizzed, pointing at the train.

"Oui, Paris," the passenger confirmed.

Feeling relieved, Nabila went back to her family informing them they were on the right train.

They only had one day in Paris. Arriving at the hotel in the afternoon, they immediately fell asleep until about eight o'clock. They went to dinner and then slept the rest of the night. The next day they visited the Louvre, walked the streets of Paris, shopped, dined at a famous restaurant, gazed at the Eiffel Tower, and then returned to the hotel to prepare for the trip to Lyon.

Fortunately, a company car was waiting to take them to Grenoble, the site of Abdul Rahman's work assignment. The driver spoke English, which was a great relief considering their previous problems with a language barrier. They met the owner of the apartment where they were going to live for the next two months. He spoke enough English for them to understand. He turned over the apartment as it was and even left all the food that was in the refrigerator.

Spending two months in France was wonderful. They marveled at the clean city and the pleasing weather. Nabila was awestruck watching a rainbow crossing the green mountains, something she had never seen in her desert homeland.

The compound where they stayed had a family swimming pool, tennis courts, schools, and markets. Nabila loved the shopping and purchased some modern clothes and accessories. Abdul Rahman worked full days while the girls and Nabila went swimming, sightseeing, and shopping. Ten days before the end of the trip, Abdul Rahman was able to get a week off to spend in Nice. They took the train without any confusion and an Italian driver transported them to the yacht. They met a middle-aged man, Mr. Alexandero, who was the yacht keeper and the cook. He did not speak English but through sign language determined if they wanted lunch. Nabila asked for spaghetti, which he understood. His spaghetti was the best Nabila had ever had, and she requested it almost every day. His delicious pasta still comes to mind when Nabila craves Italian cuisine.

Every afternoon Nabila took the girls to the beach. Abdul Rahman would not go because he did not like to miss his afternoon nap. The first time Nabila went to the beach, she was shocked to see almost all the girls sunbathing topless. Their bikinis were the size of Nabila's palm held by a strip of material between the hips in the back. Boys wore what looked like little bags covering their lower front. Some of the sun worshipers were playing cards in mixed groups and others were playing volleyball, sunning, or swimming. The next day, Nabila begged Abdul Rahman to go with them, assuring him that he would see things that he had never witnessed. Abdul Rahman refused.

"Being out of the Islamic world does not give us the permission to commit sins. Watching naked women is a sin. You know that," was all he said before he left the room.

Feeling over dressed in her one-piece swimming suit, Nabila sat in the sand with her two daughters, enjoying the sun and people watching. A man in his mid twenties approached them and greeted them, *Bon jour.* Nabila told him she only knew a little French. He sat next to her and introduced himself as Antonio. Leila decided to swim, Lamia built a sand castle, and Nabila listened as Antonio shared much of his background. He was born and raised in Nice and had travelled to many parts of the world where he learned English. He talked for over an hour before asking Nabila to dinner. When Nabila told him that it was not possible, he asked her if she could meet him the next day at the beach to swim. Nabila did not assure him that she would be able to make it. He walked with them to the yacht, and said he hoped to see Nabila the next day.

Hearing the conversation, Lamia remarked, "Wow, that man really likes you, Mommy."

The French vacation passed all too quickly. As they were leaving Nice and getting into the car, Antonio stopped by to say goodbye.

Abdul Rahman looked perplexed and asked, "Who was that man?"

Nabila told him that they met Antonio at the beach and just talked for a while.

Lamia turned to her father and said, "He likes Mommy, too."

Abdul Rahman looked annoyed, but did not comment.

While Nabila had briefly enjoyed the attention of another man, she was devoted to Abdul Rahman and her family.

CHAPTER 18

Prophet Muhammad (PBUH) said, "Food and dress are the right of slaves and servants and they should not be assigned to task which may be beyond their capacity."

~ ABU HURAIRAH

Nabila returned to Jeddah and to her past routine of school, work, cooking, and cleaning. Yasser called Abdul Rahman telling him that Uncle Saleh had left for Egypt after a fight with Amena, and she did not want him back in her house. Yasser was shouting so loud that Nabila heard every word he said. Yasser lectured Abdul Rahman reminding him that his father was his responsibility and duty to take care of him.

"You are not a good son. Why should we or our children look after him? He is only our uncle, not our father," Yasser said.

Yasser could not resist taking aim at Nabila as well, telling Abdul Rahman to keep his wife at home to care for his father instead of working in the hospital with men. He taunted Abdul Rahman by telling him he was not man enough to support his wife and that Nabila should be home looking after her father-in-law. When the phone conversation ended, Abdul Rahman looked at Nabila and asked if she heard what Yasser said. Nabila nodded, but remained silent. She did not want Uncle Saleh to live with them. She could never manage to take care of him, her home, family, and job. Nabila would not be able to cook for him with his special diet; besides, they did not have an extra room or a bathroom for him. When Adel, Abdul Rahman's brother, volunteered to take Uncle Saleh, Nabila prayed in gratitude for Allah's mercy.

Nabila's life was good but predictable. The girls were progressing with their studies, Abdul Rahman received more job promotions, and Nabila was doing well at work. Uncle Saleh, as usual, was getting ready for his summer trip to Egypt. In spite of the fact that Mansour was already a practicing doctor, he still received his monthly stipend from their savings. They also contributed a hefty summer allowance, which due to the standard of living in Egypt, his family could live on for the whole year. Nabila had to face the fact that Uncle Saleh would never stop soliciting them to support a professional doctor.

Nabila did not think about Uncle Saleh once during her glorious four-week vacation that summer in Vienna, Salzburg, and Monce, three of the most beautiful cities in Austria. The holiday was such a favorite for the whole family that Abdul Rahman discussed moving there after retirement. Soon after returning home, Abdul Rahman received a call from Adel saying that his father had an argument with his wife. Uncle Saleh did not want to live with them anymore and had decided to move back with Nabila and Abdul Rahman. Knowing that the arrangement would not work, Nabila suggested that they secure an Egyptian maid to cook and take care of Uncle Saleh. Abdul Rahman agreed and called Mansour in Cairo asking him if he could find a middle-aged woman who was strong enough to take care of Uncle Saleh. He stressed that she must be a good cook. Nabila thought it was very thoughtful of Abdul Rahman to buy and furnish a prefabricated house for his father, not too far from their own.

Thorya, the new maid arrived two weeks later. Very cheerful and talkative, Thorya was a good entertainer for the lonely Uncle Saleh. On her first day, she prepared a delicious chicken meal. For the first time in Nabila's married life, she did not have to do anything after work, but that luxury ended when Thorya moved solely to serve Uncle Saleh. All the relatives were happy to have Thorya caring for Uncle Saleh, relieved from the responsibility and frustration.

Occasionally, when Nabila's American friend, Margaret, traveled to visit her family in America, Issa would ask Thorya to clean his house and iron his clothes. He paid her handsomely. That was the beginning of the end of Nabila's peace of mind. She noticed that Thorya began to neglect Uncle Saleh to help Issa, enjoying the good money he paid her. Soon Thorya wished to work only for Issa. Nabila also noticed that Thorya spent more time with Issa's Egyptian driver, and she was certain there was something going on between them. That was confirmed when they actually married, and Thorya left to live and work with her husband at Issa's house. The family struggled with what to do with Uncle Saleh but Allelah smiled upon them when Uncle Saleh announced that he would go to Egypt for a few months. Uncle Saleh left with his pockets lined with their savings, all designated for Mansour.

Abdul Rahman surprised Nabila a few times by taking her to the beach to show her the double lands he had purchased. Soon Abdul Rahman bought several double lands; each one big enough to build duplex houses. Nabila dreamed of the day when Abdul Rahman would surprise her with a house by the sea.

With Abdul Rahman's career advancements the money began to pour in and the idea of having a housekeeper became more appealing. After all, Nabila deserved a break as she had been working for many years to help her husband and two girls. Freed from many chores, Nabila might even be able to go back to school for a master's degree. She began to look at the advantages, coming home to relax, not to scrub dirty dishes, laundry, or prepare meals. Nabila was convinced that a housekeeper would bring her the rest and comfort that she had not experienced in life.

During these years, Saudi Arabia was at its peak in resources. Many people were wealthy enough to live a life of luxury, building houses, buying expensive cars, and traveling around the world. Recruiting a housekeeper and family driver from the Philippines became the fashion for many Saudi families. Each family had at least one housekeeper and a driver. Some families had two or three. Unfortunately, not every employer treated their maids well. Nabila knew that maids were often accused of crimes in some Saudi homes. Most of these crimes were in retaliation to the mistreatment of the maid by the employer. In some cases maids would not receive their full pay and would have their passports held.

Some maids were treated like slaves, especially during the month of Ramadan when they were overworked throughout the day and into the night. Saudi families like to entertain late at night and the maids work all day in preparation for the late dinner. The guests usually do not leave before three o'clock in the morning and the maid has to clean after the party. As early as six a.m. she is responsible for getting the children prepared for school, and then returns home to resume her work. The maid rarely got more than three to four hours of sleep. Sleep deprived and angered with the working conditions some maids sought revenge through starving, hurting, kidnapping, or even killing the children of the family. Nabila's former neighbor lost a child and the maid was the prime suspect. The child was poisoned but it could not be proved as autopsies are prohibited in Saudi Arabia.

Despite the horror stories Nabila had heard, she was certain that nothing sordid would befall her family. Besides, her girls weren't children but young ladies who would soon be off on their own. Nabila looked forward to enjoying a less hectic pace and future time with Abdul Rahman now that they were financially secure. She asked her sister Ameera who lived in the Philippines to choose suitable housekeepers for both her and Margaret. Nabila was content with her decision to secure a maid and happily anticipated the arrival of the woman who would make her feel like a queen for the first time in her life.

When Nabila mentioned her decision to a friend at the hospital, Frank, a black British worker said, "Are you really bringing a housekeeper to your home?"

"Yes, what's wrong with that?" Nabila answered.

"How about your husband; don't you get jealous?" he wondered.

Nabila assured Frank that in nearly twenty years of marriage she had never felt jealous, because Abdul Rahman had never done anything that made her jealous. Thank God, her husband was not that kind of a man. He loved her too much to look at another woman. Besides, who would look at a maid?

The housekeeper was to arrive on the weekend, the second week of the Holy Month of Ramadan in 1991. At about 10 p.m., the phone rang and the caller sounded like a young girl with a Filipino accent. Nabila immediately recognized that the caller was the housekeeper who was coming to work for them. Abdul Rahman went to the airport to fetch her, and Nabila waited, watching a movie that she borrowed from the hospital video library.

After two hours, they arrived with Abdul Rahman carting a bag and the maid trailing behind him. She looked very young and thin, really under weight. Nabila showed her to her room and gave her cereal and some milk for a light snack. As the girl was eating, Nabila asked her questions, eager to learn more about her. Mara was only nineteen, but she had to record her age as twenty-six in order to obtain permission to work abroad. Mara explained that she never wanted to leave her country, but her father forced her to improve his own reputation. A person who traveled abroad to work received a special respect from family members, friends, and others in their society. She mentioned that Fay, the girl who came to work for Issa and Margaret, was her cousin.

Mara was about 5 foot 3 inches, two inches taller than Nabila. She had straight, short black hair so thin on top that her scalp showed. Nabila noticed that Mara's front teeth were not natural. She probably wore dentures, which made Nabila feel sorry for her to be nineteen and have already lost her teeth. She was wearing blue jeans and a white shirt flimsy from too many washings.

Mara finished her cereal and asked if she could go to bed. Nabila knew she was going through jet lag and that it might take her a couple of days to adjust. Mara opened her bag and took out her belongings. There were almost no clothes, only a thread-barren towel, a bottle of shampoo, shabby pajamas, and two or three pairs of plain underwear. It was evident that Mara came from a poor family.

As soon as Mara went to bed, Nabila went to the living room feeling exuberant that she was free of work and would be able to enjoy lounging and chatting with the girls and her husband. Nabila's family was watching TV, and Abdul Rahman looked up to ask if the girl had gone to bed. As soon as he heard Nabila's positive response, he suggested the girls turn off the telephone and turn down the TV because the maid needed to sleep. Mara's room was on the far side of the house and there was no way that the TV would bother her. But Abdul Rahman was adamant and surprised Nabila by demanding that she shut the hallway door as well. The door was at least six meters from the housekeeper's room, and her door was closed. How could the TV and the phone disturb her? Nabila was perplexed by Abdul Rahman's strange behavior, as she had never seen him act in such an illogical way.

Abdul Rahman's early morning routine included jogging around the compound. He put his jogging shoes on at the door and then, without realizing that Nabila was standing nearby he peaked in the housekeeper's room before he exited the house. Nabila felt a knot in her stomach. Such action was unexpected, but she did not comment. Later that day Nabila was cooking when Abdul Rahman came home. He looked for Mara and found her ironing. He questioned if Nabila made her do all the ironing without helping her. Nabila was puzzled, as Mara was just doing her job.

"You should help her," he said.

"Me help her?" Frustrated, Nabila replied, "I have been doing this ironing among all other house work along with my full time job and you never felt sorry for me or asked your daughters to help me."

Abdul Rahman walked out of the room in silence.

For the last ten days of The Holy Month of Ramadan, the girls were out of school and Abdul Rahman and Nabila were off work. Like the past two years, they decided to spend those ten days in Vienna, their favorite European city. They sent Mara to Nabila's mother's house until they returned. In spite of the fact that they returned to Jeddah at about midnight, Abdul Rahman insisted that they pick up Mara. When Nabila suggested that it was quite late and they could pick her up in the morning he did not agree and directed the driver to Rahma's house. Nabila's sister greeted them as Mara walked into the room. Mara began to cry the minute she saw them. Nabila questioned Mara to determine what caused her tears. Nabila knew neither her mother nor her sister were the cause of the problem, if there was a problem. As Nabila questioned Mara, Abdul Rahman stood nearby listening intently to Mara's explanation. During the ride home, everyone was silent. Abdul Rahman moved the phone and lowered the sound, as was now the custom when Mara went to her room. He also ordered the girls to go directly to bed, remarking it was too late for TV.

At about ten o'clock the next day, Nabila tried to reach Abdul Rahman at his office. His secretary said that he was out. Nabila was surprised because it was not like Abdul Rahman to leave his office unless he had a meeting. Later in the same day, during dinner, Mara was working in the kitchen and Abdul Rahman said something amusing. Nabila laughed and moved to get closer to tease him, when suddenly his arms spun like propellers to move away from Nabila. When Abdul Rahman continued to rebuff Nabila, it became clear that he did not want Nabila to show him any affection in front of the housekeeper.

Fay worked in Issa's house along with a new Egyptian driver called Omar. In the afternoons Omar took the two housekeepers shopping or for a ride around the city. Days later, Nabila noticed that Mara was getting many phone calls from a young Filipino man. While Mara was with her cousin at Issa's house, Abdul Rahman visited Issa. Nabila decided to go as well and chat with Margaret. As Margaret and Nabila were sipping their tea, Nabila overheard her husband asking Mara about the man who had been calling her. When Mara told him that he was a person she met at a restaurant, Abdul Rahman reacted sourly. He scolded Mara, telling her not to talk to men he did not know. The maid seemed surprised at the tone of Abdul Rahman's voice.

"But but he is from my country," Mara said shaking.

"Even so, you are not allowed to talk to a man who is not related to you," Abdul Rahman reprimanded.

Mara walked to her room in tears.

The next day, Abdul Rahman informed Nabila that he was increasing Mara's salary. Nabila thought it odd as Mara had not even finished two months of work. Abdul Rahman justified that Mara worked hard, and he wanted to show his appreciation.

Nabila could not help but angrily point out, "Do you realize that I was doing all she is doing, plus my eight hours of work at the hospital, and you never showed any sympathy for me."

"You are not suffering from poverty and didn't travel thousands of miles to work and make a living," Abdul Rahman said and stormed off to the bedroom, wanting no argument from Nabila.

It was just like the matter with ungrateful Mansour, Abdul Rahman would give Mara the increase whether Nabila agreed or not.

After working at the hospital for five and half years, Nabila submitted her resignation to start her university studies. Nabila's ambition to have a master's degree outweighed her love for the hospital job. Part of the university application form required Abdul Rahman's signature. At eleven a.m. Nabila phoned Abdul Rahman at his office to see if he could meet her to sign the form. Abdul Rahman was not there, so Nabila asked the secretary if he knew where Abdul Rahman was.

He said, "Mr. Abdul Rahman went home for a family matter."

The secretary's answer left Nabila with doubt; why would Abdul Rahman go home and say it was a family matter? Nabila called the house but no one answered. Suspicious, Nabila dialed Issa's home to ask Margaret to check on Mara. Nabila waited on the line while Margaret searched for Mara.

When Margaret returned she said, "Mara was in her room talking to the master."

Nabila was appalled, as her husband would never walk into a servant's room. She became jealous and mistrustful of her husband. Her misgivings increased when she told Abdul Rahman that she had called his office and he was absent. Abdul Rahman's response offered no clue that he was at home.

Abdul Rahman only said, "You know I am very busy."

Nabila could not believe what she heard. Abdul Rahman would never hide anything from her. He was honest and sincere. He even used to call Nabila to tell her when he would not be in the office in case she needed him.

Alarmed, Nabila went to Issa's house and talked to Margaret about the incident. Margaret told Nabila that Abdul Rahman actually came home every day at about that time while Nabila was at work. *What was going on?* Nabila asked Margaret if she would allow Mara to stay at her house as soon as she finished her work. The next day Nabila asked Margaret if anything happened while she was at the university. Margaret reported that when Abdul Rahman came home and did not find Mara, he came to Margaret's house. Angry, Abdul Rahman insisted that Mara remain at his home.

There were days when Nabila's family was chatting and laughing, and for no reason, Abdul Rahman would leave to be with Mara. Nabila confronted Abdul Rahman about it more than once. She told Abdul Rahman that she pitied Mara and did not want her to lose her job. Mara needed the money to support her family, and they were supposed to help her. Abdul Rahman innocently wanted to know what he was doing that bothered Nabila.

"Don't give her too much attention," Nabila said. "Remember she is only three years older than your daughter. You are forty-five and she is only nineteen."

When Abdul Rahman inquired what he was to do, Nabila set firm expectations.

"I want you to leave her alone. Let her do her job without you talking to her. She is here to work, to make her living," Nabila replied.

Nabila decided to send Mara to sleep each evening with her cousin at Issa's house.

Unfortunately, Nabila's efforts to keep her husband away from Mara were fruitless. Mara was also becoming less of a help to Nabila. With guests coming for dinner one evening, Nabila called Mara to assist with the meal. She looked everywhere for her, but Mara was not around. Nabila thought that she might have run away, which was common as many housekeepers left a residence for more money. Some maids even ran away from employers to become prostitutes to make more money. Despite being treated well, some maids abused the children in the family by hitting them and teaching them profanity and bad habits. Various scenarios crossed Nabila's mind, including the notion that someone may have kidnapped Mara.[1] When Nabila saw Abdul Rahman entering the house, she frantically ran to tell him that Mara was missing.

Abdul Rahman looked straight at Nabila and said, "I took her out because she was tired of the house work."

Nabila steadied herself, willing her brain to process what she had just heard.

"WHAT?" she screamed. "What do you mean, you took her out?"

Abdul Rahman shrugged, saying that Mara worked so hard that he thought she deserved a break. Nabila tried to make him understand that she had needed Mara, as she was entertaining. Nabila reasoned that Abdul Rahman should have at least told her Mara was leaving.

Abdul Rahman coldly informed Nabila, "No, I don't ask for your permission. You are not her sponsor. Why must I get your permission to take her out?"

Nabila greeted her guests that evening in an exquisite dress stained with tears.

CHAPTER NOTES:

1 Saudi Arabia does not comply with international standards for eliminating trafficking and is not making significant efforts to prosecute and punish trafficking offenders or significantly improve victim protection services (2011).

A story garnering headlines featured a Saudi man attempting to sell his son on Facebook for approximately $20 million to avoid 'living in poverty.' The man claimed trafficking his son was the only option to continue providing for his wife and daughter since his illegal business was shut down.

CHAPTER 19

Command the Muslim men to keep their eyes low and to protect
their private parts that is much purer for them; indeed Allah is
Aware of their deeds.

~ AL NOOR 24:30

For *Hajj* vacation, Issa and Margaret and their friends Shaza and Don joined Nabila's family traveling to Nairobi, Mombasa, and Mount Kenya on a safari. Leila and Lamia were particularly excited as Nabila discussed the coming trip. Abdul Rahman wondered aloud where Mara would stay. When Nabila suggested keeping Mara at Rahma's as they did before, Abdul Rahman announced that they would take Mara with them.

Nabila seethed. "Why? Why should we take a maid on our family vacation? She is not a member of this family!"

Abdul Rahman accused Nabila of having no mercy on the poor. He rationalized that Mara had seen nothing in her life and that it would do her good to travel and see different parts of the world. Nabila could not believe it; her husband wanted the maid to accompany them on their vacation. It did not take a psychic to figure out that it would not be a pleasant trip.

On the plane, Issa, Margaret, and their son were in the front seats of the plane. Shaza, Don, and their three children were seated two rows from Issa's family. Lamia and Leila occupied the two seats in front of Abdul Rahman and Nabila. Mara sat next to Leila. Nabila noticed Abdul Rahman stood up frequently to glance at Mara, which irritated Nabila. At the hotel Abdul Rahman's interest in Mara increased. Mara became the center of his attention. At mealtime, he would call her to come to the table before any of the others arrived.

The hotel rang a special bell whenever wild animals came near the building and could be observed from the wide windows. Whenever the bell sounded, Abdul Rahman would call Mara to join him in watching the animals. He did not bother to call Nabila or want her to join him. All Abdul Rahman cared about was Mara. Even during sightseeing, he would call to Mara and take her picture in various poses at different sites. At the end of the trip, he had many more photographs of Mara than of the girls and Nabila.

Nabila could not trust her thinking. She felt like a ping-pong ball smacked back and forth across the net. In previous discussions with some of her friends, Nabila was the only one who defended her husband, telling everyone that she had never felt jealous because Abdul Rahman loved her so much and never gave her a reason to feel jealous. Her friends complained that all men are cheaters, no matter how beautiful his wife is or what she does for her husband. Men always cheat. *No, Abdul Rahman was completely different from the average man.* No matter what happened between them, he would never look at another woman. Nabila had the ideal, role model husband. Then the ball would jump across the net. Was she wrong in judging Abdul Rahman? Was he just trying to help their poor maid have a better life?

The ten-day vacation ended. On the return flight, the plane landed in Sudan at about five p.m. They had to exit the plane and take all their property because the plane had a mechanical problem. They found themselves in an abandoned airport isolated from the rest of the city. There were no airport personnel, no people except the passengers from the plane. Even the crew from the flight was absent. The passengers clustered in groups waiting for an official. Children were hungry and crying; everyone became frustrated, as there was no water or food to eat. It was ten o'clock, and no one came to help. When a man in a uniform walked by, he was mobbed by the crowd. He was mistaken for an airport worker, but he knew nothing about their situation. During the long wait, Nabila kept her eyes on Abdul Rahman. She watched him casually walk around in a circle and come back to where Mara was sitting. Nabila's daughters were making the best of the detour with Margaret and Shaza joking and laughing oblivious to all the troubles around them. Nabila was alone, and their laughter added to her misery. Nabila could not listen to them having fun while she was so depressed and uncomfortable with Abdul Rahman's disloyal behavior.

She wanted to close her eyes to dismiss this nightmare. But she could not blink an eye and just stared as Abdul Rahman continued to circle around Mara, an animal and his prey.

Most of the passengers stretched out and used their luggage as pillows. Nabila's daughters, the other children, Margaret, and Shaza were still sitting in a corner of the hallway. Issa and Don were near the edge of the gate chatting and trying to determine the problem with the plane. Abdul Rahman did not return to sit with Nabila; instead he seemed magnetized to Mara. Each pang of jealousy rooted Nabila to the ground and rendered her incapable of looking away. Nabila watched her husband of twenty years, the father of her children, slip away.

At about midnight, a pilot appeared. The men in the crowd scurried to talk to him, hoping that the pilot had an answer. The pilot was barely visible as all the male passengers surrounded him. The pilot indicated that the situation was beyond his control, and they would need to wait for those in authority to send help. However, the men got frustrated and started to shout at the pilot that there was no one to complain to and nothing to eat or drink.

"We are not animals. You dumped us here with no water or food, not even a bathroom," the men shouted.

The pilot tried to calm the crowd by promising that he would test the plane and see if it was good enough to fly to Jeddah. The announcement gave the passengers hope that someone was trying to do something about the situation. The pilot circled overhead twice and flew closer for the landing. As the plane touched down, they heard an explosion. Fortunately, the explosion was no more than a tire that blew out as the landing gear malfunctioned.

The passengers were relieved when the authorities brought in sandwiches and bottles of water. An official arranged lodging, and a bus was in route to take passengers to a hotel. Finally, at three o'clock in the morning the bus dropped off their group at the hotel. The driver informed them that he would return at nine a.m. to transport them back to the airport.

Nabila's family was promptly on the plane the next morning but exasperated as the plane lingered on the ground for another two hours. Again, there was no one to ask about their plight. The heat inside the plane was unbearable. People complained to the attendant serving breakfast, but she would not answer any questions. Soon after the flight attendant picked up the breakfast trays, a pilot informed the passengers that something was wrong with the plane and that they would have to exit the plane with their luggage. They waited another two long hours before reboarding the plane that finally returned them to their home.

Nabila's life in Jeddah changed after the vacation. Abdul Rahman decreed that Mara would be responsible for the cooking. Nabila was disheartened as she prided herself in being an exceptional cook. Mara was inexperienced at cooking, and her first meal prepared on her own was a disaster. The girls were not happy, and Nabila was too hurt to say anything.

In the middle of the day, Nabila could not find Mara. She was not anywhere on the property. Her woman's intuition was telling her that something was going on. She hoped and prayed that Mara was not with Abdul Rahman. Nabila was tortured with worry and jealousy. *Oh Allah, please do not let it be what I think*. Nabila prayed as she had never prayed before. However, Allah did not answer her prayer as Nabila saw them both coming up the walk. She was devastated. She could not take it anymore and began to shout at Mara for not letting her know where she went. Mara turned and looked at Abdul Rahman for support. Abdul Rahman's anger matched Nabila's, but his turned violent. Abdul Rahman raised his hand and struck Nabila across the face.

Abdul Rahman yelled, "I heard her coughing last night, so I took her to see the doctor." He continued to slap Nabila on her face and head.

Mara stood by the door watching and waiting.

It was not just the physical abuse; each day Nabila suffered as Abdul Rahman put the maid first, over her. Nabila was neglected, mistreated, and abused by her husband. She told Abdul Rahman repeatedly that she did not need a maid. She could just be a homemaker and do all the work herself. She tried to convince Abdul Rahman to send Mara back to her country. Whenever Nabila mentioned that Mara must leave, Abdul Rahman took Mara's side saying she had not done anything wrong. He accused Nabila of not having the heart for the poor and making Mara work while Nabila watched TV. Desperate, Nabila called the immigration office and asked how to break the servant's contract and send Mara back to her country. The office informed Nabila that only Mara's sponsor, Abdul Rahman, could deport her.

Nabila lived in misery, unable to escape her husband's infatuation with the housekeeper in their home. Relatives and friends had servants in their houses, but none of them had problems. Why her? She could not understand why her husband was interested in a young Filipino girl close to his daughter's age who was not from his culture, religion, or class, which was very important in his country. Abdul Rahman did not even know Mara's background or about her life in her own country. Nabila could not accept that Abdul Rahman had changed. He frequently became violent, assaulting Nabila, and making her miserable by his cruelty and abusiveness. He would not accept anything Nabila had to say. Abdul Rahman yelled, insulted Nabila, and criticized her in front of the girls.

He would point to the ugliest and most wicked character on television and tell the girls, 'Look, this is just like your mother.'

Their relationship worsened every day; he avoided talking to Nabila. She insisted Abdul Rahman deport Mara, but all her demands were ignored. It was impossible to convince Abdul Rahman to send Mara away.

Abdul Rahman would say, "Why would I do such a thing to the good girl? She has not done anything wrong. You are the one who has no mercy on this girl."

Abdul Rahman and Nabila battled until their marriage was in ruins. To prevent her husband and Mara from getting together while she was out of the house, Nabila took Mara everywhere with her, and sent Mara to the neighbor's house, with her cousin, in spite of all Abdul Rahman's objections.

Six months passed and Abdul Rahman spoke to Nabila less and less. He was fixated on Mara and gave Nabila no credence. Nabila felt like a stranger in her own home, and she was supposed to be the mistress of the house. In spite of all her torture and suffering, Nabila kept it inside, refusing to tell any members of her family. She suffered alone from the humiliation. Her daughter, Leila, was the only one Nabila felt she could confide in, cry with, and explain her feelings. Nabila thought being close to her daughter's age would help Leila to understand her better. Leila would listen to Nabila's concerns, but didn't offer a word of support or any comments. Abdul Rahman had somehow managed to convince the girls that he was justified in his actions.

Abdul Rahman's actions diminished Nabila's trust, but she never gave up. She was determined to fight for her marriage and continued to beg Abdul Rahman to send Mara back to her country.

"Please, Abdul Rahman, for Allah sake, send this girl away from our house."

Finally, Abdul Rahman agreed to send Mara back to the Philippines, but dismissed any hope of reconciliation. "Okay, I will send her back, only to prove to you that she is not the reason for our unhappiness. I want to prove to you that we just can't live together any longer."

However, Abdul Rahman's promise to send Mara away came with a price. Mara was not the only one to leave the family home. Abdul Rahman insisted that Nabila leave as well. While Nabila was heartbroken she agreed to the separation, believing that with Mara far away Abdul Rahman would come to his senses and wish for his wife to return.

Housing costs were soaring and tenants were expected to pay the rent up front for the entire year. Nabila had received the 50000 riyals from the government awarded to all citizens who graduated from college. Now that money would need to be used to rent an apartment. In addition, Nabilia had to tap her savings to purchase basic furniture needed for an apartment.

Nabila wanted to live close to her mother, but unfortunately, residing with her mother and sister was not a possibility because they were constantly arguing. Fatima had inherited her father's aggressive personality and as always Rahma was the victim of the abuse. With her brother's help, Nabila was able to rent a place in the same building as her mother. Living next door provided more than enough drama for Nabila whose mental state was as fragile as a china cup.

Nabila had only been in her new apartment for a couple of weeks when she received a call from Adel's wife. Nabila was shocked at her sister-in-law's revelation half way through their phone conversation. Abdul Rahman had not kept his word. Instead of deporting Mara as he had promised, she had been staying at Adel's home. Of course, by custom, Adel could not refuse his older brother's wishes. Now that Abdul Rahman had succeeded in evicting Nablia, he summoned Mara to live with him. When Nabila found out she had been deceived she was not about to honor her side of the agreement. She believed that as long as she was still married and had committed no wrongs, she should live in the family residence. So she returned to the house, confronting both Abdul Rahman and Mara. After much turmoil, Abdul finally agreed to deport Mara, and Nabila abandoned the apartment and moved back into their unhappy home.

Nabila wanted to be sure that Abdul Rahman was really going to send Mara away so she called Margaret to ask if she could borrow her driver to go with Abdul Rahman to take Mara to the airport. When Abdul Rahman and the driver returned from the airport, Nabila quizzed the driver if Mara actually left the country. She was relieved when he said yes; however, Nabila was not happy when he revealed that Abdul Rahman rewarded the girl with a few hundred riyals on her way to the plane.

Nabila thought Mara's departure would restore harmony in her home. Unfortunately, her relationship with Abdul Rahman worsened. Abdul Rahman severed contact with Nabila, even electing to sleep in another room. In all of their married life, her husband had never left her bed, not for a single night. Abdul Rahman slept on a floor mattress in the guest room. Nabila tried to talk to him, telling him how much she missed him and how much she wanted him back in her bed.

Abdul Rahman responded with insults. "I don't miss you and I don't even want you around."

Nabila knew Abdul Rahman could easily divorce her. It occurred to Nabila that perhaps Abdul Rahman was abusing her only to force her to ask him for a divorce to avoid feeling guilty. He would have an excuse to answer others who would seek the reason for their divorce after years of marriage. Abdul Rahman could easily say, "She asked for it," and Nabila would get all the blame for destroying the home and the family. So because of this, Nabila specifically did not mention the word "divorce" to Abdul Rahman and tried her best to overlook his behavior. During the months that passed, they lived as strangers. There was nothing left between them, as Abdul Rahman would not accept anything from Nabila. Her attempts to talk to him on many occasions resulted in more insults and rejection.

Abdul Rahman would come home from work and eat, then disappear to his private room to listen to newly purchased love songs. Whenever he needed anything, he would call his daughters to ask Nabila. He would not talk to Nabila directly. When the phone rang and the girls were not at home, to avoid talking to Nabila, he would tell the caller that Nabila was not there.

Uncharacteristically, Abdul Rahman received presents on Christmas and Easter. Nabila knew the presents weren't from their friends, because none celebrated Christmas or Easter. Even Christians were not permitted to celebrate either holiday in Saudi Arabia. Every time he received presents, Nabila's stomach would clench in despair. She knew they were from Mara. The pain of betrayal is like no other.

When Nabila found an application for an Indonesian domestic helper lying on the dining table, she asked Abdul Rahman if he was thinking of recruiting another maid. She pleaded with him not to do it, repeating that she did not need any help. Nabila assured him that she would take care of everything herself.

"She is not going to be for you. She is going to take care of the girls and me," he replied before fleeing the room. "We can't be without a maid. The house is only clean and organized when we have a maid in the house."

Nabila could not believe that Abdul Rahman could honestly deny her efforts and hard work for all those years. When love dies, must all resemblance of truth perish as well?

Nabila hired a local Somali woman, Selima, thinking Abdul Rahman might approve of her work and ignore the idea of recruiting a maid from another country. Selima handled the job well, but Abdul Rahman did not like her. When Selima got sick, Abdul Rahman refused to take her to a doctor, or give her the money to pay the medical bill. Selima stayed for a little over a month, before Abdul Rahman brought an Indonesian woman, Zolekha, home and adamantly introduced her as the new house cleaner. Nabila was disappointed to let Selima go and the poor woman could not understand the reason for her dismissal. Selima begged Nabila to keep her so she could support her three children. Nabila explained to her that Abdul Rahman was the one in charge, and she had no idea he had recruited another maid. Nabila was comforted to see that Zolekha was a middle-aged woman but still active. At least Zolekha was capable of caring for the house, though no one could restore it to a happy home.

*As a three-year-old in her red party dress for the Eid
Holiday, the biggest celebration of the year.*

As a young teenager pictured two months before her wedding.

Nabila was born in her parents' home at the top of this mountain. In the late '80s, the royal family acquired the mountain, building a large palace overlooking the Great Mosque in Makkah.

Their wedding celebration in Egypt complete with a belly dancer.

Performing traditional prayers. Women are covered from head to toe to perform Islamic prayers five times daily.

Faithfully reading the Quran each day.

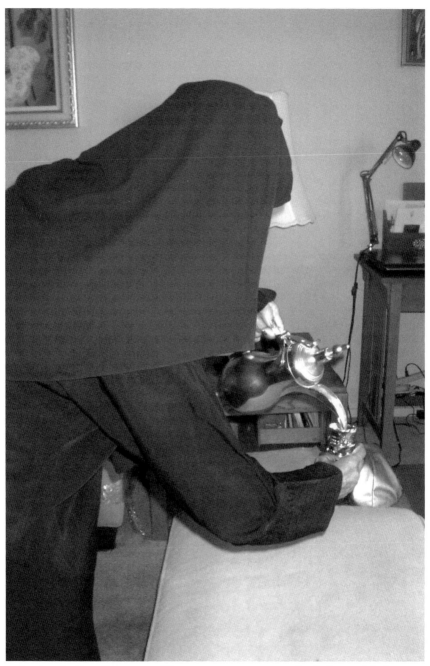

Serving Arabic coffee to guests. This is an important custom for the hostess. The hostess always serves the coffee with her right hand.

A page of the Quran, Muslims most respected book. The Quran contains the valued principles that Muslims abide by governing their daily lives.

Saudi Arabia was full of rapid changes during this time period. During King Khalid's reign from 1975-1982, he revolutionized the structure and educational system of the country and developed a friendly foreign policy with the U.S. In 1979, two events occurred which threatened the royal regime and had a long-term impact on Saudi foreign and domestic policy. The Shi'ite minority, in the Eastern Province housing the prized oil fields, staged several anti-government riots in the region in 1979 and 1980, prompted by the neighboring Iranian Islamic revolution. The riots, coupled with the seizure of the Grand Mosque in Makkah by Islamist extremists, caused the royal family to respond with a much stricter enforcement of Islamic and traditional Saudi norms in the land.

Under King Khalid's power the country assumed a more influential role in regional politics and international economic and financial affairs. Islamism continued to grow in strength and Crown Prince Fahd was chosen to oversee the aspects of the government's international and domestic policies.

During the 1970s and 1980s, more than 45,000 Saudi students traveled to the United States for study. The discovery of oil in Saudi Arabia prompted more than 200,000 Americans to relocate to work in the industry.

Before King Khalid death in June of 1982, a preliminary agreement was formed on the partition of the Saudi-Iraqi neutral zone. The agreement was finalized in 1983.

During the1970s and '80s Saudi Arabia became the world's greatest producer of oil. The economy was greatly impacted by the wealth generated by the oil industry. King Fahd, who succeeded his brother Khaid to the throne in 1982, made certain the oil revenues were controlled through the government. At the same time Fahd maintained a policy of close cooperation with the United States and increased purchases of advanced artillery from the U.S. and Britain.

Saudi values were impacted by increased wealth, the cities' expansions, influx of foreign workers, mass public education, and media accessibility. However, changes in the government did not keep pace with the country's improvements and the royal family continued with a lock hold of power. This has led to disaffection among many Saudis who seek greater participation in the country's government.

Saudi Arabia joined the anti-Iraq Coalition after the Iraqi invasion of Kuwait in 1990. Because King Fahd feared an attack from Iraq, he requested that American and Coalition soldiers join Saudi troops in the Kingdom. Unfortunately, allowing outside forces to be based in the country sparked an increase in Islamic terrorism in both Saudi Arabia (1996 Khobar Towers bombing) and in Western countries, with the 9/11 attacks in the U.S. being one of the most horrific.

While Saudi Arabia was extremely wealthy, the country's economy was weak and unemployment high. This contributed to civil unrest and discontent with the royal family. The royal family's response was to make limited changes to superficially appease dissenters.

When King Fahd suffered a debilitating stroke in 1995, Crown Prince Abdullah assumed daily operations for the government, continuing a domestic policy of minor reforms. He did, however, execute a major foreign policy move by distancing the Kingdom from the U.S. This was evidenced in 2003, when Saudi Arabia declined to support the U.S. and its allies in the invasion of Iraq. But because of mushrooming terrorist activity in 2003 such as the Riyadh compound bombings, the Saudi government increased action against terrorism.

Upon King Fahd's death in 2005 his half-brother, Abdullah, ascended to the throne. King Abdullah focused on moderate reforms in limited deregulation, foreign investment, and privatization of the country's precious commodity of oil.

King Abdullah, still in power today, has taken a diligent approach to deal with Islamic terrorism. He has ordered that force be employed by the country's security forces to contain extremists. In February 2009, the king proposed governmental changes for improvement for the judiciary, armed forces, and various ministries as well as replacing extremist individuals with more moderate officials.

CHAPTER 20

*If ye fear a breach Between them twain, Appoint (two) arbiters,
One from his family, And the other from hers; If they wish for
peace, God will cause their reconciliation.*

~ AL NESSA 35

Abdul Rahman's cousin, Yasser, invited Abdul Rahman and Nabila for lunch in Makkah. The family there did not know of their marital problems until Nabila called Uncle Hassan seeking advice to deal with Abdul Rahman. During the call, Nabila sobbed so heavily that she was not able to explain anything to him over the phone. Uncle Hassan was kind and understanding and asked Nabila to wait until she got to his house to discuss the problem.

During the two-hour ride to Makkah, Abdul Rahman was listening to a tape and practicing how to speak Tagolog language in thirty days. Nabila was burning inside and could not hold off her tears. She wiped them away with her tarha. Certainly, he had to realize how much he hurt her. Nabila's emotions fluctuated between sorrow and anger. Furious, Nabila questioned why she had to put up with all the pain just to stay with a man who did not want her. *Why don't I ask him to divorce me?* While Abdul Rahman was listening to the tape, Nabila contemplated what her life would be like if she got divorced. Nabila knew as a lone woman in her country no one would rent to her. None of her brothers would take her, because they had family responsibilities of their own. In Islam, the next guardian to the father is the brother, but the fact is that most brothers do not want to be bothered. Besides, none of the wives would accept Nabila in their houses. Where would she go? Nabila was still teaching at the university holding an hourly teaching job, not enough to support her. The girls would be living with their father, which upset Nabila. Her thoughts zigzagged between trying to restore her marriage and figuring out how to end it.

Their cousin Yasser met them at the door of Uncle Hassan's house. They greeted the women and children with the traditional kiss on each cheek and shook hands with the men.

Nabila's family surrounded the plastic sheet spread on the floor for the main meal of rice with two large roasted legs of lamb and a side dish of pickles. No spoons or any other utensils were present, so Nabila requested them for the girls and herself.

Knowing that Yasser was always traveling to the Far East to recruit maids and drivers, Abdul Rahman asked him if he could find a maid that could cook Arabic food. Abdul Rahman said he was planning to move to his new home at the Prince's Project soon. This news jolted Nabila into the realization that he was planning to leave her.

Soon after the meal, Uncle Hassan called Nabila to the other room. She silently prayed to Allah that Uncle Hassan would be able to help. Nabila told him how Abdul Rahman hurt her and that she was in a quandary as to what to do. Uncle Hassan called for Abdul Rahman and asked Nabila to leave the room. Nabila sat with the women and Yasser. They had no idea what Nabila was going through, but quizzed her when they saw her wet face. Nabila gave them a brief account and Zain, Yasser's wife, was shocked at her tale.

"But Abdul Rahman loves you so much. He wouldn't do that to you," Zain said in denial.

Each of the women had an opinion.

"Men are deceivers," one declared.

Another asked, "How can anyone trust a man?"

"What happened to all the love he had for you?" she wondered.

"Don't worry, men often do that, but he will come back to you. He loves you too much to leave you," supplied the oldest woman there.

"Inshaa Allah he will," Nabila responded, hoping he would come back to his senses.

Soon Nabila heard Uncle Hassan calling her. The women all encouraged Nabila and gave her hope that Uncle Hassan would put an end to her misery with Abdul Rahman.

As Nabila walked into the room, Uncle Hassan stood up, took her hand, and pulled her toward Abdul Rahman saying, "I talked to Abdul Rahman, and he showed a great love for you; so now I want you both to kiss and make up and go home happily."

Abdul Rahman obliged and kissed Nabila on the head.

As they left the house, the family was happy to see them back together. They cheered, and Zain kissed both of them on the cheek, advising them to take care of each other.

Then Zain turned to Abdul Rahman, "I know you always loved your wife and she loved you very much, and neither one of you complained about the other throughout those long years together. What happened?"

Her older daughter replied, "They must have been envied by the evil eye, Mother."

At Uncle Hassan's, Nabila felt the stress that she kept inside give way only to return during the drive home. Abdul Rahman had not said a word to her, and she did not bother to talk to him thinking they would have much to say when they returned. At home, the girls went to their rooms, and Abdul Rahman dressed in his house clothes and watched TV. Nabila went to clear the kitchen, still hoping Abdul Rahman would talk to her, but nothing happened. Abdul Rahman went to bed earlier than usual, and Nabila was delighted when she saw him in their bed. Later, when Nabila awoke chilled from the air conditioner, she quickly turned it off.

Abdul Rahman spoke up. "See, everything is up to you. I have no say or opinion on anything."

"What is it? Nabila asked surprised.

"You did not ask me if it is all right to turn off the AC. I have no opinion on anything. It is always your word against mine. I am going to sleep in my room," he said.

He left the room, and Nabila knew immediately that he was making any excuse to stay away. He really did not want to preserve their marriage, but could not admit that to his older uncle. It was all an illusion to delude the family.

Abdul Rahman and Nabila lived shackled in a meaningless marriage. Nabila continued cleaning, cooking, and looking after the girls. Abdul Rahman maintained his regular routine of work, home for a meal, and listening to his love songs. At the end of the day, Abdul Rahman went directly to his private room. They did not communicate; whenever Abdul Rahman needed something, he would ask one of the girls.

Time passed, but Abdul Rahman's unloving actions toward Nabila did not. She tried to keep her anger in check, frightened that he would divorce her. She had hypothesized about what she would do, and was convinced divorce would end her life. As a Saudi woman, Nabila would not know how to live alone. She had never faced life by herself. Before marriage, her father and brother took care of her, and then she married at the age of fifteen. She was paralyzed without a man around as Abdul Rahman took care of everything in her life. Nabila did not know how to write a check or use an ATM card. She had blindly depended on Abdul Rahman and could not imagine an existence without him. She had spent most of her life with Abdul Rahman and had passed no milestone without him. Everywhere she went, either at home or around the world, was with him; Nabila had no memories that he was not a part of. She was convinced he loved her very much. Everyone they knew throughout their lives had envied Nabila for having a great husband. She could not accept that Abdul Rahman had changed and their lives would never again be intertwined with love.

Nabila put great hope in Allah and prayed faithfully. When she could no longer keep reality at bay, Nabila succumbed to the fact that she would live the remainder of her life as a divorced woman. Why was it so difficult to break up or leave a man who treated her so bad? Could her love for this man be so strong that she was willing to do absolutely anything to bring him back and restore their life together?

The way Abdul Rahman was treating Nabila was all pointing to the fact that he wanted her to take action, but Nabila refused. If Abdul Rahman wanted out then he was going to need to take responsibility for his actions and work through a suitable arrangement for all involved. Nabila moped pathetically, but she never lost her feistiness for justice. She believed the day would come when Abdul Rahman would deeply regret his infidelity.

Even if divorce was Nabila's only reprieve, she might not be able to survive alone in a country where women in general, and divorced in particular, were treated less than a second-class citizen. Society had no mercy on any woman, especially a divorced one. Nabila concluded that divorce would guarantee loneliness, the absence of her girls, and the loss of her home.

A woman is the loser in any Saudi divorce. Men are without blame in the society. No matter how bad the husband is, the woman is always at fault for the divorce. The wheels of justice are broken for Saudi women. In desperation, Nabila sought the advice of one of the religious leaders at the court in Jeddah. She explained how Abdul Rahman was treating her and how he was interested in the Filipino maid. His response buried Nabila with despair.

He said, "It must be your fault. If you were a good wife, your husband would not turn to another woman."

Nabila needed to talk to someone besides her daughters, who were not able to make her feel any better. Nabila felt they both took their father's side. She called her two closest sisters, Ennas and Shaymaa. Both her sisters' husbands had worked with Abdul Rahman, but Shaymaa's husband had left the job to take care of his own private business. Nabila was hardly able to complete a sentence. She was stuttering, trying to control her tears, pouring forth the sordid story of Abdul Rahman and Mara. Her sisters questioned Nabila's account as they both viewed Abdul Rahman as an ideal husband and father and wondered why he would still be acting distant, as Mara had been gone for some time. They both advised against Nabila asking for a divorce to make it easier for Abdul Rahman to exit the marriage. Shaymaa wondered aloud if Abdul Rahman was still in touch with Mara. Nabila had not considered that possibility and the idea destroyed her. However, when Ennas said her husband was unsure why Abdul Rahman would send presents and chocolate with every worker who traveled to the Philippines, Nabila's heartbeat quickened. A suspicion evolved and soon became an obsession to know the truth.

Nabila had to know if Abdul Rahman was still in touch with Mara. What she imagined could not be worse than finally knowing the truth. She did not know if he had received any letters as all mail was delivered to the post office box, and women were not permitted in the post office.

Ennas offered some insight explaining. "Usually men hide their secrets in their cars because they know women have nothing to do with cars."

Nabila decided to search her husband's car for any evidence of his contact with Mara. She set the alarm for five in the morning, an hour before Abdul Rahman got up. She found the key and walked outside to the car that was parked a few steps from the house. Nabila's hands shook as she opened the glove compartment. Nabila found five handwritten letters neatly stacked and knew immediately they were from Mara. Her heart felt like it was pumping out of her chest as she walked back to the house. Nabila returned the car key, and hurried to her room with the letters. She locked her door and turned the light on very low, enough to read the letters. The stationery showed a naked man and woman holding hands, kissing, and about to make love. Through the letters, Nabila learned Abdul Rahman had bought Mara a house with a telephone, so that she could call his car phone. He also had been sending her a monthly allowance, sent her to college, and even bought her a coffee bean farm to start her own business. This was beyond anything Nabila could have fathomed. *Who was this man I still called my husband? Where was my cousin, my love, my husband who had cherished me for years?* Nabila sank to the floor, drowning in a pool of deceit.

Nabila heard his footsteps heading toward the bathroom, at about seven a.m. as usual.

She suspected there would be more unrest when he found out she took the letters. She waited in her room until Abdul Rahman left the house to go to work.

Nabila was severely wounded by her discovery but still able to fight for her marriage. She decided to send Mara a letter telling her if she had any respect for Abdul Rahman or any feelings for him, she should leave him alone. Nabila explained that he was a man of a great position in the government, and his reputation was very important to him as well as his family. Keeping in touch with him could cause him to lose his job and might bring about a scandal that Nabila was sure Mara would not want for him. Nabila did not sign the letter but enclosed a copy of Mara's letters to let her know she had them. Nabila kept the original ones. She was hoping her appeal to Mara for Abdul Rahman's well being would be heeded.

Days passed and fortunately Abdul Rahman did not look for those letters, at least not in the house. He looked a little worried, but did not inquire about it.

However, one day when Nabila was typing papers for work, Abdul Rahman passed by and said, "So this is the machine you used to type everything on." Nabila immediately knew that Mara had told Abdul Rahman about the letter Nabila wrote to her.

Two years had passed since Mara left Jeddah. Abdul Rahman and Nabila were still not speaking with any good will. She had tried uncountable times to talk to Abdul Rahman hoping he would listen to her, but there was no change. However, Nabila never felt that she could give up. She always had hope that she would be able to revive her relationship with Abdul Rahman if she kept trying.

Nabila's stress escalated as Uncle Saleh decided to come back and live with them. As he greeted Nabila, he commented, "I came to live here for the rest of my life." With Uncle Saleh present, they needed a driver. Abdul Rahman decided to hire the Yemen's driver, Othman, to drive the girls to school and spend his free time with Uncle Saleh. Uncle Saleh began to complain that he sometimes needed Othman, but he would not be around to help him. Abdul Rahman decided to recruit another driver from Indonesia to keep Othman with his father, and the new driver transported the girls.

Nabila occasionally used the new driver, but the driver was rude to her. Aware of the problems between Abdul Rahman and Nabila, the driver often refused to transport Nabila. Once he stopped in the middle of the road and said, "I will not drive you anywhere. Get out of the car, or find someone else to drive you. Mr. Abdul Rahman does not want you. He even wants me, and doesn't want you."

When Nabila complained to Abdul Rahman about the driver he said, "That's because you overwork him and don't treat him right."

The driver gave his side of the story, and Abdul Rahman responded, "Don't listen to this woman. She is crazy."

Nabila was devastated that Abdul Rahman humiliated her in front of the driver. "You tell the driver, who works for us, I am crazy? How do you think he will feel about me?"

Abdul Rahman said he had to try to make the driver feel better because Nabila did not treat him well.

"Make him feel better?" Nabila asked "What about me? How do you make me feel in front of him? Did you ask me what happened?" she asked with frustration.

Nabila explained to Abdul Rahman that the driver said he only worked for Abdul Rahman and that he was not supposed to drive Nabila anywhere. He said he was doing it as a favor for Abdul Rahman, and to stop to pick up a friend of Nabila's was not part of his business. Nabila wanted Abdul Rahman to tell the driver he was wrong instead of telling him she was crazy. Nabila was humiliated and angry with Abdul Rahman for taking the servant's side against her.

The next day, Nabila summoned the driver, but he refused to drive her. Nabila informed him that it was his job to drive, and if not, she would cut his monthly salary. The driver was livid and began attacking Nabila. Leila was at a distance listening to the exchange. When she saw the driver hitting Nabila, she called her father. Nabila retreated to the house and called her brother, Aneese, who came immediately. Aneese took off his *egal*, the black round supporter of the Arab men's head cover, and struck the driver. Then Aneese took the driver to jail. At last, Nabila found someone who would stand up for her. Although Leila had called her father at work and explained what happened, Abdul Rahman did not bother to come home. His only response was to repeat that Nabila overworked the driver.

Aneese came the next day to tell Nabila the driver was still in jail and officials would deport him. However, Abdul Rahman wanted Aneese to release the driver by submitting a forgiveness form, because Abdul Rahman wanted the driver to come back to work. Shortly, two police officers arrived with the driver who had his hands cuffed behind his back. They came to the driver's room, packed all his belongings, and headed to the airport. Unfortunately, the other driver, Othman, quit as he could not deal with Uncle Saleh.

Less than a month later, Nabila was at the fruit shop and to her surprise, spotted the same driver who had attacked her. He had returned with his wife and baby to the country, and Nabila's daughters ran to welcome him and admire the baby. Nabila was angry with her girls, as they showed no feeling for her circumstances. Abdul Rahman had actually brought the driver and his family back into the country. Nabila called Aneese and he explained that many workers return to their country and change their passports to come back under a different name. With the help of her husband, the driver had outsmarted Nabila and returned against her wishes.

CHAPTER 21

A Muslim must not hate his wife and if he be displeased
with one bad quality in her, then let him be pleased with
another that is good.

~ AL SAHIH

Nabila's oldest brother, Aneese, had just come to her rescue the month before so she was surprised to see him on her doorstep. He had come to confront Nabila about her problems with Abdul Rahman and wondered why she had not told anyone in the family. He had found out through Issa's cousin that Abdul Rahman and Nabila were having a difficult time. Nabila was ashamed to discuss her marriage with her brother.

"Oh, my brother, I am so hurt by this man, and I don't know what to do. I tried my best to make him come back to his senses, but I am failing. I don't know what to do," Nabila said.

Aneese wondered what had happened to change Abdul Rahman. Instead of being forthright, Nabila had hidden the truth and protected Abdul Rahman and his reputation. Aneese was outraged that Nabila would attempt to protect Abdul Rahman after all he had done to hurt her. Aneese decided he would talk to Abdul Rahman privately.

The girls were old enough to know that their parents' marriage was in trouble. Leila was in college and Lamia was in high school.

Once Nabila asked them, "What do you think of what your father is doing?"

They both looked at her without saying a word.

Nabila asked again, "Do you want the woman who worked for us a maid, cleaning our bathroom, who is completely different from our society, our religion and our social status, to take my place and be your stepmother?"

Leila's eyes met her mother's and she said, "If that's what he wants."

"It's his choice," Lamia joined in.

Nabila quizzed, "You really do not care to what is happening to me, and you are old enough to see what he is doing to me. Do you see how he hurts me?"

Nabila was crushed by the boulder of apathy and lack of support from her daughters. They were fully entrenched in the Saudi traditions and way of life. The girls walked in their father's footsteps and they left Nabila to cry alone.

Aneese returned the following day after meeting with Abdul Rahman. Aneese said, "Abdul Rahman wants out of this marriage."

Nabila's brother told her to forget about Abdul Rahman and live her life.

Aneese made it very clear. "This man does not want you. Don't you have any dignity and respect for yourself? He doesn't want you."

Nabila was in denial and tried to dispute what her brother was saying. "Is there really dignity between a husband and a wife?" She still believed Abdul Rahman would come back to his senses. She knew her husband very well; he just was not like that.

As Aneese was leaving, he said, "I am telling you again, this man does not want you anymore. You better leave him."

As a last resort, Nabila decided to go to her father for advice. *May Allah help me and support me.* But as Nabila prayed, it was Aneese's voice she heard in response: 'I am telling you, nothing will bring him back.'

Aneese and Nabila drove to Makkah to see their father. With the help of her brother, Nabila was able to tell Saad about her marital problems. Saad was astounded to hear Nabila complaining about Abdul Rahman.

Saad said, "What happened? You both were doing fine. I have never heard you complaining about Abdul Rahman, and I have never heard him complaining about you. How did things get so bad between the two of you?"

Nabila sighed, hardly believing herself that it could all be true. She never wanted anyone to know about her husband's behavior, as Nabila was ashamed and wanted to shield Abdul Rahman from scrutiny. Abdul Rahman had always been above reproach, and Nabila believed that he would return to that stature.

"The housekeeper? Is that possible? Abdul Rahman goes after a Filipino maid in the house?" Saad said, unconvinced.

Everyone assured Nabila that Abdul Rahman was not that kind of a person and that he soon would come to his senses. Saad agreed to speak with Abdul Rahman to hear his story. Saad and Aneese met with Abdul Rahman at the prefabricated house where his father had lived when he was in the country. Neither Nabila's father nor her brother wanted Nabila to be with them during the confrontation with Abdul Rahman. Nabila knew Abdul Rahman would say anything he wanted, and she could not defend herself. Nabila was sure he would make up stories to convince Saad and Aneese that she was the one at fault.

Many women told Nabila that some men go through a crisis, and they usually end up coming back to their wives. Words like that encouraged her, offering hope. Others were surprised that Nabila was able to endure the continued torture from a man. It was easy for anyone to advise her to leave him. However, Nabila just could not think of leaving him and being a divorced woman. Nabila had coped with too many difficulties, humiliations, disgrace, abuse—both physically and verbally—and she was willing to put up with a lot more to get her husband and former life back. Two hours later, Saad and Aneese returned.

"What do you think, Father?" Nabila asked anxiously.

He looked at Nabila for few seconds and said, "Abdul Rahman told me everything."

Nabila was not sure what he meant by everything, suspecting he had lied or omitted things too private to tell her father. Saad looked very unhappy about what he had heard from Abdul Rahman. Nabila asked if he believed all he had heard.

"I don't know what to believe anymore. What I heard from Abdul Rahman was completely unexpected. I could not say anything, but listened to his complaints against you," her father said.

Nabila flung herself on the sofa and bawled. Unable to comfort Nabila, Saad returned to Makkah, and Aneese tried to convince Nabila to leave her husband. Nabila begged her brother to divulge what Abdul Rahman had said.

Aneese complied. "Among many other stories, he said you do not give him sex, and that one day in America, he had to beat you up and throw you out of the house because you were not obedient to him."

"Can you imagine I was beaten and thrown in the street in the middle of the winter because I said no?" Nabila angrily replied, remembering the scene.

"Yes, he told us that," Aneese agreed. Abdul Rahman also recited Prophet Muhammad (PBUH) saying, 'if a man wants his wife for sex, even if she was on a back of a camel, she must get off the camel to obey her husband's desire for sex.'

"So he is really looking for a machine, not a human. He was never like that before. He is so full of hate and rejection for me now," Nabila acknowledged.

Aneese shared that Abdul Rahman also complained that Nabila did not want to serve his father.

"I am not married to his father. I have enough work outside the home, inside with the kids, and I have no help. When he finally got rich, instead of honoring me by hiring a housemaid to help me, like the rest of the people in this country, he disgraced the family. He made her the woman of the house and I was the servant. I was beaten, kicked out of the house, and insulted verbally in front of her to show her how much he hated me," Nabila explained with bitterness.

Nabila told Aneese how Abdul Rahman gave Mara so much money that she became well known and respected because of her wealth in her poor country. As for Nabila, Abdul Rahman refused to pay for anything she needed. He said Nabila was not a good wife, and that he would only feed her and give her shelter as long as she was still his wife. Nabila had to save money for dental exams and doctor appointments. Aneese questioned her insistence to stay with such a husband. Nabila used her hurt to fuel her anger. She did not intend to make it easy for Abdul Rahman; he would have to take responsibility for his decision and actions.

Each morning Nabila read the verse of the Quran about the relationship between a husband and a wife: 'and He ordained between you love and mercy' (Sora Al Rom verse 20-21). Looking at that verse, and reviewing her marriage, she often wondered, *Where is the love that was between us? How did it disappear so suddenly?*

Chapter 22

And your Lord has decreed that you worship none but Him. And that you be dutiful to your parents. If one of them or both of them attain old age in your life, say not to them a word of disrespect, nor shout at them but address them in terms of honour.

~ Al Isra 17:23

One evening Nabila overheard Abdul Rahman talking to Leila about the fellow who was seeking her hand in marriage. He was telling Leila that the suitor was not from their country and that he could never have a decent job to make a good living. Foreigners could only work as laborers and he had no degree to help him have a good life. Leila had told her father about her wish to marry the young man but kept it a secret from Nabila. Leila did not want Nabila to know, thinking Nabila would not accept him.

When Nabila confronted her daughter, Leila said, "You wanted me to marry someone educated with a position and a good job. You are always against my wishes."

Shocked Nabila responded, "Have I ever stood against you? I thought you were my best friend. What is happening to this family? Why are you turning against me at a time when I need your support the most?"

"When I tell my friends about you, they tell me I have the worst mother," Leila continued, attacking Nabila.

"Is that really you saying that? You see what I am getting from your father!" Nabila cried. "I can't believe I am attacked by the two of you. Don't you have any mercy on me? I am your mother! What is it that I have done to you to make you hate me?"

Nabila had to fight both her husband and her daughter with no support from anyone. Abdul Rahman had managed to turn both the girls against their mother. Leila began to spy on Nabila by listening to her phone conversations and asking the drivers questions about where she went and what she did. Leila reported everything to her father. Nabila found threatening notes on the mirrors in the bathroom saying, "I am recording all your phone calls, and I will use them against you. I will not only report it to my father, I will also send it to your brothers, and the whole family will know everything about you." Nabila did not know what caused her daughter to turn against her but often wondered if Leila felt she needed to take sides, or competed against Nabila for Abdul Rahman's unconditional love and attention. Did Leila really believe all Abdul Rahman said against Nabila? Leila was not a young girl; she was in college, and had witnessed the abuse, along with her sister. Leila had become immersed in the Saudi culture, believing her mother had no right to dignity.

It was one thing to handle the abuse from Abdul Rahman, but from her precious daughter as well? Leila would not discuss her issues with Nabila and eventually they came to the point that they stopped talking to each other. Nabila's self-esteem plummeted, and her life was beyond any resemblance of its former state. As much as Abdul Rahman scorned her, it was nothing like the hatred Leila lashed. Nabila could never fathom how her own flesh and blood could treat her with such scathing disrespect. Filled with despair, Nabila sunk to the floor with the Quran in her hand. She opened it, read aloud, and prayed deeply from her heart that Allah would help her. Nabila felt she was fighting the whole world and sorely losing. She needed a stronger power beyond human capacity to sustain her. The Quran and prayers were her only comfort. She was devout with prayer, praying days and nights for insight. *Oh, my God, if I could only know what to do or how to survive without a man in this country, I would leave immediately. But where would I go and what would I do?* Nabila knew her husband did not want her in his life anymore. Her older daughter was following his abusive actions, hateful and trying to force Nabila to leave. Lamia was distant, whispering a lot to her sister. The girls shared things, excluding their mother. Nabila was a stranger within her family, the puzzle piece that did not quite fit.

In the midst of Nabila's heartbreak, her father became very ill and needed her to take him to the hospital. He refused to be admitted that day saying that the government was going to buy his old house to build a palace, so he must sign for the money. He promised to return as soon as he finished the transaction. The hospital was in a state of despair about to close its doors for good. They were not serving any meals to the patients. There was only one doctor, a general practitioner in the hospital, who came occasionally to see the patients. Because of the shortage of nurses, Nabila decided to stay with Saad to help as long as she could. She took a few days off to care for her father, cooking for him every day. He was not alert most of the time and sometimes failed to recognize Nabila. When Nabila tried to talk to him about the past and the years they spent in Egypt, he would ask her how she knew all that information. She repeatedly reminded him that she was his daughter.

Saad was restless at night, tossing and turning, and the doctor could do little to help him. He sometimes cursed Nabila and hit her with his fists, but she knew the violent behavior was the result of his disease. Nabila was torn, as she did not want to take Saad home because of the situation with Abdul Rahman. At the same time, she could not take him to his home with his Egyptian wife, because she would not be able to stay with him. Her brothers and sisters tried to come and visit him as well. After ten days, the doctor discharged Saad because the hospital was closing. His wife Soso took him home, and said she would take him to Egypt as soon as he felt better.

After Saad's release from the hospital, Nabila kept trying to telephone him, but would only reach his wife. Days later, Saad called to tell Nabila that his wife forced him to sign legal papers turning over all his money and the house to her. He believed that she took advantage of his sickness to get his signature on the papers. When Nabila talked to Soso, she denied everything. Soso claimed Saad was unconscious most of his time, and when he was alert, he was hallucinating and did not know what he was saying. Some of Saad's neighbors said that he was losing his mind, because he told them that his wife was stealing his money. Soon Nabila heard that Saad left for Egypt with Soso and their children.

In the summer, Nabila convinced Lamia to travel with her to Egypt to see Saad. Nabila had a difficult time finding his residence, but the taxi driver finally pulled up to a high rise in a low class residential area. They lived in one of the buildings that Nabila's stepmother had purchased. Soso led Nabila to where her father was laying unconscious.

He had declined in the few months since Nabila had seen him. She bent down and whispered, "Father, Father, it's me, your daughter." She held his hand hoping for any reaction from him, but there was no response. Lamia was standing by the door, too fearful to come any closer. Nabila kissed Saad's forehead, and called to Soso. Saad's wife confirmed that he had grown increasingly ill since they arrived in Cairo. She added that the doctor could not do anything more to help him. Saad would not eat and she could do little more than moisten his lips with water.

In her grief, Nabila called out to him again, "Father, Father, can you hear me?" She held his limp hand and rubbed it, but Saad did not rally.

Nabila asked Soso to bring a glass of water but neither of them were able to get him to drink. The water trickled out of the corner of his mouth. Overcome, Nabila laid her head on Saad's chest and sobbed. She sensed he was leaving this world. She was losing all the people in her life that mattered, and she could not fathom how she could possibly go on without Abdul Rahman, Leila, and now her beloved father.

In August of 1994 Nabila's father's body was brought to Jeddah for the funeral. Nabila's mother, Rahma walked up to the coffin and sat near her deceased husband. Nabila overheard her mother whispering, 'I forgive you for all that you have done to me. May Allah forgive all your sins and you rest in peace.' Rahma prayed for Saad. Maybe it was the emotion of the day or all she'd been through, but Nabila was infuriated with her mother's response. How could Rahma forgive Saad? *I will never forgive Abdul Rahman for what he did to me. I don't think there will ever be peace.*

CHAPTER 23

Lodge them [in a section] of where you dwell out of your means
and do not harm them in order to oppress them.

~ AL TALAQ 6

Each year was a rerun of the one before. For six years, Abdul Rahman and Nabila rarely spoke to each other. Nabila buried herself in her work as a full time high school teacher as well as working part time at the university. Lamia was in her last year of high school, and Leila was in her third year in medical school.

Everyone went his or her own way in the household; Nabila was no more than a servant. Abdul Rahman approached Nabila one day with talk of starting a restaurant business. Because he needed workers, he thought it prudent to travel to recruit them from Manila. Knowing Abdul Rahman never traveled without her gave Nabila hope that he had decided to take her along on his trip. Abdul Rahman quickly squelched that idea, informing Nabila that he was traveling alone. It soon became clear to Nabila that Abdul Rahman was going to see Mara in Manila. The days of Abdul Rahman traveling only with his wife and family were part of his other life in the distant past. Nabila reminded Abdul Rahman that she had begged him to go on trips offered through his job to make more money, but his answer was, 'not without my family'. Could this really be the same man?

Nabila discovered that Leila was going to take care of all her father's private business while he was away. *Why couldn't Leila see that she was encouraging him by taking care of his job while he was with the other woman? Didn't that send him a message that she approved of his affair?* Leila contended that she was only taking care of the paperwork until he returned. Nabila was angered that Leila was so naïve to believe Abdul Rahman's reason for the trip.

A week passed since Abdul Rahman had gone to Manila, and the family had not heard from him. Nabila was overwhelmed with the desire to know his whereabouts. She called every five star hotel in Manila, but his name did not appear on their registers. Finally, after ten days, Abdul Rahman called. When Nabila answered the phone, he asked for Leila, giving her his return flight and time. At the airport, he hugged the girls but kept Nabila away with his hateful stare. With one daughter under each arm, he turned his back to Nabila. She lagged behind them like a dog and not one of them turned around to see if Nabila followed.

For years, Abdul Rahman had a locked safe box where he kept money and other valuables. Since Abdul Rahman had returned from Manila, Nabila noticed he seemed possessive of the key. He even went so far as to take the key to his room and put it under his pillow when he went to sleep. Curiosity and suspicion got the best of Nabila as she was determined to find out what he was hiding.

Nabila waited until about three o'clock in the morning when she was certain Abdul Rahman was in a sound sleep. Quietly, she tiptoed into his room. As Nabila stared at her husband, she wondered how they had come to a place of such mistrust. She reached carefully under the pillow and fished out the key. Nabila did not know how she got the courage to take such action but she was desperate to know what was going on behind her back, and lucky enough not to wake him. Nabila wasted no time in opening the safe box. A few letters fell out of the box as well as some Filipino newspapers held together by rubber bands. The papers written in Tagalog included one with her husband's picture in it. However, it was the thick brown envelope stashed in the back that caught her eye. Nabila's hands were shaking as she emptied the envelope, revealing the contents that would ultimately ruin her life. There were pictures, many pictures that left no doubt of an affair. The photos showed Abdul Rahman with Mara hugging and kissing. In some, Mara was sitting on Abdul Rahman's lap as they fed each other. The pictures were private and real. Nabila knew they were real, because she had seen that look in Abdul Rahman's eyes before. It was the way he used to look at her. Nabila's eyes blurred, blinded by the truth. *Ya Allah, ya Allah, Oh my God, it cannot be true. Oh, please God let it be a nightmare and wake me up, please, please.* Nabila gagged on the revelation but was forced to swallow the truth.

Immersed in prayer and sorrow for hours, Nabila arose to find it was not quite dawn. She forced another glance at the pictures, keeping six as proof of the affair. She slid the rest back in the envelope, replaced them in the safe box, and locked it with the key. No matter how she tried, Nabila could not get the images of them together out of her head. Nabila's body recoiled as each frame played in her mind, and Nabila thought she would surely die of heartbreak.

Time was passing quickly, and Nabila needed to calm down to be able to replace the key before Abdul Rahman awoke. Nervously, Nabila managed to return the key as Abdul Rahman slept. She went back to bed but her tears kept her from any rest. Later, Nabila heard him coming toward the room so she covered her face with the bed sheet and pretended to sleep. Abdul Rahman performed his prayer, dressed, and left for work.

Nabila pulled herself out of bed, unwilling to face the day. She stumbled to the bathroom, leaned against the sink, and looked at her reflection in the mirror. She willed herself to function, even though her heart had been trampled. Nabila thought of her country's position on adultery. The sharia required substantial proof of adultery or intercourse. Four witnesses must attest in court that they witnessed the crime, and if such an accusation is not validated, the witnesses are then liable to be punished. Executions for adultery were rare but stonings were more common to humiliate the offender. Nabila doubted that there would be any witnesses to testify, and besides a man of Abdul Rahman's position would surely go unpunished for his actions. While Nabila dwelled on Abdul Rahman's adulterous affair, she was suddenly struck by a far worse possibility. What if Abdul Rahman married Mara?

Nabila hastily dialed her mother. As mothers often can, Rahma recognized the sadness in Nabila's voice. She said Nabila's sisters, Fatima and Najat, were there and to come over.

Nabila did not hold anything back from her family this time.

Nabila showed them the pictures and asked, "Do you believe this? Do you think he married her? Won't anyone help me and tell me what you think?"

Nabila's sadness gave way to a frenzy of madness; she had to know the truth. She carried on, asking each one what they thought was going on between Abdul Rahman and the Filipino woman who was their maid six years ago. For some reason now it seemed important to get it all out, all the doubts and fears she had withheld so no one would know and Abdul Rahman's precious reputation could remain intact. Her mother and sisters gaped at her listening to Nabila's recount of the sordid affair.

Her sisters called their husbands and other sisters and brothers and the whole family gathered at their mother's house. Nabila held center court screaming and waving the tell-all photos.

"Tell me, do you think they are married, because Abdul Rahman was never with any woman like that, and he would not do it unless they are married. What do you all think?"

No one spoke. They were as confused as Nabila was, looking at each other and not knowing what to say. Finally, Nabila's brother tried to comfort her telling her to wait until she found out the truth. But the photos were her truth, and what was she to do if they were really married?

"If he is married to her, then low class and dirty housemaids are his level and you would be too good to be with such a man," her brother replied. "Whether he is married to her or not, you should not live with him any longer."

Where would she go? What would she do? Always questions without answers. All Nabila had done was wallow in her grief. She desperately needed to do something, but could not think. She had to get away to clear her head. Nabila took the pictures and left the house without another word to her family. Her situation was beyond talk. She asked the driver to stop at the mall near her house. Inside the mall, Nabila looked for a photo shop and copied the telling pictures. Nabila did not know exactly why she needed a copy of the pictures, but her subconscious mind was forming a plan.

At home, Nabila tried to act as natural as possible. She did not say a thing to her daughters, as she did not trust them to tell them about the pictures. When Abdul Rahman came home for lunch, he seemed troubled. Nabila suspected he looked for the pictures and found some missing, but he could hardly ask the girls or Nabila about them. She hid the originals at one of her relative's house and kept the copies with her. Nabila was still not sure what she was going to do with them, but she believed the pictures were the key to stopping her husband from seeing Mara. It became her sole challenge. She wanted her husband back and would do anything to get him back. She was willing to forgive Abdul Rahman and start over again. They could do it; they just needed Mara out of the picture and then Abdul Rahman would think sensibly again. Nabila stared at the photo of Mara and Abdul Rahman kissing and knew what she had to do.

A Filipino friend at work had a brother who worked for a popular magazine in Manila. Nabila asked her friend for a favor and Nabila would pay for it. Nabila explained how a Filipino maid tried to destroy her marriage by stealing her husband. The friend was sympathetic and agreed to help. Nabila's plan for revenge was to give the pictures of Abdul Rahman and Mara to the magazine with the caption: 'A distinguished Saudi man is spending a holiday with his Filipino maid in Manila, leaving his family in Saudi Arabia.' Nabila's friend agreed to the scheme but noted that it would cost some money, not for her, but for the reporters of the magazine. Nabila handed her the address, the pictures, and a good amount of money. Nabila also told her to send a copy to her husband's address. In that instant, Nabila just wanted Abdul Rahman to feel the pain of the betrayal that she had been forced to live with the past few years.

At that time, Nabila had a Filipino driver whom she did not really know well. He approached her in what appeared to be concern.

"Madam, I am sorry; I don't want to interfere in your life, but why does Mr. Abdul Rahman treat you so cruelly? You are a good woman. The Filipino woman is not like you."

Nabila immediately reacted when he mentioned the Filipino woman and asked how he knew of her.

"Sorry, Madam, but every time a Filipino worker goes to Manila, your husband sends presents to her. Almost all Filipinos know the relationship between your husband and Mara," he explained.

Nabila burst into tears.

"Madam, I can help you if you allow me," he said.

Nabila asked, "What can you do to help me?" What could anyone do to help her? It was useless.

"Well, it is easy in my country. I can pay someone to throw acid on her face, and that should take care of your problem, or even hire someone to kill her," he replied.

At that moment Nabila recognized her limitations. She could never physically hurt Mara. Nabila could not kill a bug, let alone a human. Allah would punish her for such an act. All she wanted was to keep Mara out of their lives. Nabila wanted her life with her husband back. There had to be a way to get rid of Mara, but not by killing her. God forbid.

Abdul Rahman was not himself. He would go to work for a few hours and come home looking stressed and worried, but saying nothing. Eventually, he confronted Nabila. Abdul Rahman looked tired and defeated when he asked if Nabila had seen the pictures stored in the safe. Nabila trembled, fumbling with her hands to hide her nervousness. She inquired what kind of pictures he was looking for.

"Some pictures I took while I was in Manila," he said, "If you must know, they are pictures of my engagement to Mara. I am planning on marrying her," he explained plainly with no concern for Nabila's feelings.

Nabila looked at him in disbelief through teary eyes and quietly asked, "What about me?"

"You will be here and she will stay there. I will not bring her to this country as everyone will treat her with disrespect because she was a maid in this house," he said.

Nabila inquired about his position in the government and how he could face the people there. She hoped to give him the message that what he was about to do was occupational suicide.

"Do not talk about my position and how people are going to react to what I plan to do. I am going to resign, so no one will say the manager did this, the manager did that," he shouted loudly, covering his ears with both hands.

Nabila continued, "Well, do you really think resigning will stop the people from talking about you? This is going to be a big scandal in Jeddah at least."

Abdul Rahman turned his concern back to the pictures, indicating he must find them before they got in someone else's hands. Nabila suggested he left them in Manila with Mara, but Abdul Rahman said no, as

Mara had copies as well. Nabila speculated that Abdul Rahman could have dropped them somewhere or perhaps someone stole them from him. Abdul Rahman wondered why anyone would steal pictures.

"Men in your position usually have enemies. They could be someone you refused to hire, or you did not promote for some reason," Nabila explained.

It was killing Nabila carrying on a sham with Abdul Rahman, but she seized the opportunity to continue.

"Look, Abdul Rahman, you have no mother or sister to talk to, and you and I grew up together. I am going to talk to you now, not as your wife, but as a friend. I have been trying to save this marriage for the past six years. If you don't want me, I can't force you into it. If you really want another woman, she should not be Mara. She was a maid in our house; all the neighbors and people at your work are aware of that."

Nabila reminded him that according to their culture, he was destroying himself with this relationship. He could get the best woman from a respectable family, whether Saudi or any other nationality, and society would accept that. Nabila recognized it was common to have more than one wife, but also important to know the woman well who would carry his name.

Abdul Rahman didn't look at Nabila, but he did seem to be listening. What Nabila said to him was not what she wished for him to do, but she thought it might be the only way to get him to stay away from Mara. Then she would deal with other issues if needed.

As Nabila checked on the overcooked meal, she prayed to Allah that Abdul Rahman would consider what she said. Nabila turned the stove off, collapsed in to the nearest kitchen chair, and cried. She willed herself to look at Abdul Rahman across the room. He was staring out the window, running his fingers repeatedly through his hair as he often did when he was in deep thought. Nabila wiped her tears away and prepared lunch. Then Nabila heard him call her name. She held her breath bracing herself for what Abdul Rahman would say.

Guilt or reason must have influenced Abdul Rahman to reconsider his marriage to Nabila. He announced that he would go to Manila and explain to Mara that everything was over between them. "I am not that kind of person. I don't want any troubles in my life."

As soon as he said that, Nabila felt, at last Heaven had opened its arms for her. She ran to him, gave him a joyous hug, kiss, and said, "I will go with you."

"Go with me? I am telling you, I am going to talk to her to break off this relationship, and you want to go with me?" he quizzed.

Nabila suggested sending Mara a letter instead, to which Abdul Rahman agreed. He said for Nabila to mail it and put any address to receive the reply to prove that he was serious about it. Nabila sank to her knees, clinging to Abdul Rahman and sobbing with relief. She raised her head and Abdul Rahman kissed her on the forehead.

The reunited couple had lunch with little conversation. While Nabila was stacking the dishes in the dishwasher, Abdul Rahman handed her an envelope and then walked away. It was a letter to Mara, telling her that things were not going to work out between them and he wanted to wish her the best. Nabila mailed the letter, laboring over what Mara might say in response. Days later, Mara's letter arrived, addressing Abdul Rahman as Mr. instead of, 'My love,' as in her previous notes. Nabila should have been relieved, but unfortunately, that was not the only piece of news they received.

The copy of the Manila magazine with Abdul Rahman and Mara's pictures reigned at the top of the stack of mail. Nabila hid it along with the pictures in her closet. She was sure Abdul Rahman also got his copy. Nabila waited anxiously to see Abdul Rahman's reaction to his pictures published in the magazine, a plan Nabila had foolishly enacted weeks before. Surprisingly, he didn't react right away to news, or at least Nabila did not notice any reaction from him.

Abdul Rahman vacillated between the husband he had been and the man he had become. But Nabila felt that she finally succeeded in getting her husband back when he suggested a vacation in their favorite city, Vienna, Austria. The ten days in Vienna was a second honeymoon for them. Abdul Rahman was lovable and considerate, willing to do anything that would make Nabila happy. He surprised her with everything she liked, taking her to the best restaurants in the city, ballet, concerts, movies, and theaters.

Unfortunately, Nabila's happiness did not last. A few days after their return from Vienna, Abdul Rahman changed again, like a chameleon in the sun. He left their bedroom and went back to his isolated room, deserting Nabila for a reason she did not understand. Whenever Nabila tried to talk to Abdul Rahman, he rejected her violently. He would hold Nabila's arms and push her away telling her he did not want her in his life. Without any explanation, Abdul Rahman would kick and hit Nabila and try to make her leave the house.

Nabila discovered the reason for his behavior when she checked his car again for any new letters from Mara. While Abdul Rahman was at the mosque, which was only across the street from their house, Nabila found love letters that Mara sent while they were away on vacation. In the last letter, Mara accused Nabila of paying someone to put pictures in a magazine and that she would do her best to prove it. Mara said she needed one hundred thousand Saudi riyals to find out who actually did it. Mara added that Abdul Rahman and she must get married for revenge against Nabila. One hundred thousand Saudi riyals was a large amount of cash for any Saudi family, and worth more in a country as poor as Manila. Nabila was sure Mara was just trying to get a good sum of money for herself. She left Mara's letters, as if their contents could not haunt her if they remained buried in the glove box. Obviously, Mara had planted the seed that Nabila was responsible for Abdul Rahman's disgrace in the press.

Days later, Nabila tried to engage Abdul Rahman in conversation as he sat in the garden sipping his tea. She settled in next to him, but he did not give her any attention.

"Abdul Rahman, let's just talk for a minute," she tried.

"I have nothing to talk about," he said rising to walk toward the house.

Nabila wanted to discuss their marital problems and work toward a resolution. Abdul Rahman had started up the path to the house before he stopped and slowly turned to face her.

For once, he looked straight at Nabila and said, "I know you did it. Didn't you?"

"Did what?" Nabila choked.

"You are the one who plotted to put my pictures in the magazine in Manila."

Caught off guard, Nabila managed to scoff at Abdul Rahman's accusation and asked where he would get such information.

"From your own daughter; Leila told me."

Nabila felt like she'd been stabbed. The words cut deeper than any
wound she'd ever had. Nabila's daughter spied on her and uncovered the
information as to Nabila's plot. Abdul Rahman exploded with rage and
struck Nabila across the shoulder. The blow to her body was nothing
compared to the sting of his words. "Do you think I don't want any more
children? I do want more children, but not with you." Abdul Rahman
stormed out of the garden and out of their marriage.

Life became meaningless. It was easier for Nabila to think of her husband dead than to see him leaving her for another woman. As for Leila's
betrayal, it was unprovoked and unimaginable. Nabila was not certain that
there could ever be resolution with her first born.

Devastated, Nabila went to visit her oldest brother Aneese's family hoping to find solace with their innocent children. As she was relaxing with
the children, Nabila noticed Aneese at the entrance door, and unexpectedly, Abdul Rahman appeared. He glanced at Nabila and was about to
leave, but Aneese insisted that Abdul Rahman come in, hustling him to
the upper floor of the house. Abdul Rahman's presence ruined the few
pleasant moments Nabila had with the children. After Abdul Rahman
left Nabila asked about the purpose of his visit.

"I hate to tell you, he wants you out of the house. He came here to ask
me to tell you to leave," Aneese said unhappily.

Nabila's words came spilling out. "I don't know, where will I go? You
know how it is here; no one will rent a place to a single woman. I know
the girls will stay with their father. I just have no place to go."

Nabila reminded her brother that she worked very hard in the United
States and went to school at night just to save money. "When we returned
to Saudi Arabia, I worked for over five years at the hospital. I gave Abdul
Rahman every penny I earned when he was in need. Now that he has
become rich, the first thing he wants to get rid of is me. I helped him
to save money to buy several plots of land and hoped he would build a
house in the nicest district of Jeddah. He decided against my wishes to
build a cheap old-fashioned house in the Prince Project in the middle of

the desert, which I would never live in. He built it for the Filipino maid, not for me. I do not know what to do with my life. I have been with him since I was fifteen-years-old; I am almost forty now. How am I going to start my life over?"

Nabila barely took a breath. "He took care of everything. He never gave me a chance to depend on myself. I don't even know how to write a check or get money from the bank or an ATM machine. How am I going face all the problems as a single woman in this country without a man to support me and take care of me? I don't know how to handle things here. What am I going to do; where will I go?" A dam of tears was all that stopped her words.

"We all can help you as much as we can," her brother said in a pitiful way and his wife supported him.

"Let's be frank," Nabila said. "Who is, at this time and age, free to help his sister? You have a wife and children to take care of, and so do my other brothers. Besides my other sister, who never had a man in her life, and my mother, who is deserted by our father, who has the time to take care of them? A man can only do so much. I am going to have to depend on myself, which I have never experienced."

The ride home was like a funeral with Nabila depressed and crying. As she looked out the car window to keep her tears away from the driver's sight, she spied Abdul Rahman driving past. He glanced at her without expression and then returned his eyes to the road. *Oh, where is all the Love you had for me, Abdul Rahman? What happened? I still can't believe you are doing this to me.* She watched his tail lights vanish in the thick desert air.

CHAPTER 24

... either take them back on equitable terms or part with them on equitable terms; and take for witness two persons from among you.

~ AL TALAQ 2

It was clear to Nabila that Abdul Rahman was going to divorce her, and he would never accept reconciliation. She was forced to think seriously about her future, where she would go and what she'd do. That same day Abdul Rahman approached Nabila with a file of papers. His eyes were glued to the floor as he said, "Here, I got you a good job as a teacher in a public high school. You will be working for the government and you will get good pay."

Nabila reached for the file, unsure of its contents and Abdul Rahman's offer. "But I already have a job."

"Yes, but you are not making enough money working at the university for a few classes a week. This is a good job for you," Abdul Rahman responded.

Nabila stared at Abdul Rahman, listening and wondering why he was doing this for her.

"I was hoping that one day you would thank me for all my effort to help you to get to the position you are in and ask me to quit working and stay at home and rest since you are able to support me now, but you are offering me another job? Why?" Nabila asked through her tears that could not be contained.

Abdul Rahman only replied, "You must go tomorrow morning to the assigned school and give this file to the director of the school."

The next morning, Abdul Rahman insisted that Nabila go with him to the school and give the file to the director. They had an argument in the car as she tried to convince him she did not want the job. Teaching high school girls was not her choice, besides Nabila was tired of working all those years. Nabila knew for sure he wanted to get rid of her, but at the same time, he wanted to guarantee a source of income for her. Nabila was angry and hurt but went inside the school and met the director, although she did not give her the file.

When Nabila returned to the car she handed Abdul Rahman the file and said defiantly, "Here it is; I am not going to work for that school."

Abdul Rahman said, "You will be sorry," and drove Nabila home.

About a month later, on Ramadan Eve (the fasting month in the Islamic religion and the best holiday of the year), Abdul Rahman and Nabila were still not talking much. Nabila was in the kitchen preparing for the big meal of Ramadan's Sahoor, which is a meal Muslims eat before sunrise to fast for the rest of the day, when Abdul Rahman passed through the kitchen.

Inspired by the holiday, Nabila kindly suggested, "Listen, Abdul Rahman, this is a holiday and the best time of the year. I really wish you would forget the past for this month, and let's have a good holiday as a family."

Nabila came closer to kiss Abdul Rahman, but he pushed her away and stammered, "You're divorced." He rubbed his face, and it was hard to tell if he was feeling sorry or glad it was over.

Nabila was stunned and started shaking. "Oh no, you don't mean it, do you Abdul Rahman? Tell me you don't mean it."

Abdul Rahman's acid words were the weapon that crushed Nabila's love. Then he ordered her to leave his house.

Nabila steadied herself and tried to absorb the tsunami of emotions. "Leave your house? First, this is not *your* house; it belongs to the government. Second, I am supposed to stay here for the next three months of the iddah."

Abdul Rahman informed Nabila that there was no iddah.

No iddah? What could he mean? Of course there was iddah, the period for possible reconciliation, after talaq, the statement of divorce.

Unbelievably, Abdul Rahman claimed, "I have divorced you twice before; therefore there is no iddah."

"Oh my God help me. Ya Allah, what is this man doing to me? Help,

Ya Allah, help me please. I can't take all this!" Nabila cried and screamed to Allah.

Abdul Rahman left Nabila in her misery and went to his room. Nabila continued crying deep from her heart and prayed and prayed to Allah for help.

Nabila expected Abdul Rahman to leave her, or at least suspected it would happen. But when Abdul Rahman actually uttered the words "you are divorced," she was unprepared for it. All these years Nabila was in denial believing that Abdul Rahman would never leave her. Nabila was so sure Abdul Rahman loved her too much to consider divorce. She could not understand what happened to all the love that he had for her. Can love change so quickly into hate only because a man becomes interested in another woman? Another man would have a relationship with a woman he was interested in for a period of time, and then he would come back to his wife. Abdul Rahman was a man who went by the rules of Islamic books. He would not just have a relationship with any woman. Marriage was imminent if Abdul Rahman was involved with a woman. Therefore, he would marry the maid, whom he brought to the house, supposedly to honor Nabila. How ironic that his high ideals and integrity did not keep him from having an affair while he was married, but ruled that he should marry their maid.

A few hours later, trying to understand her fate, Nabila went to Abdul Rahman's room. He was sitting on the floor reading the Quran, which was his habit after prayers.

Puzzled, Nabila asked, "When did you divorce me the first two times, Abdul Rahman?"

Abdul Rahman looked at her with hate. "Why do you ask about something that happened years ago?

Nabila was confused when he said, "years ago."

"Yes, do you remember when Leila was two-years-old, sick in the hospital? I told you not to give her the ugly toy and that if you did, you would be divorced. You did not listen to me, because when I came back into her room, I found the toy near the baby's bed. So that was the first divorce," he explained.

Nabila hurriedly responded, "But I didn't. A nurse did it thinking the baby would like it when she woke up. I did not have a chance to move it back; you came back immediately after the nurse left."

Abdul Rahman was not interested in any explanation and remained adamant that it was the first divorce.

"The second time was a secret divorce; you didn't know about it," Abdul Rahman revealed.

Incredulous, Nabila shrilled, "What, you divorced me and returned me back as a wife without telling me? What is that supposed to mean?"

Nabila was frustrated and annoyed with Abdul Rahman's faulty explanations. She questioned the laws of the land that governed her marriage. Is it possible that a man can divorce his wife and have sexual intercourse with her to keep her as his wife without telling her? Nabila believed that could never be part of her religion. Where were her rights? Didn't she get the opportunity to decide if she wanted to stay with him or leave him? It just could not be true.

Abdul Rahman became irritated and started to yell, "I never wanted you from the day I married you. If you think I did not want any children, you are wrong. I did not want any children with you."

"Then why did you keep me this long if you really did not want me from the first day you married me? You could have divorced me years ago," she said.

"I wanted you to raise the kids. They are grown now. They don't need you anymore," Abdul Rahman answered.

"Raise the kids?" Nabila asked with agony and frustration. "What about my life, my youth, and my good years that you have wasted? I could have had the kids I wanted. Did you ever think of my life and me? You are telling me you kept me to raise your kids, after all the trust I had and believed every word you said to me. You have deprived me of my best years, my desires, and my right to have more children, and the good life that I thought I had with you. Why are you doing this to me? You were the ideal husband and father. You never made me feel that you never wanted me or that you hated me. Did you have to wait until this housekeeper comes to clean our bathroom to realize that you never wanted me?"

"It did not have to be her. It could be any other woman," he said. "Besides, I did not do any more than what other men do."

"Other men? What kind of man would do this? Now at my age, where will I go? Who will take care of me? I am a woman in this country; we are paralyzed without a man. What am I going to do all alone?"

Abdul Rahman suggested Nabila go to her family.

"My family? I've been married to you for twenty-five years! My father is dead; my mother is very old and lives with my sister. My other brothers and sisters have their own families and their own problems. None of them would take me. They would have taken my mother if they were able. So who is my family? This is my family," Nabila said.

As Nabila wept, Abdul Rahman touched Nabila's shoulder and said, "Be strong. Face the facts."

The next evening, Abdul Rahman suggested a living arrangement. He would use half of the house and Nabila would use the other half, but Nabila would still be cooking for him and the girls.

Nabila responded in anger. "Me, cooking for you and the kids; why? You did not hire me to be your cook. Besides I may find another man to marry me."

Abdul Rahman shouted, "Marry you! Who would marry you? You are too old to get married again. You are almost forty now. You think you can find a man! Keep on dreaming. No one wants you. No one will ever want you."

Nabila's body ached with a tornado of emotions. She was destroyed by his scathing words. Nabila had to surrender; Abdul Rahman left her no hope. She tried her best to save her marriage. With all her effort, Nabila failed and Mara won the battle. Mara had Abdul Rahman, the new house, and all the money that Nabila helped him save. In addition, Mara came after Uncle Saleh's death. She did not have to go through any problems with Abdul Rahman's father or deal with Abdul Rahman's job stress.

According to the practice in Saudi Arabia, when a woman gets a divorce, no matter how long she was married to her husband, she gets none of his money or his property. Nabila started her life with Abdul Rahman in near poverty, and when he became rich, twenty-five years later, she had no right to any of his money.

Who would believe Abdul Rahman, with his advanced degrees and high status in the country, would turn to a Filipino housekeeper, who was almost his daughter's age? Mara came from a completely different culture, and Abdul Rahman knew nothing of her background or her past. He claimed he wanted to save her from poverty. Feeling hurt Nabila had told him, "You're allowed four wives, so why don't you save four poor Filipinos!"

Nabila's two grown daughters, who had heard their parents were divorcing, were as silent as stones. Nabila kept wishing that one of them would support her just once, but they never did. The girls were products of their upbringing and accepted the harsh realities that befall women in Saudi Arabia. Nabila not only lost a husband, but her family was destroyed. The girls' allegiance was to their father and their mother remained the outsider.

When Abdul Rahman returned later that evening, he shared that he had consulted the highest religious court to see if there was a way to void the divorce. Nabila was immediately cheered believing that Abdul Rahman had reconsidered.

"So what did he tell you?" Nabila asked optimistically.

"He advised me to find another woman to marry. I told him everything and he confirmed it is valid for a divorce. So you and I are officially divorced. I only need to go to court a get the divorce papers."

Nabila's heart ached. *Oh, merciful God, help me, help me to accept my fate, and be with me when I am alone,* Nabila prayed to Allah.

Nabila tried to appeal to Abdul Rahman. "You know in your heart that I have no place to go. I am asking you— begging you—if you would just give me one piece of all the land that we have. I will try to manage to build a small place for me to live, because otherwise I don't know where to go."

"No, Allah will help you. You don't need anything from me," Abdul Rahman answered.

Nabila's emotions yo-yoed between hurt and anger. She had done nothing wrong. Instead, she had worked hard for years, turning over her wages to her husband. Is that the reward for years of devotion to a man and his children?

Nabila continued, "I was a servant in this house for you, because I thought you were worth my efforts all these years. I was waiting for the day to quit my job and have you take care of me, but I guess it will never happen. I saved you money and when you became rich, you took all my investment in this family to give it to the dirty, toothless, street woman who came to work as a maid. Now you throw me out in the street to the wild dogs to chew on my bones."

Nabila stormed out of the room but then, desperately, returned to propose another deal with Abdul Rahman to find a place to live.

"Would you give any of the land to your daughters? Then I could manage to build a place under their names to live. The deal would not be for me, but for your daughters. They will need it in the future," Nabila tried.

Abdul Rahman refused, "No, may Allah be with my daughters. They do not need anything from me. I gave them an education and that is all they need."

On the morning of July 13, 1997, any hope Nabila had was extinguished. Abdul Rahman, accompanied by Nabila's brother, delivered the divorce certificate. Nabila had been married on July 19 and divorced on July 13, almost twenty-five years later to the day.

Before leaving, Abdul Rahman turned to Nabila's brother and said, "Now, I want you to be a witness. I have divorced your sister. It is not her business what I do or where I go. She must not interfere in my life."

Nabila turned to Abdul Rahman, trying hard to control her shaky voice, but unable to control her tears. "Do you think this piece of paper will erase twenty-five years of my life and all the years before that we had together?"

Abdul Rahman said nothing as he walked out of their house. Nabila collapsed on the nearest sofa and sobbed. Her brother tried his best to calm her, but her daughters stood by as statues, unwilling or unable to comfort her.

In her waking hours, Nabila walked and talked in a fog of disbelief. She was not able to sleep much and when she did, she awoke believing it was all a nightmare. She was tortured thinking of her husband being with Mara. Nabila prayed and prayed. *Allah, the most merciful, have mercy on me. I am suffering and I cannot deal with it without your help. Help me, please. Mighty Allah, I need your mercy on me.* Nabila found some comfort in the TV and the light in the bedroom. She kept them on all night. Since that day, Nabila has not been able to sleep in the dark.

Everywhere Nabila went was a place Abdul Rahman and she had been together. Every street and every path was marked with their footsteps. Nabila thought they were inseparable with an unbreakable bond from childhood throughout adulthood. *Is it true that Abdul Rahman and I are not together any longer and forever? No, it cannot be. He will come back to me, because he misses me; I know he will.* Even after the divorce, Nabila waited for Abdul Rahman to return. She was lost without him, not knowing where to go or what to do. He was her security and her provider; Nabila refused to accept her fate. She believed this transformation was not really Abdul Rahman. It was if a disease had inflicted him for which there was no cure. Nabila wanted to believe Abdul Rahman still loved her. *What happened cannot be true. He will come back. I feel it and know it; he will. I just have to be patient.*

The girls and Nabila stayed in the same house. Abdul Rahman paid for the car and the driver, but Nabila couldn't help but wonder how long she would have his assistance. After all, it was not their house; it belonged to the ministry. Eventually she had to leave, but to where?

Nabila was confused and afraid of the future. The girls were young adults, and they would soon be married. Nabila would be struggling in a society that did not accept a single woman living alone, and even worse, a divorced woman living alone. She started making plans to leave the country, thinking that would be the only way to live a better life. America was Nabila's choice, since she had lived there for a few years and spoke the language. However, to do so, she had to save enough money and get her citizenship. Despite the darkness that enveloped Nabila, she was formulating a plan to survive.

CHAPTER 25

*Divorce is twice. Then, either keep [her] in an acceptable manner
or release [her] with good treatment.*

~ AL BAQARAH 229

Nabila's brother suggested Nabila take the girls to Cairo to help ease her pain. A Saudi woman could not leave the country without permission from the father, a brother, or if married, permission from the husband. Nabila's brother gave permission for Nabila to travel. As soon as she boarded the plane, Nabila was overwhelmed with memories of the many trips that she had taken with her husband and family. Nabila began to cry again. All she could think of was Abdul Rahman sitting beside her on every trip, but he was not there. Abdul Rahman was in the arms of another woman.

The trip to Egypt did not soothe Nabila. Everywhere she went brought more memories of her good life with Abdul Rahman. Sitting in a restaurant, Nabila would point to a chair and say, "This is your father's chair. Look, it is empty. He is not here with us."

As always, Nabila saw no reaction from her daughters. The girls were still not really talking to Nabila, but she had to take them with her because there was no way her brother would allow her to travel alone. Nabila was surprised that the girls agreed to the trip. At the beginning, Leila almost refused, as she wanted to take care of her father's business while he was away. The girls were totally under their father's influence and indoctrinated in the cultural ways of their society.

The three were in Egypt for about two weeks when the girls received a call from Abdul Rahman indicating he had returned to Jeddah. The girls begged their father to come to Egypt for a couple of days. Abdul Rahman finally agreed to come for one day. Nabila was secretly pleased that he would travel to Egypt. She did not see him, but knew he was in a nearby hotel. When Nabila and the girls decided to go to the theater, Abdul Rahman went as well. The girls sat with him, and Nabila sat far away from them. During the intermission, Nabila was surprised to see her cousin's son and talked to him awhile.

Two days after her return to Jeddah, Nabila's older brother visited. He demanded Nabila's passport. Nabila was perplexed as to why Aneese would take her passport, but she relinquished it.

"You will never leave this country again. I am taking your passport and I am going to keep it with me," he said.

Clueless as to what she'd done, Nabila asked for the reason.

To Nabila's surprise, Aneese said, "You are divorced from Abdul Rahman, and according to Islam, you are not supposed to see him, and he is not supposed to look at you. Don't you know it is a sin for both of you even to meet after a divorce? I am going to the airport and sign a paper that you are not allowed to leave the country from now on."

Nabila questioned how he knew that she had seen Abdul Rahman. He indicated that they were seen in the same place; her cousin's son must have seen Abdul Rahman at the theater. Nabila felt overwhelmed with despair and out of control of her life. She began to have dizzy spells, stopped eating, and lost a lot of weight. She was not able to concentrate on work. *How am I going to leave the country now that my brother is in control of me and is holding my passport?*

Nabila's only entertainment was to visit family or neighbors, but it was embarrassing and disgraceful listening to comments about what her husband had done. She eventually stopped going to the neighbors. Visiting family offered some pleasure, but she could not always control her emotions. They kept saying, "You have to forget it. Don't think about it." She wanted to, but did not know how. Nabila was tortured. She could not sleep or eat. Everything she did, she imagined Abdul Rahman there. *Would someone tell me how to forget him and let go? I want to, but I cannot.* Nothing helped her pain.

Nabila neglected her home. She was barely able to cook small meals for the girls. Even the red Bleeding Heart vine plant that Nabila had for years started to die. The plant had survived moves and many changes, but it was as if it had given up living now that Abdul Rahman and Nabila were apart.

Nabila was unable to tell anyone she was divorced. Friends would visit and innocently ask for a connection to find a job that Abdul Rahman could provide. Nabila could not accept her cruel fate. She used his name and talked about him as if he were still with her. Finally, Nabila figured the only way to survive was to try to get the job at the school that Abdul Rahman had suggested. She took the file and pushed herself to go to the university and submit her resignation. From there, Nabila went to the high school to secure a job she did not want.

The school resembled a prison with high, thick cement walls. All the windows were closed, as each room had a window unit air conditioner. Nabila walked into a large barren yard and saw a few girls sitting on the floor chatting. They were wearing long yellow uniforms that covered their ankles and their arms. The *Khala*, the woman, who is usually the wife of the guard outside the school, was the connector between the school and the guard. The male guard cannot enter the girls' school, and guard's wife does not deal with all the men outside the school.

Nabila asked the Khala to direct her to the principal, Abla Adeela. The principal was a middle-aged woman, good looking, and well dressed. Nabila supplied her paperwork and told her she came for the teaching job, hired by The Presidency for Girls' Education department. Nabila filled out all the information they needed, including the guidance portion. She was to list one of her brothers, but Nabila wrote down her ex-husband's name, phone number, his title, and his address. The dress code called for her dress to cover her ankles and the sleeves to be to the wrists. Pants were prohibited, and Nabila's face had to be covered before entering the school and leaving the school.

Due to the harsh climate in Jeddah, the schools started at half past seven. Teachers had to be in school twenty minutes earlier than the students. The school day ended at half past twelve. On Nabila's first day, the principal handed her a schedule, and asked her to help with the *taboor*, lining up the girls to get them ready for their classes. Then Nabila was to go to her classes to introduce herself to the students and try to get to know them.

The bell rang for the students to line up for an orderly entrance, but the girls did not move. The teachers had to go to each group of girls, "Yallah, yallah, twabeer, get up and go to your line." Nabila noticed that this task took at least fifteen minutes. Once organized in the lines, one of the students would read a few verses of the Quran, and Hadeeth, (Prophet Muhammad saying). After that, a teacher would give daily instructions to the pupils. During this time, the girls were not paying attention. Instead, they were busy chatting with their friends, while the teachers were doing their best to keep the students quiet to listen to the Morning *Eza'a*, (morning broadcasting). Announcements were part of the first class, which made many teachers reject teaching first period complaining it was too short for their lesson.

After the taboors, the students walked with their teacher to the classroom. Nabila entered her class with about forty-five girls. The room was too small for that many students. Some other classes had more than fifty girls in a classroom. A student had to push her chair into another student just to be able to stand up to answer a question. Nabila introduced herself to the girls and began to ask a few questions to test their knowledge about the subject matter. The pupils raised their hands and shouted all at the same time, "Me, Me, teacher." While many wanted to respond, their answers were rarely correct.

While answering one of the girl's questions, Nabila felt dizzy and was about to collapse. Two of the girls brought Nabila a chair and a drink of water and soon Nabila was feeling better and able to continue class. Incidents of feeling faint were frequent during her first few of months of work.

During the morning break, Fosaha, that was about thirty minutes long, the girls went to the commissary to purchase something to eat. Standing in a line waiting a turn was not the norm. Instead the mob of students, one on top of another, stuck their hands into a small window to the Khala waving money and shouting, "Ya Khala, Ya Khala, I want the cheese and the soft drink." The Khala could only serve a few at a time, despite their deafening shouts. The food sold at the commissary was full of carbohydrates and sugar, bread with feta cheese, croissants loaded with butter, small cheese pizzas, and sweets of all kinds, candies, brownies, cakes, and soft drinks.

Nothing was fresh or warm, quite unhealthy food for young people. After thirty minutes, the bell rang and the teachers, again, had to go through the same procedure of herding the young girls to their classes.

A second break started at about noon, a 'prayer break.' This break was about twenty minutes, enough for the girls to perform ablution and pray at the school mosque. After prayer it was even more difficult to focus the girls on their studies.

At the end of the day, one of the teachers stayed at the gate from inside the school to be sure the girls made it safely to their families' cars. It was part of the guard's duty to know who was picking up the students. The girls could only leave with a father or a brother or a person whom the father had assigned for his daughters. When a family member came to pick up a girl, the guard would call the name of the father or the family's name over the microphone. The girls' first names were not announced over the microphone, especially in the presence of men. The teacher in charge was to be certain that the girls were completely covered from head to toe with the black abaya before leaving the school.

The dizziness continued, and Nabila was losing her concentration. Her thoughts were scattered. She would be doing one task and thinking of other things. Toward the end of the month, the teachers were supposed to give a monthly exam and evaluate the students. Nabila would prepare the students' exams, grade them, and submit them to the office of revision. The office complained that Nabila had errors in her work. Simple tasks on the papers were incorrect. The director advised Nabila to pay more attention to her work, since she was new and that may affect her evaluation. Nabila decided to do most of her work at home to give it more focus; however, the result was the same. She was not able to concentrate enough to do the job correctly. She prepared lessons at home, but the assistant who evaluated the lessons often found parts missing.

Sometimes Nabila wondered how the students had made it to the twelfth grade. Some of them were unable to write their names correctly. They were not able to do simple tasks and they were unwilling to try. Their concentration in class was almost zero. All they cared about was socializing with their friends. They depended on one or two good students' papers for their homework or on the teacher to pass them. Many teachers gave passing grades to avoid any problems with the school administration.

Every morning Nabila watched many students gather around the excellent students to copy their homework. When Nabila checked one of the twelfth grade student's papers, Nabila asked her if she needed help. The girl refused and insisted on trying again without help. Soon she returned to show Nabila her work. Unfortunately, her papers were still full of mistakes. Nabila tried again to help her. Again, the student refused help and insisted on doing it herself. However, when she brought back her work for the third time with the same mistakes, Nabila made her explain her responses.

The girl was upset, "What is it with you, teacher? Three times you tell me it is wrong, and every time I copied it from different girls in class, and you are still telling me it is wrong. What am I supposed to do?"

Maha, one of Nabila's students, told her that a few students were complaining that they did not understand the lesson. When Nabila retaught the lesson trying to help those who were having difficulty, they turned to Maha, shouting at her that they did not want their teacher to know and that Maha had no right to tell. The girls did not care if they understood the lesson; they only came to school to have fun with their friends.

The principal often attended classes to evaluate the teachers as well as the students. She approved of Nabila's teaching style. The principal talked with the students in Nabila's class. Two students told her they were in the school only because they were bored at home, and it was their father's desire to give them an education. The principal gave them a short lecture about the importance of education in their lives.

Nevertheless, one of the girls said, "But we will get married and our husband will support us."

Students depended on others to do the work. Nabila explained to the class that they should do their own work and if they needed any help, she would be happy to sit with them, one on one to tutor them. However, the girls didn't readily accept the assistance and kept on copying from other girls.

Nabila was determined to change the school culture. She identified girls who were weak in the subject and persisted in tutoring them before or after school to improve their academic performance. Soon the students' grades improved, and they began to like the subject as well as their teacher. Nabila's concentration had improved as well; school during the day and preparations of lessons at night kept her mind busy. The dramatic improvement of the students' grades encouraged the principal to send Nabila a letter of thanks and to select her as the outstanding teacher of the year. Since teaching was one of the few jobs for any woman in Saudi Arabia, all Nabila's sisters were also teachers. They had similar experiences with many academically weak junior high as well as high school students in public schools.

Some of the teachers did not care if the students truly learned. One of those teachers, Miss Huda, was the students' favorite, simply because she gave them high grades without any effort from the students. During one of the school recesses, a worker came to the teachers' room to ask Miss Huda to dictate the students' grades to the computer specialist.

Miss Huda turned toward the computer specialist and said, "Give them all high grades."

A teacher, Khadeja, looked at the teachers next to her and said, "Don't you have different levels of students? They can't be all the same." The comment did not deter Miss Huda.

Miss Huda was dubbed Miss Vanity. She kept a mirror on her desk, where she constantly checked her appearance. Even when someone spoke to her, she focused on her reflection, checking her makeup and her hair, which she changed the color of every few weeks. All she cared about was what the students thought about how she looked.

The most generous teacher was Miss Afaf. She offered her classes to any teacher who wanted them. She was often too tired to lead a class, but her students were always excellent students. Frequently, the assistant came to the teachers' room looking for Miss Afaf; she would find her sleeping under her desk. The assistant had to wake her up to get her to go to the class. "I am so tired. Please find another teacher who can use my class," was her usual response.

Miss Fayza, on the other hand, was always absent. She came to school only one or two days a week. With all her absences during the year, her students' grades were suspiciously high.

Many teachers came to school completely unprepared. They would scramble to write lessons when they saw the supervisor or the *Abla Adeela* coming to evaluate them.

The Presidency of the Girls' Education prints and offers compulsory books for each course, yet the office of school administration as well as the principals and their assistants insist that the teachers not teach everything. They ask the teachers to give the students a few simple questions from the books with the answers for all the exams and the finals. If the students are required to write paragraphs, the teacher must write them for the students and revise them with the students several times to help the students memorize them. In that way, the students are able to write them on the exam papers. The exams must be secret and treated as important documents that no one has the right to view except the teacher of the subject.

The school assistant and Nabila were always butting heads. The assistant insisted that the students had to study specific questions in order to pass the finals, and Nabila was not willing to give any students questions from the final. Nabila would simplify the course and give a study folder, but never the exact questions and answers. Nabila put a lot of effort and time into creating the most simplified course that she hoped the assistant would not reject or criticize.

However, the assistant looked at it and stormed, "All that? It is too much. No wonder your students do not pass your exam. No, no, this is not accepted."

Nabila took it to the principal and told her, "I put so much effort to make this folder for the students, which will help them to study better, but the assistant did not agree."

The principal examined the folder and agreed with the assistant.

"But the Presidency of Girls' Education offered all these books for that course. I am supposed to teach all these books, and they are supposed to study them," Nabila said.

She acknowledged the books but cautioned that Nabila must make the girls pass.

"Then, why do I have to work very hard preparing the lesson every night and teach the whole course if I am going to give them a few questions with their answers at the end of the semester?" Nabila continued, "And why does the government spend so much money to print all these books for the students? Why don't we make it easier on ourselves, as teachers, and only teach them what they are going to have on the exam, and ask the government to save the money from printing all those books?"

Abla Adeela did not like Nabila's response. "Just go and do what I told you. Give them a few questions and the answers like the rest of the teachers."

Nabila insisted on giving the students folders, and did not give them the questions with the answers. In class, she explained her method of structuring the finals and the study guide. With the exception of a few students, the girls did not object. Nabila made it a little easier by limiting the paragraphs to three, and choosing one of the three subjects for the finals.

One week before the finals, the staff had a teachers' meeting with the director. She emphasized the secrecy of the finals. She also warned the teachers against cheating. Teachers were supposed to check each student before she entered the exam hall to be sure she did not carry anything that would help her to cheat. They were to check the students' desks for any written materials or papers. During the meeting, most of the teachers were not listening and were conversing with each other. The principal slammed her ruler on the desk to get the teachers' attention and stop them from chatting during the meeting.

On the day before the finals, the teachers arranged the students' seats for the tests. Most of the teachers placed every two seats close together. Nabila objected as that arrangement would help the students cheat from each other.

The teachers said, "Let them pass the finals, if that is going to help them."

During the exams, Nabila walked around the classrooms. She noticed many teachers, who were supposed to supervise the students, were at the door of the classroom chatting with other teachers and the students were on their own copying each other's answers.

After the finals, the teachers gathered in groups to correct the papers. Teachers were not allowed to be alone with the papers to avoid any teacher from correcting the students' answers and increasing their grades. Yet once the principal saw that some students did not make good marks, she tried to force the teachers to increase the students' grades. Nabila had a student who did not make the passing grade. The social advisor asked

Nabila to pass the student who needed six more points to pass. Nabila tried to explain that the student wrote so little that she could not increase her grade.

"But this student has not passed for the past three years. Haram, (mercy) pass her," she said.

Nabila convinced the social advisor that there was no way she could pass the student. The advisor finally left, went to Nabila's co-worker, and asked her to pass the student. When she found there was no hope, she went to complain to the principal.

Upset, the assistant caustically approached the teachers, "You enjoy seeing students fail, don't you?"

Nabila responded, "I hope this student will turn out to be your children's teacher someday if you keep on passing her when she is failing."

The assistant looked at Nabila with venom. "My children go to the private school and they are taught by good teachers." She gave Nabila another dirty look and left.

After correcting all the papers, which took almost two weeks, the principal approached the teachers carrying ten exam papers. She directed Nabila to take another look at them to pass the students. Nabila took the papers without any comment. Nabila knew that those particular students could never pass the exam. Nabila suggested that the students would have a second chance with the makeup exam.

"Just look at their grades and try to increase them," the principal said in an authoritarian manner.

"But I cannot do that," Nabila said looking at her co-workers for support. Nabila asked her co-worker, "What are we going to do? Those girls could never pass."

When Nabila gave the principal the bad news about the students, Nabila was asked to make their exams oral exams and try to increase those grades.

Nabila said, "But the girls are not here for me to give them another chance on the oral exam."

Nabila refused to add points to any student's grade before she had legal approval from the Education office. The principal was not happy with Nabila's decision.

When the first semester was finally over, Nabila wanted to take the first step toward her plan of leaving the country and securing her American citizenship. She needed a relative who was over twenty-one and American born to apply for a green card in America. The only person who could really help her was her older daughter, Leila but Nabila's relationship with Leila was still strained. She appealed to Leila to accompany her to the American Embassy and Leila agreed, nodding her head, not saying a word.

Nabila's hurt eased during her working hours; however, it became worse as soon as she entered the house. Nabila needed to occupy herself after school hours and the evenings. By the second semester, she was ready for any distraction. The university offered graduate courses for women, and Nabila thought of enrolling to occupy her time and get a degree as well. Moreover, she was thrilled to join a health club opened for women for the first time in Saudi Arabia. Exercising was hard in the beginning but was much less painful than Nabila's emotional trauma. She was working during the day, exercising after school, and studying at night. Whenever she had time away from her studies, on weekends, and during vacation, she exercised at the health club. Nabila became obsessed with working out. She felt her stress melt and could temporarily keep her mind off her heartache. Nabila was exercising three to four hours a day, and when she had time, she would work out twice on the same day! Friends and instructors advised her to slow down, but Nabila continued the hectic pace. The health club even requested that Nabila substitute for instructors as she had become quite fit. They offered her a job as an instructor, but Nabila declined.

Nabila wanted to continue her education, so she applied for master's degree courses. During Nabila's interview with the dean of the university, she discovered that all the courses were from eleven o'clock in the morning until three o'clock in the afternoon twice a week. The dean advised her to talk to her school principal to request release time twice a week to attend classes. The principal encouraged Nabila and agreed to release her two days a week to pursue her degree.

The university needed instructors to teach level-one English. Nabila offered to teach the class after finishing her teaching duties at the high school. Nabila immersed herself in work to keep her mind fully engaged and off her troubles.

Since there was no mix between genders, Nabila received instruction in her master classes through a closed circuit television from the men's university branch. The female students were able to see the male professor, but the professor could not see the students. There was a microphone for each student for discussion or questions. All notes and handouts from the men's department were delivered by Khala, the housekeeper, who passed them through a small window to the women's classrooms.

Two years passed and no one at the university finished a master's degree. Many of the students in Nabila's master's degree program had been struggling with the program for four years. The girls in the program were very smart and a promising group, but they never seemed to advance at the Saudi university. Nabila had taught students at the university, and they had left the country for a higher degree. Some of them returned with an MA and others with a PhD, while Nabila was still trying to earn an advanced degree.

Day by day, Nabila's desire to leave the country increased. Neither her brothers nor anyone else would stop her. America became Nabila's refuge. Her plan was to apply for a leave of absence as soon as the girls were married. As for the master's degree courses, Nabila knew it would take years in Saudi Arabia to finish. She would save enough money to finish a master's degree in the United States. Once Nabila received her degree and secured a job, she would resign her Saudi teaching position. Nabila's only obstacle was retrieving her passport from her brother.

Nabila had not been close to her older brother since he had seized her passport two years ago. However, she knew she had to convince him to return her passport if she had any hope of travelling to America. Determined, she went to visit her brother. The servant opened the door at his residence and Nabila asked to talk with her brother. Her brother appeared surprised to see Nabila and greeted her with a kiss on the cheek. After curiously inquiring about his family, Nabila immediately asked for her passport. Nabila's request caught Ameer off guard as he had no ready response as to why he should not return it. Besides, his anger at Nabila had subsided over the years, so he fetched it from his safe and gave it to her without comment. Relieved, Nabila thanked him and headed home. Nabila hugged her passport and believed that her dream plan just might work.

As Nabila returned home, she saw Leila standing at the door talking to her father. Nabila noticed Abdul Rahman was carrying a travel ticket. When Abdul Rahman saw Nabila approaching the house, he immediately got in his car and drove away. Nabila did not want to talk to Leila, but she could not stop herself from asking if her father was traveling to the Philippines. Nabila felt the familiar stab of chest pain when Leila affirmed her guess. Nabila wished Leila would have lied to spare her the agony of thinking of Abdul Rahman and Mara together. She spent another turbulent night unable to block the images of the couple. Nabila never wanted to hear another thing about Abdul Rahman. She did not know why she asked. She seemed to devour every bit of information about Abdul Rahman's activities, but it only caused her pain. Work and study filled Nabila's days but the nights were empty allowing too many opportunities to envision them together. *When will I be over him? Why does it take so long?*

One evening Nabila dreamed that Abdul Rahman had a new baby girl. She awoke thanking Allah it was only a dream, and prayed it would not become a truth. It was devastating to imagine Abdul Rahman having a baby with Mara. The TV chattered and the light burned all night, every night to keep Nabila company in her misery.

The next day Nabila and the girls were watching TV when Nabila recounted her dream. Lamia glanced at her sister but neither commented. A few months later, mid evening, Nabila heard a knock at the door. Lamia answered the door and returned to say that her father wanted to talk to Nabila. Nabila had no idea what Abdul Rahman wanted to talk about after two years of divorce. She met her former husband at the front door. He was wiry, refusing to sit, and pacing back and forth, wearing an imaginary groove in the walkway. Nabila assumed he was worried that a member of her family might see him in her house.

Abdul Rahman said, "You know, you kept your head up in front of everyone, and here I am down to hell. I know I should have given it longer thought before I got involved, but it is too late now."

Nabila sighed, "Yes, it is too late. You had six years with her and now you think you should have given it more thought!"

Abdul Rahman removed a picture of an infant from his wallet. He said, "Well, anyway, I have a baby girl now. She looks Filipino, like her mother."

Nabila felt dizzy. "Oh, my God, you had a baby with her? Ya Allah, Mercy on me. You told me you would never have children with her. She really knew how to hold onto you by giving you children. Believe me this is not going to be the only child."

"No, no, this was only an accident," he said.

Nabila fought to maintain her composure, but struck out, "Is that what you came here to tell me? It is too late. You left nothing between us. You have made the biggest mistake in your life. You ruined my life, your daughters' lives and that woman, too. You stopped her from having a normal life with someone her age. This kid and all the kids that I am sure you will have are going to be, for the rest of their lives, the kids of the maid carrying your name. Most of all, you ruined your life and your reputation. Aren't you ashamed and embarrassed for what you did?"

Abdul Rahman, looking for some redemption, shared that when he told his father he was getting married, he congratulated him. His father did not say it was the wrong thing to do.

Nabila said, "Your father hated me. It was his pleasure to see me hurt. Just go and leave me in my misery. I had more than enough from you. May Allah make it easier on me, and help you for what you will go through."

Her resolve collapsed and Nabila wailed with fresh pain. Abdul Rahman knew there was nothing he could say to appease Nabila. The cancer of his actions had sickened her; there was nothing he could do but walk away. Nabila's roller coaster of emotions was heading toward anger as she rejoined the girls in the living room and through tears informed them they had a baby sister. The troubling news enveloped her and she lashed out at her daughters.

"Are you happy about it? Or you still have no opinion about it? Doesn't it bother you in any way? I can't believe you have nothing to say about it. You see how much I am hurt. Doesn't that bother you? Don't you have any feeling for me? If it were not for me, you would be living with her. I am protecting you by keeping you with me in spite of all you do to me. You two have no feelings for your mother, because if you did, you could have told him you don't like the way he treated me and you could have stopped this marriage."

"Mommy, Mommy, listen to me," said Lamia, putting her arms around

Nabila. "He told us about the baby. We were surprised when you told us about your dream, because it was the same day the baby was born. We decided not to tell you because we didn't want to hurt you."

Nabila was not comforted by Lamia's words. "Stay away from me. You could have done a lot for me or at least supported me, talked to your father to tell him what he was doing was wrong, and that you would not accept any of what was happening to me. You do not know what I am going through. I am hurt from him, from your sister, and even from you."

As time went on, Nabila had two more dreams about Abdul Rahman having children with Mara. Both dreams held true and were confirmed by Lamia. Nabila's rage surfaced as she had violent dreams where she was beating Mara and slapping her face, overcome by hate and revenge.

Disheartened by her failed marriage and tense relations with her daughters, Nabila had little to uplift her outlook. Only after her father's past urging to secure her education resounded in her mind was she prompted to focus on her plan to get to America. She asked Lamia to remind her sister of the appointment at the American Embassy to apply for Nabila's green card. On the way to the embassy, Leila and Nabila did not speak. At the embassy, the officer handed Nabila the forms and took her Saudi passport and Leila's American passport. They waited an hour for the officer to return with the official file. He advised Nabila to call the American Embassy in Riyadh to schedule an interview. Nabila had to go to a specified hospital to get a blood test and a few days later, she was flying to Riyadh for her appointment at the American Embassy. It took over two hours before an officer called her to raise her hand to swear to the information. Then he gave Nabila a large envelope to take to customs in the U.S. airport within four months. Reaching out to Lamia, Nabila asked if she would like to go with her to the U.S. Nabila proposed they would go to Disney World and to visit their former residence where Lamia spent her childhood. Lamia was delighted with the idea.

On the plane, Nabila's mind once again wandered to her previous trips in happier times with Abdul Rahman by her side. She was never a single passenger on any trip; he was always with her. She had never felt more alone.

At the airport in the United States, she submitted the envelope to a customs officer. He issued a green card and told Nabila she must not stay out of the states for more than eleven months a year or she might lose her green card. This was unexpected. Nabila could not move full time to the United States, as she had not saved enough money. She decided the best way was to enter America every ten to eleven months, get her driver's license, and keep it valid. Since dual citizenship is not permitted in Saudi Arabia, Nabila had to go to the U.S. through Egypt, which did not require a visa from any of the Arab countries. Just to get out of Saudi Arabia was a struggle, as her brother had to accompany her to the airport to sign her out of the country as his responsibility. Nabila and her brother had to face many difficult situations at the airport just to allow her to travel. Nabila felt sorry to put him in such humiliating situations to help her.

Most the officers in charge of signing women out of the country appear either very prejudiced against women, or they want to demonstrate their power over women. They do not favor women traveling out of the country alone, and they try to complicate the process, resulting in women forfeiting traveling abroad.

Nabila experienced horrendous problems trying to exit her country. On one trip to the U.S. Nabila waited until well after midnight for her brother to gain permission to sign her out. Since women were not supposed to be walking around in front of men, Nabila stayed seated watching from afar. Nabila saw Samir pacing in several directions waiting for the officer in charge to return to his office. He was supposedly in the building but had not answered the previous three pages. Another officer could not substitute the clearance process. Nabila was concerned that she would miss her flight. Samir checked each office for the officer, but to no avail. Finally, two officers tried to help Samir. The two officers and her brother searched for the missing officer, circling the office area at least four times.

Then the two officers left and Nabila's brother came to tell her that no one could locate the officer in charge. They had to wait, hoping he would show up before the plane left. Twenty minutes before take-off, the two officers called Samir to come to the office. He finally got to speak to the officer in charge, but the officer wanted an official approved divorce document. Otherwise, her brother had no right to sign Nabila out of the country. Nabila covered her face and cried in defeat. Nabila had no way to get it from her home. Her brother knew she was disappointed and decided to try again to convince the officer. It took about seven minutes before he returned with a smile. The officers had changed shifts, and the next one on duty did not request the divorce decree. He only asked Nabila's brother to sign the form. *Al hamdllah.* It took great patience to remain hopeful.

There were a couple of years when Nabila had to go only for the weekend to the United States in order to keep her green card active, and return to her job through Egypt to avoid answering the Saudi Arabian Immigration officer's question, "Where did you come from?" However, days before any trip, Nabila had to be prepared for the worst, as they might not let her go. The officials could stop her because she had a green card. They could do anything to keep her from leaving the country. It was all in the hands of the Saudi Immigration officer, not the law. Whatever the officer on duty chose to say or do determined Nabila's eventual departure.

Nabila learned her lesson and decided to carry her divorce document with her whenever she traveled outside Saudi Arabia. It seemed the officers always concocted something to complicate the exit procedure. On one trip, Samir had Nabila's divorce document with him to prove her marriage status and his own ID to prove he was her brother. The officer looked at all the documents, and turned to Samir asking him for Nabila's father's death certificate.

"How do I know that her father is dead if you don't have the proof?" the officer asked.

"But I am her brother, and I am in charge of the family. This is my ID to prove to you," Samir said with annoyance.

The officer insisted Nabila could not leave until her brother brought proof of her father's death.

"But we have no time now to go and bring the death certificate. I am the guidance and in charge of my sisters after my father's death." Samir tried to convince the officer.

"Unless you bring your father's official death certificate, she will not leave. How do I know your father is dead? He might be alive and then he is the only one who can get her out of the country," explained the officer.

Samir tried again. "Okay, let her go this time and next time I promise you I will bring all the papers."

The officer ignored Samir, pulled a chair to the outside, and sat watching the people walking around. Nabila called to her brother and told him not to humiliate himself any longer. Nabila suggested that she would just change the flight to another day. However, Samir wanted to try again.

He went back to the officer. "Please, please let her go this time. She is going to miss her flight. If we had the time, we would go home and bring to you, but time is too tight. Consider her your sister. You wouldn't like it to happen to your sister."

Nabila was watching from a distance. Samir begged the officer.

"My sister would never dare to travel alone," the officer said and repeatedly refused to let Nabila go.

The flight announced its last call to Cairo, Egypt. Samir gave up and turned to leave when the officer smiled and called to him, "Okay, she can go."

Samir came back frustrated and cursing the officer, but Nabila finally got on the plane a few minutes before it took off.

Nabila's married sister also had trouble traveling abroad. She was going with one of her brothers on vacation when her husband took her to the airport to sign her out of the country. The officer stood with the three of them and asked her husband, "You agree that your wife travels with her brother?"

"Yes, I do," answered her husband.

Then the officer turned to her brother, "You agree to take your sister abroad without the company of her husband?"

"I agree," answered her brother.

Nabila's sister, a mother of four grown children, had no voice in the matter. She looked at the officer, her brother, and her husband. "Doesn't anyone want to say something to me?"

Grown women simply had no say as to their travel abroad. A colleague at work found this out when her two-year-old became ill. When the father took the child to see the doctor, the doctor advised the father to admit him to the hospital. The father disagreed with the rest of the family on which hospital they should admit the child. There was an argument between the two families. The father decided to take his child and fly to another country without informing any member of the two families, not even his wife. When the mother found out, she arranged to join her child and her husband. To her surprise, her husband had left an order banning his wife from traveling outside Saudi Arabia. No one was able to get her out of the country to be with her child.

In another instance, when Nabila's brother was out of the city and became quite ill, he fell into a coma. His wife could not travel to the hospital to be with him because he could not grant her permission to do so. Her son needed to take the doctor's report to the Saudi embassy to receive permission to transport his mother to the hospital.

Another colleague's husband asked her to prepare his formal clothing to attend his friend's wedding. After attending the wedding, the husband disappeared for four days. The wife frantically tried to locate her husband. She finally found out that the wedding was actually her husband's own wedding and the four days of disappearance was his honeymoon with his new wife.

Many Saudi men have used this travel restriction[1] for women to inhibit their wives, sisters, and mothers' freedom.

CHAPTER NOTES

1 In November 2012 the press reported that all Saudi women who attempt to cross the country's borders are now monitored by government officials, who alert the women's male guardians by cell phone text. This practice has been met with outrage from civil rights activists both within and outside Saudi Arabia.

CHAPTER 26

And give the women (On marriage) their dower
As a free gift; but if they, Of their own good pleasure,
Remit any part of it to you, Take it and enjoy it
With right good cheer.

~ AL NESSA 4

After her graduation from the university, a man sought Leila's hand in marriage through her father, and she agreed to marry him. While Lamia was at the university, she had some training at a hospital in Jeddah where she met a college educated young man. He proposed marriage to Lamia. Nabila was happy to hear her two daughters were being married, but worried about what she was going to do after their weddings. Nabila could never stay in the house and the car and the driver were not hers. She had a little over fifty thousand dollars in her savings and thought it might be the right time to move to America.

Like any other mother, Nabila wished to give her two daughters wedding parties, but their relationships were not normal mother-daughter relationships. Nabila saw Leila's wedding dress lying on the bed and was saddened that she had no part in her wedding plans. Nabila hoped there would be a party, but soon heard that Leila was traveling to the U.S. with her new husband, where her in-laws lived.

As for Lamia, in spite of the fact that the wedding was in one of the nicest hotels in Jeddah, disorganization was the theme. The invitation cards strictly forbid children under twelve from attending the wedding, and guests were to be at the wedding hall no later than nine o'clock in the evening. None of the guests arrived before midnight and the wedding hall was filled with children, including screaming infants. The wedding was chaotic as the children were out of control and the parents did not care. Nabila had to plan something to occupy the children. She had them sit on chairs and asked them to wait while she went to get presents and games. The children were obedient and under control until three of the groom's sisters intervened, "Why are you sitting here? Go play and enjoy yourself. This is your uncle's wedding."

The children shouted whooping calls and flew like birds around the guests. Nabila saw there was no way to control the children or the in-laws who were joining her family.

Wedding parties are the most formal parties in the Saudi society. The party is separated by gender. Female guests are involved in the main celebration. They dress up in the fanciest clothes, especially the young single girls, hoping a mother of eligible bachelors might notice them and choose them for their sons. Loud music is provided by a men's orchestra in another room, but women do not see the musicians nor can the musicians see the women. The bride does not join the party until the early morning hours. During the party and before the bride shows up, the girls dance together throughout the night. As soon as it is the time for the bride to join the party, which is about three o'clock in the morning, the dance and the music stop, and all guests wear their abaya to cover themselves as the groom joins the party.

A group of about six black women give a special drumming and sing traditional songs; it is very difficult for most people to understand the lyrics of the songs. The musicians lead the bride and the groom through the aisle to their seats on the stage. Small girls holding the bridal dress, children carrying flowers, and close family members follow the bride and groom to the stage.

As they sit in their special seats, sisters and female relatives of the groom dance in front of him on the stage. Soon, one of the groom's sisters or his mother brings his gold presents and a dowry attractively displayed on a fancy serving cart. Then the groom begins to dress his bride with all the jewelry on the cart. They exchange their drinks and move the rings that were on their right hand onto the left hand. It is the sign that they are married. Soon after, the drumming starts again, growing louder and louder. All these events take place without males in the room with the exception of the groom. Minutes later, however, the males of both families come to congratulate the couple, dressed in formal outfits, meshlah, the outer robe worn over the traditional white thoub men wear in Saudi Arabia. The meshlah is usually made of an expensive material in either black or brown. Embroidery in gold thread decorates the front of the meshlah along the opening of the robe. The cuffs of the robe repeat the same gold design. The head cover, *ghotra*, is made of expensive white material and the head cover, egal, is black and round, worn on top of the head to hold the ghotra.

The male members of the family kiss the bride and pose for pictures, and then they leave. When it is time for the buffet, the bride and the groom lead the way to the buffet and cut the cake. Then either they both leave together or the groom leaves, and the bride remains with the female guests to have dinner and to dance with the girls. As soon as the groom leaves, all women remove their abayas, and join the dinner and dance until daylight.

At religious weddings, however, the groom never enters the wedding hall. The party takes place among women only. There is no orchestra at religious weddings, only drumming, and girls dance moving their shoulders but not the lower half of their bodies. The gold presents and a dowry are visible at the party without the presence of the groom.

When it was dinnertime at the wedding, Nabila noticed there were not enough utensils or plates for the number of guests. The Egyptian wedding supervisor apparently did not do a good job of arranging the dinner table. Nabila complained about things that were not done to her request or as they should be. The supervisor became upset and annoyed with Nabila's complaints.

"Too many complaints! Who are you to complain like that? I am going to call the bride's mother to come and talk to you," stated the wedding supervisor.

Nabila looked at her, confused. "What do you mean? Don't you know I am the mother of the bride?"

The woman and her helper were surprised to discover that Nabila was the mother of the bride, but their service did not improve despite Nabila's vocal displeasure. When the bride and the groom reached their chairs, which usually takes about thirty minutes for them to walk slowly through the aisle with the drumming, the supervisor of the wedding was supposed to turn on the disco lights and colored bubbles to highlight the stage around them. The supervisor, however, turned the disco light and the bubbles on almost ten minutes before the two arrived at their chairs.

After the wedding festivities Lamia and her husband left for their new home. Nabila could not help but recall her own marriage and wished that her daughter would fare better in matters of the heart.

With Lamia married, it was the right time for Nabila to leave the country. She took a six month leave of absence from her teaching job as a trial period and dropped out of the master's program at the university in order to finish it in the United States.

When Nabila went to the registration office at the university to secure her records, the woman at the desk told her to "come tomorrow," and Nabila informed her that she was leaving the country in a few days. ("Come tomorrow" are the most common words used by workers in the country, no matter how high or low their status.)

"You can't come tomorrow?" she asked Nabila.

"I wouldn't have the time in the next few days," Nabila answered, knowing the clerk would have no problem giving it to her immediately.

The clerk rose with a sigh, opened the drawer, and retrieved Nabila's file. It was that simple.

Nabila's sister recommended that Nabila meet her friend, Haneen, who was on a scholarship in one of the largest U.S. cities, New York. Nabila contacted her to get all the information she needed about the city, the university, and the cost of living. Feeling positive about her plan, Nabila transferred money to a bank in the states and was soon ready to leave.

Even though Nabila was about to embark on a new life, she felt depressed. Her world had changed completely. She had been content in her marriage and never imagined its demise. She grieved for the son she never had. She was bitter that she did not receive any money, which she had spent twenty-five years helping Abdul Rahman to save. It all went to the woman who came to work for her. Nabila wanted to grow old with her husband, but it would never happen. Even her two daughters turned against her, poisoned by their father's lies and reinforced by the practices of a society unfair to women. Nabila's choice was to struggle in Saudi society alone, or leave her family and friends to survive.

As much as Nabila needed to go she still yearned for her past life. *Oh, Abdul Rahman, how can you do this to me? I am lost in this world. Is this what I deserve, abandoned after all these years? Where had all the love you had for me gone? Is it possible that a man who loved so much can hate so much? I wish you would come back to me, Abdul Rahman. I still want you, and need you badly in my life. Yes, I will forgive you if come back; just come back.* Nabila continued talking to Abdul Rahman in her mind. She knew she needed to forget him; after all, it had been over four years. But how could she get over him? Nabila was haunted by her former image of a loving husband who no longer existed.

The eighteen-hour flight to the United States did little to dispel Nabila's troubles. Once in New York, Nabila met Haneen and tried to focus on a better outlook. She rented an apartment for three months next to Haneen. As they became acquainted, Nabila shared the story of her failed marriage. Haneen repeatedly reminded Nabila that she was forever talking about her former husband.

"You must let go and live your life," said Haneen.

Nabila wished it were that easy. People did not understand how much she longed to forget, how she wished for a pill that would void her mind of thoughts of Abdul Rahman. Yes, Nabila had known other women who had to fight through the pain of divorce, but when it was happening to her, the lonliness was so acute that it was impossible to feel outside her own heart. Haneen eventually married and moved out of the city, and Nabila was alone again.

Nabila tried to acclimate to the city. She enrolled at the local university, took driving lessons, and bought a car. Between the tuition, the car, and the rent, her money was steadily shrinking. Six months had transpired and the Education office in Saudi Arabia called asking if she was returning. Nabila had only two weeks to return or she could lose her job. Nabila called the office and explained she needed one more year to finish her master's degree. The authority agreed to extend the leave for six more months, the maximum limit for any leave of absence.

The Gulf War started and all the Saudi public schools closed for four months. All the teachers were paid for those months except those who were on a leave of absence, like Nabila. Rapidly running out of funds, Nabila's only hope was to secure a scholarship. She called the Saudi Embassy in Washington D.C., requesting a scholarship to finish her master's degree and the embassy quickly sent the registration form. As Nabila was completing the application, she came to a question which destroyed all hope for the scholarship. 'Who is your male guardian with you in the U.S.? Send a copy of his visa and a copy of his passport.'

Nabila called her brother Samir and explained the requirement of his presence as guardian in order to secure a scholarship.

She asked him, "If I get you an acceptance from one of the Language Colleges, do you think you could get a visa to the U.S. and come for few a days?"

Agreeing to the plan, Samir traveled to the U.S. but he could not stay more than a few days because he had to go back to his work. Nabila sent a copy of his passport and his visa to the embassy. A few days after Samir left the United States, Nabila received a warning that her brother had a visa, but never showed up at the institute. Now considered an illegal alien, Samir had to report to the institute or he would be reported to the Saudi Embassy. Nabila's scheme failed, and she gave up hope of a scholarship for lack of a male guidance.

In the midst of trying to prove guardianship, Nabila received a phone call from Lamia. She told Nabila that Uncle Saleh passed away after a long illness in the hospital. Even though he had treated Nabila terribly, she still felt sorrow about his passing.

Paying for school tuition, books, rent, and a car depleted Nabila's funds. The only job available paid minimum wage at the university, and she worked for a few months before finding another job. Although working at a boutique only paid minimum wage, Nabila was able to work more hours and substitute for others working during holidays. She made enough to finance her degree, finishing the entire course load in less than two years. She only needed to write a thesis, which would take another six months. But then Nabila received a warning letter from The Presidency of Girls' Education in Jeddah to return within two weeks to work or resign. Unfortunately, she could not afford to lose her job. She had come so close to earning her degree but her efforts were in vain.

Whenever Nabila faced a hardship she thought of Abdul Rahman. If he were here, he would have used his connections to extend Nabila's leave. *Oh, how I wish you were with me, Abdul Rahman.* It had been years since they were together, but Nabila still envisioned him as her knight to right the wrongs in her world. *I must get over him, I must.* Nabila tried again to extend her leave, but the director at the Presidency of Girls' Education refused, suggesting Nabila return and request a scholarship to King Abdul Rahman-Aziz University to finish her program.

CHAPTER 27

Read and your Lord is Most Generous, Who taught man (reading and writing) by the pen, Who (besides that) taught man (all that) which he did not know.

~ AL ALAQ 96:1-5

With nowhere to live, Nabila returned to Jeddah and had to stay with Lamia and her husband in a small apartment, next to Lamia's in-laws. Lamia was pregnant with her first child and trying to make it through her junior year of university studies. Unfortunately, Nabila could see that her daughter was not happy with her husband; she referred to him as a mother's boy. He worked from eight-to-five every day, and when he returned, he went directly to his mother's apartment, leaving Lamia alone. He would call Lamia to bring food to his mother's house, but never asked Lamia to stay for a meal with them. Lamia felt neglected and deserted while her husband tried to please his mother.

During the three months Nabila spent with Lamia, she found Lamia's husband to be a good man, but his mother had strong control over him. She was able to force him to do almost anything she desired. He put her first over anyone else in his life, in fear of his mother's anger.

The simple one-bedroom apartment where Lamia lived had no phone. The only phone was in the mother-in-law's apartment. Whenever Lamia received phone calls, she had to walk to the in-laws apartment to answer her calls. Once Nabila received a call, but was not able to immediately respond. Nabila had just gotten out of the shower, and did not want to keep the person on the phone waiting for her to get dressed and walk to the other apartment. Nabila asked if they could send the phone over since it had a long cord. Later in the day, Nabila overheard Lamia arguing with her husband over that phone call. Poor Lamia had to apologize to her husband's mother because Nabila had inconvenienced her.

Nabila knew she had to move to her own apartment. To avoid a scandal of a divorced woman living alone, Nabila recruited a housekeeper to live with her. She found a driver, a middle-aged Pakistani, her first experience with drivers after her divorce. Nabila had to pay two thousand Saudi riyals for a visa for a maid and five thousand riyals to the recruiting office. It took about three months for them to arrive from their country.

Nabila was about to face many problems living alone. There was nothing for her to do but to deal with them as they came along. What she encountered was completely unexpected. Since public transportation did not exist for women, hiring drivers was the only recourse. Women were beaten, used, humiliated, threatened, harassed, and some were even raped by drivers.[1] There was no place to complain, and no one punished a driver for his wrongdoing with women. Drivers knew how much women needed them; therefore, they were able to do whatever they pleased. They knew females in Saudi Arabia had no recourse, and if job conditions did not please them, they simply left to work for someone else.

Private houses all over Saudi Arabia were built to accommodate a driver living on the premises, but a driver's room did not exist in an apartment building. Women or families living in an apartment sometimes had to rent a room for the driver. Nabila had to get the owner's permission to build a room behind the building for her driver, and equip it with everything he needed.

Nabila's issues with housing a driver were not her only concern. The process of earning an advanced degree had been fraught with problems since the beginning. Nabila took her file to the director of the department at the university. The director looked at it and informed Nabila that her major was not available at the university or at any university in Saudi Arabia. She indicated that Nabila would have to change her major.

"But I have finished all the requirements of my degree in this field. I only need to write my thesis or take my comprehensive exam. I can't start from the beginning," Nabila pleaded.

Nevertheless, that was the director's only advice. As Nabila was walking out of the office, she ran into some of the friends who were in her earlier master's degree program. They told Nabila that they were still struggling with their program. They truly thought that it might take a few more years for them to get their degree. All the girls were perplexed as to why there were so many obstacles to obtain a master's degree in Saudi Arabia.

"Things are so complicated here," said one of the girls. "If I were you I would return to the U.S. and never come back."

"I wish I could. I would not be here an extra minute," Nabila responded.

When Nabila recanted her plight to her brothers and sisters about the university, they encouraged her to go ahead with a new major.

"You will have a degree even if it is not in the major you wanted. You never wanted to be a teacher anyway, but you ended up as one. Think of it this way, almost no one gets what he wants, especially in this country. You will be one of the first groups to have a master's degree," Samir said, trying to convince Nabila. "Isn't it better than going back to teaching after finishing all those courses with no master's degree? If I were you, you are getting paid anyway. I would accept any major if I can walk out with an extra degree and get a break from teaching."

Nabila agreed and returned to the director the next day. She gave Nabila a major choice and told her that she must take at least one undergraduate course as a refresher course. Nabila was incredulous that she would be taking classes with undergraduate students. However, she took the course prescription and her records to the class instructor, Dr. Kawther. Nabila requested that the instructor review her course work taken in the states to see if credit could be granted for some of the courses toward the MA program. After reviewing the records, Dr. Kawther surmised that Nabila would be much more advanced than the students in her class. She suggested that Nabila did not need to attend classes, but should just take the exams and the finals. Nabila was delighted with her suggestion, as it would give her more time to focus on the MA program. However, a few days later, Nabila was summoned to the director.

As Nabila walked into the office, the director asked in an unprofessional manner, "Where is the file you told me you would bring to me to see the courses you had covered in the U.S. school?"

"I handed it to you before I left your office," Nabila answered, trying to control her temper.

"No, you did not. If you did, where is it?" she questioned Nabila.

Nabila offered to make another copy.

"Yes, do that and bring it as soon as you can. The men's department is asking about it, and I told them you haven't brought it yet," the director responded.

Nabila tried to remind her that she handed it to her and then Nabila was given the undergraduate course paper to give to Dr. Kawther.

Aggravated, Nabila left her office. Nabila brought her a second copy the next day. The director opened it, looked through the papers, and put them on her desk. Nabila hoped she would not complain again.

However, when Nabila stopped by the director's office later, she shouted at Nabila, "How many times do I have to ask you to bring the names and the grades of the courses you have taken at the university?"

"Oh, my God, I gave it to you a second time," Nabila said.

The director huffed, "They are not complete. How can we credit those courses if you did not bring them?"

Nabila restated that she had brought them to her office.

"Not complete. You said you have finished the entire requirement. I do not see the grades of all the courses. You have to be more careful. I will have to report it to the men's department and that would affect your grades," the director scolded.

She treated Nabila like a kid in grade school. Nabila took the file from the director and looked at it carefully. It was complete. Nabila decided not to talk to her any further and requested the folder under the guise that she would complete it. Nabila gave the folder to her driver to deliver to the men's department. Then Nabila called the men's department to verify they received the complete folder. Nabila asked if they would examine it and inform her if there were missing papers. The department confirmed that all Nabila's papers were complete and they would credit many of the courses Nabila had taken in the U.S. They said Nabila needed to talk to the director to assign one of the doctors to follow up with preparation for her thesis within two weeks.

How Nabila hated to go back to the director's office and ask her to assign a doctor to supervise her thesis.

"How can I assign you a doctor when I just heard that you are not attending the undergraduate course, and Dr. Kawther is not happy about that," the director said in a shrill voice.

"WHAT?" Nabila shouted, "Dr. Kawther told me that I was much higher than the girls' level in her class, and she wanted me to come for the tests only. Those were her words."

Nabila felt the director wanted her out of the program. "Would you assign a doctor soon?" Nabila asked trying to control her temper.

"The only doctor who would supervise your thesis is my relative, Dr. Anar, but she has no time for you," the director said.

Nabila asked what she was supposed to do if Dr. Anar could not help. Her retort was to ask someone in the men's department. Many Saudi people, especially those with high positions, like to hold on to their status and fear competition. Nabila surmised this doctor was the only one with the same major as Nabila and may have thought Nabila would be competitive with her; thus, she tried her best to avoid Nabila, or anyone, who would threaten her status.

Nabila could not understand why, with the support of the director, she refused to supervise her thesis. If Abdul Rahman was with Nabila, he could have gone to the men's department and settled the matter in minutes. Now Nabila had no man to stand by her and support her in what she was doing. Nabila almost gave up on her master's program, but decided to keep trying as long as she had time left on her scholarship.

As a last effort, Nabila decided to seek help from the dean of the University. She called every morning and afternoon, but he was never there. When it was hopeless to find the dean, and time was running out, Nabila went back to the director and asked her for help, explaining how time was shrinking to finish her degree.

"This is your responsibility to find someone, not mine," she said. "Go to Riyadh. You don't have to have someone here."

Nabila called the university in Riyadh to speak to the dean but was not able to locate him. Instead, the director of the department advised Nabila to try again with the doctors in the department in Jeddah, because she would not be able to travel to Riyadh as often as needed for the program. Nabila felt like a hamster on a wheel. She wasted lots of time going from one doctor to another looking for someone to supervise her thesis. The

Presidency of Girls' Education had given Nabila only two years of leave to finish her degree. She felt that there was a plot arranged between the director and her relative to get Nabila out of the program. Eventually, the director informed Nabila that her relative Dr. Anar had agreed to supervise Nabila until she found someone else. She followed up with Nabila for about a month, but she was not easy to find. She was always too busy, out of the university, or absent for the day.

The last time the supervisor met with Nabila, she discussed several major points and indicated she was impressed with Nabila's knowledge about the subject. The supervisor encouraged Nabila to talk to the director to get an extension to finish her MA program.

Full of hope and enthusiasm, Nabila asked the director if she would write a letter to the Presidency of Girls' Education to extend her leave to finish the program. Nabila's good spirits plummeted when the director said, "What extension are you talking about? Didn't you know you are out of the program? You better go back to your job."

Nabila had progressed in the program and was clueless as to what would prompt the director to discontinue her program. The director claimed that Nabila ran out of time and she left the room ending the conversation. Desperate, Nabila called the Presidency of the Girls' Education asking them to give her extra time. They said they could only extend Nabila's scholarship if the director of the department requested the extension. Their answers destroyed all hope for receiving a higher degree. With all the obstacles and the time Nabila wasted finding someone to supervise her thesis, the director was able to remove Nabila from the program for no reason. Crushed, Nabila had no choice but to return to teaching.

Nabila's teaching supervisor recommended that she consider teaching twelfth graders to prepare for college. Nabila was pleased with the idea, thinking the girls would be serious about their studies. The supervisor also advised Nabila to go back to the United States to finish her MA. Nabila told her that she could not leave her job, and the supervisor was sympathetic. She suggested a university where Nabila could complete her thesis so she would not have to forfeit her previous work. It had been a long time since anyone encouraged or believed Nabila could complete her studies. Nabila attended an American university during the summer for three years and she eventually earned her master's degree in 2000.

With an advanced degree, Nabila could take a teaching job at the university, but thinking of the director of the department discouraged her. She decided to continue teaching in public schools even though her pay was not substantial. Nabila had to closely monitor her money as she was part of the shrinking middle class in Saudi Arabia, dividing the rich and the poor even further.[2]

Nabila's focus shifted from teaching to Lamia, who was ready to have a baby. Nabila took Lamia to a private hospital in Jeddah, which she believed was one of the best hospitals in the city. Lamia was in labor for about twelve hours, when the gynecologist found out that the baby was not in the right position for delivery. The doctor needed Lamia's husband's consent to perform a cesarean section. Nabila waited for over two hours for the doctor to return and Nabila's son-in-law to show up. During those two hours, Nabila tried to locate him but was not able to find him anywhere, not in the hospital, not on the phone, not even at his mother's house. Another hour passed, with Lamia in great pain and the doctor still had not returned. The nurse paged him two more times. The doctor finally came to tell them that he could not locate the anesthesiologist, and that if he could not be brought in soon, Lamia would have to transfer to the nearest hospital. Distraught, Nabila insisted that they provide an ambulance to transfer her daughter to another hospital. They called the ambulance but it was not equipped with the materials needed for Lamia's condition, and there was no nurse to accompany Lamia to the other hospital. Frightened, and having no man around to help, Nabila called one of the government hospitals to send an ambulance as soon as possible. Within five minutes, the ambulance was there. Nabila waited outside the delivery room and prayed for Lamia and the unborn child. While she was deep in prayer, her son-in-law appeared.

"What happened?" he asked anxiously.

"I looked for you everywhere I could think of to come and help me. They needed you to sign the consent form," Nabila explained, trying to hide her anger.

"I did not think you would need me, so I thought I would spend some time with a friend," he explained.

Their conversation was cut short when the doctor emerged from the delivery room with the comforting news that the newborn and mother were in good condition.

God did not give Nabila the son she had always wished for, but He rewarded her with a healthy grandson, named Faris. Nabila loved him from the first minute she laid eyes on him. Two months after the delivery, Lamia had to return to the university. Nabila took care of the baby during the day and Lamia took him home at night.

Nabila took the baby to her workout at the women's gym. She kept him in a high chair in the exercise room. Faris sat there happily watching the women dancing and listening to the music. She took him shopping, to visit friends and family, and toward the end of the school year, she brought him to school with her. Faris became an important part of Nabila's life; she loved that child so much that she was consumed with making him happy. The love she felt for her grandson warmed her heart as it did when her children were young. Weeks later, Lamia called to tell Nabila to keep Faris during the day and night as her problems with her husband had escalated. Although Lamia was unhappy, Nabila was jubilant to have time with her grandson. She was so attached to the baby; he kept her company and filled her empty life with love. Nabila was only separated from Faris during her working hours when Faris stayed with Leila or the housekeeper.

When Faris was three-years-old, Lamia graduated from the university and decided to take Faris home.

"I am going miss him so much, Lamia," Nabila said as they were leaving.

"But he is my child, Mother," said Lamia.

"I know that, but I am so used to him. It breaks my heart to see him leaving," Nabila cried.

Lamia was kind enough to bring Faris to see Nabila every afternoon. His presence was the highlight of Nabila's day.

Lamia became depressed because of her marital troubles. Her husband Hamid left her alone day and night. She would awake in the middle of the night to find Hamid missing from their bed. Lamia turned to religion, praying day and night for help. Some of her female friends took advantage of her vulnerability and pressured her to become involved with a fanatic religious group. The religious sect changed Lamia. She spent most of her time with the religious women, so she resigned from her job at the hospital. Lamia became devoted to a new mission—converting Christians into Muslims.

By the time little Faris was five-years-old, Lamia hired a Pakistani to teach him to recite and memorize the Quran. Soon Faris was in kindergarten during the day, and studied the Quran in the afternoon. He would spend a day of the weekend with Nabila, but Lamia made it a rule that he must come home at a certain time for his Quran lesson. The lessons continued for over a year. One day, Faris asked Nabila if he could skip the Quran lesson that day. Nabila told him it was up to his mother, but she would try to convince Lamia. Nabila took him home and told Lamia that Faris needed a break from the afternoon religion lesson.

Lamia shouted at Faris, "No, you must continue with the lesson. Do you understand?"

Nabila tried to explain to Lamia that he would be taking lots of religion classes and Quran lessons, and if she kept on pushing him into religion, she might drive him away from it. But Lamia strongly disagreed.

Nabila remained silent as she watched Lamia push the boy into the Pakistani teacher's room. A tear stung Nabila's cheek when she peered through the classroom window at Faris sitting on the floor rocking forward and backward as he read and repeated the Quran verses.

Faris was also made to pray in the mosque for every prayer, and at the age of six, Lamia forced him to fast the Holy Month of Ramadan. Nabila visited Faris several times during Ramadan and saw the child returning from school weak from fasting all day. The minute Faris arrived home, he collapsed on the sofa, tired and frail. Lamia never gave the child a break. Nabila tried to make Lamia understand that Faris was only six and according to Islam, he was not obligated to fast until after puberty, but Lamia would not listen. Lamia believed her child had to faithfully practice to be a good Muslim.

Time passed all too quickly and Leila was expecting her babies, twin girls, while Lamia was having her second child, another boy. Lamia requested that Nabila suggest a name for the new baby boy. Fortunately, things went all right in the delivery room with Lamia and the child. The baby's father agreed on the name Nabila had chosen for her second grandson, Emad. Both Faris and Emad had a special place in Nabila's heart. Nabila remembered her own grandmother used to tell her that grandchildren are even more precious than your own children.

When Leila was ready to have her twins, she called Nabila to go to the hospital with her. It was about 2 a.m. Nabila was with Leila in the delivery room, waiting anxiously. A few hours later, the gynecologist called the pediatrician on duty, but she was not able to be located. She was paged several times but was not available. Disgruntled, the doctor inquired if he could request another pediatrician because the babies were about to be delivered. The pediatrician on duty showed up just then. She meandered into the delivery room carrying a cup of coffee and smacking her chewing gum. The pediatrician talked to Leila, trying to convince her that taking the back injection for delivery would be best. The pediatrician refused to relinquish her coffee cup, even when the doctor needed her assistance. Despite her unprofessional behavior, the adorable twins arrived without trauma.

Nabila adored her four grandchildren. They helped Nabila to forget her problems with their mothers. She welcomed the two families to her house only to be with the wonderful children. They filled her life with great love. Nabila believed that her two daughters had changed after having their own children, especially Leila. Leila wanted to live close to help Nabila and convinced her husband to move and live in the same building as Nabila. Both daughters left the children with Nabila during the weekend and came once a week to have a meal with Nabila. Lamia and Leila were finally repairing the broken relationship with Nabila that had plagued the three women for years.

Yet it seems that Nabila and her daughters would always be at odds with each other.When Lamia got pregnant for the third time, Nabila was delighted, but her happiness dissolved when Lamia said she would name the baby after her father, Abdul Rahman. Nabila was crushed and asked if this was to please Abdul Rahman. Lamia said that her father was always asking, 'Aren't any of you going to name a child after me?'

"And you wanted to please him, do you not?" Nabila asked. "Doesn't that, in your opinion, tell him that you did not care what he had done to me? You still honor him. Do you think it would be easy for me to call my grandson using your father's name?" Nabila asked. Nabila was devastated at the thought of regularly repeating the name.

Leila tried to make Lamia change her mind about the name. She even appealed to Lamia's husband, Hamid. He said they would decide later as it was a few months until the baby was due. Nabila knew Hamid was siding with Lamia, since he could have easily forced her to change the name. Nabila cut ties with Lamia over the name issue. She refused to go to the delivery or even talk to Lamia. One of Nabila's sisters talked to Hamid explaining that Abdul Rahman had hurt Nabila very much and to give his name to a new grandson showed that Lamia did not care how badly he upset her mother. Hamid did not seem to care and acted as if he had no opinion on the subject.

Seven months after the birth of her third child, Lamia could not cope with the problems with Hamid. Lamia wanted a divorce. Hamid did not want to divorce Lamia; however, with Lamia's insistence he agreed and offered her the house and to keep the children with her. But Lamia desperately wanted out of the marriage and to get away. Uncharacteristically, she left the house and the children with their father.

When Nabila received a phone call from her son-in-law, Hamid, she went immediately to see him. With Lamia gone, she was worried about the children being alone with the housekeeper, who knew nothing about children. When Nabila arrived, the two boys ran to greet her. Shortly after, six-year-old Faris scrambled up the steps and returned with the baby, Nabila's third grandson whom she had never met.

Proudly, Faris said, "this is my new brother."

Nabila held the infant against her chest and sobbed. She could not resist loving this child, no matter what his name may be. The baby appeared hungry so Nabila went to the kitchen and found milk and cereal for the baby. Then Nabila talked to the boy's father for an hour about his failed marriage. Hamid explained that he never wanted to divorce Lamia, but she insisted. It was mid afternoon, so Nabila took the boys to the store to buy groceries for the family. A forlorn Faris did not talk much and did not want to eat anything. When Nabila asked Faris if he missed his mother he shook his head and burst into tears. Nabila could not help but weep with him.

CHAPTER NOTES:

1 Women are not the only group that is met with sexual violence in Saudi Arabia. Pressure from online campaigns have called for the investigation of sexual abuse of children in Saudi Arabia. A report published in the Okaz daily newspaper in April 2011 confirmed that Riyadh had recorded 583 cases (404 boys and 179 girls) involving rape, physical and sexual torture, and violence of children over the previous three years.

2 Recent statistics in Saudi Arabia showed a decline in the average family income and an increase in unemployment for both Saudi males and females, even though they may have college degrees. A many as 89 percent are in debt with credit cards and bank loans.

CHAPTER 28

Good deeds properly, sincerely and moderately and know that your deeds will not make you enter Paradise, and that the most beloved deed to Allah's is the most regular and constant even though it were little.

~ SAHIH AND BUKHARI

After six years of service, Nabila's Pakistani driver decided to take six months vacation to visit his family. Nabila tried to talk him into taking only one month, but he said his working visa did not expire for another seven months and he did not want to change his plan. Nabila had to recruit a husband and wife to work as a driver and a housekeeper, paying four thousand Saudi riyals for the visas and ten thousand to the recruiting office. For over three months while Nabila waited for them to arrive, she had to depend on taxis, the neighbor, sisters, and brothers for transportation.

At last, the housekeeper and the driver, middle-aged Indonesians, arrived in Jeddah. Nabila had to pay another 600 Saudi riyals for working permits and 600 for the driver's license. While the house worker was doing a fine job, the driver was never available when Nabila needed him. Nabila questioned the housekeeper as to his whereabouts and she usually said he was in the mosque praying.

Nabila had to talk to him. "Listen, Ya aboya. I do not mind you going to the mosque, but you must tell me before you go. I don't want to look for you when I need you."

The driver was upset. "No, I don't have to tell you. If you don't find me, you know I am praying in the Mosque."

Days later, Nabila reminded him, "You must tell me when you go to the mosque. I don't have to look for you every time I need you."

The next morning, both the driver and the housekeeper were gone. They were Nabila's first experience with runaway servants. Nabila had to recruit another couple and thought that workers from the Philippines would be more reliable. Nabila believed the key factor in those servants being good workers was the presence of a man in the family. Nabila had never had a problem with runaway drivers or abuse of her car when she was married. There is always abuse of single women from all kinds of workers.

Once again Nabila shelled out money for the fees for recruiting a new couple from the Philippines. The driver and housekeeper were not related and only met when they came to work for Nabila. The housekeeper took great care of the apartment, and Nabila found her to be honest and sincere. With a private driver and a housekeeper, Nabila could finally relax.

During this time, Leila arrived from the U.S. alone. She asked Nabila if she could live with her until her husband returned. Nabila agreed, but worried that there would be some troubles with the arrangement. Tensions between mother and daughter seemed to flare easily.

Feeling a sense of freedom with the presence of a private driver, Nabila re-enrolled in the health club. She worked out daily, never missing a day for two months. The only health club in Jeddah had two sessions, morning to three in the afternoon for women, and four in the afternoon to nine in the evening for men. One morning as Nabila approached the entrance to the club the guard stopped to tell her the club closed. The Motawes (religious police) ordered the health club closed to women. The rumor circulated that a love letter was found in one of the lockers addressed to a woman. The police punished all members of the club for the action of a man who disobeyed the laws of their culture.

In the past, there was a venue for women to gather and entertain, trade recipes, and chat with families. Religious lectures or other useful talks of interest were given to females, such as raising children. Much to Nabila's horror, a man dressed up in women's clothing, covered with an abaya, had entered the women's hall causing problems. The next day the Motawes closed the hall for women.[1] Once again, the women received the punishment instead of the man who committed the infraction.

Three months passed, and Nabila was headed to work. She looked for the driver but he was not in his room. She called his cell phone but it was turned off. Instinctively, Nabila knew he had gone to work for someone else. Nabila had to take a taxi to work and when she returned she went to look at his room. All the furniture, the television, and all the pots and pans were missing, including the cell phone. He left nothing but the refrigerator. Nabila had to supply the room with everything again for the next driver.

Nabila had to work with a recruiter to secure a driver. But the recruiters were unscrupulous and matched legal drivers to other families who would pay them more money than their contracted family if the driver gave the recruiter a monthly fee. It worked both ways, as many families, especially women, were desperate for legal drivers and unable to afford recruiting one from abroad. They were willing to grab any driver with a legal visa to work for them; at the same time, legal drivers also looked for the best offer. Drivers ran away from their sponsors to make more money elsewhere under the sponsor's name. Nabila offered workers more money than what the contract stated, but they still found better offers with other families.

Finding a taxi in the morning was very difficult. Nabila had to walk about half a mile every morning to get to the main street, and wait for over thirty minutes to find a taxi. She had to scout for a local driver until she could afford the charges for another working visa to recruit a driver. Local drivers were notoriously untrustworthy; they never worked full time and asked for more money than foreign drivers. Their aim usually was to work for women, only to have a car under their control.

The best way to find a local driver was to ask people if they knew someone who wanted to work as a driver. Nabila found a Pakistani who had a free visa. With permission and payment of a monthly fee to his sponsor, the driver could work anywhere in the country. These kinds of drivers usually asked for more money in order to be able to pay their sponsors. Feeling desperate, Nabila hired him for the money he bargained for, thinking it would be temporary until she recruited another driver. The next morning Nabila gave him the car key and he started the car. It quickly became evident that he did not know how to drive. He moved forward only to jerk the car backward every few feet. Nabila felt like she was riding on the back of a frightened camel, bolting in the middle of heavy traffic. The drivers in the cars behind hers were honking, cursing, and yelling insults. Nabila had to convince the driver to park the car close to the sidewalk;

then she took the keys and told him to leave. She abandoned the car and took a taxi to school.

Unfortunately, the taxi driver was new in the city and had never worked in any Arab country. He did not speak Arabic or English. He also did not know any streets in the city; he only knew right, left, and straight. Nabila had to direct him using those words.

When they approached the government gate where Nabila worked, he said, "No, no, no licenses, no registration card."

He dropped Nabila off outside of the compound and she had to walk the rest of the way. It was absurd that a cab company recruited and hired a taxi driver who was unable to speak any languages except his native tongue, was unfamiliar with the streets in the city, and had no driver's license or registration card!

Despite Nabila's horrendous experiences, she kept trying to find a driver. She decided to try hiring a Saudi who would come in the morning and leave in the afternoon. He came on time the first day and went home at about three in the afternoon. He left Nabila his home phone number in case she needed him later in the day. At about five o'clock in the afternoon, Nabila looked out her window but did not see her car. Nabila called him and asked about the car. He confirmed that he had it, and Nabila questioned why he had taken her car.

"Well, I need the car in the evening. You don't need it until the morning, and if you need to go anywhere, I will take you," the driver replied, acting as if the car was now his property.

Oh, my God. Nabila asked him to bring the car immediately to the house. Her unfortunate experiences confirmed that local drivers want to work to have a car at their disposal to use for their own purposes.

Many drivers do not like to work for women who are knowledgeable about cars because they cannot take advantage of them by charging them more for gas or oil that they do not need. Nabila had a driver who insisted on changing the oil every week. When Nabila refused to change it that often, he got mad and shouted, "You don't know about cars. It is very important to change the oil every week. I will not work for you. You don't change the oil; the car will not be good."

He left Nabila after a brief employment.

Nabila had no choice but to keep searching for a local driver and settled on a Pakistani named Khan, who had a free working visa. He was working very well and on time, but he tried to cheat on gas. He would take thirty Saudi riyals and fill the car with only twenty. Nabila did not want to lose him and go through searching for another driver, so she decided to go with him to get gas or an oil change. The driver and Saudi society discouraged this action as Saudi women by customary law did not frequent the fueling centers.

After working for several months, Khan met another Pakistani working for Nabila's ex husband who was making almost twice as much as he was. Khan began to complain to Leila, "Your mother does not trust me. She thinks I was a thief. Why must she go with me to get gas or to change the oil?"

Leila told Nabila that Khan disliked working for her.

Nabila wondered, "Why is he with me if doesn't want to work for me? Why doesn't he leave? He complains to you, but he never told me he doesn't want to work for me."

After several conversations complaining to Leila about Nabila, the driver left. Again, Nabila had to search for a taxi every morning. It was frustrating having her two cars parked near her apartment building, and not being able to use them. In the afternoon, Nabila had a long walk out of the compound where she worked to get to the main street to find a taxi. She waited for twenty to thirty minutes in the hot Jeddah sun for a taxi to pass by the deserted area. As much as Nabila hated the process, she knew she had to recruit a driver from abroad again. However, while she waited for the three months to pass, Nabila had to look for a temporary driver. She asked several people and faced humiliation standing in the street asking every driver if he knew a driver who wanted to work. Each one of them promised they knew a driver. They acted so positive as they exchanged phone numbers with Nabila. But when she called them she received false promises. Nabila finally found a driver who looked younger than her daughters, and she thought she could treat him like a son. Nabila was pleased with his driving and took him to buy some clothes and every-thing he needed for his room.

One morning Nabila received a telephone call at work from the driver saying he had a car accident. When Nabila inquired about his location, he was in the southern part of the city, far from Nabila's home and work. Nabila did not understand why he was in that area and took a taxi to the scene. Nabila found the car smashed like an accordion in both the back and the front. The driver had vanished and left the car keys on top of the car. The auto was beyond repair and had to be towed. The men at the towing company asked Nabila if she had a man to take care of the car but with no one to help she had to trust them to take the car to the junk yard.

Nabila returned home disappointed and depressed with no solutions to resolve the issues with drivers. When she arrived, the guard told her that the young driver and a friend had been there with a truck. He stole everything in the room, the mattress, the pillows, the gas stove, the dishes, the pots and pans, and the TV. He only left the refrigerator and the window air conditioner. Nabila cried, defeated. *Oh please Allah, help me. I cannot deal with all these problems.*

Leila's husband returned from the United States and they moved to another apartment on the next street. One day as Nabila was returning from work, she passed by Leila's building and spied Leila leaving in a car with the Pakistani driver, Khan. Apparently because he was unhappy working for Nabila, Leila had arranged for Khan to work for Abdul Rahman and did not seem to care that her mother was without a driver. When Nabila confronted Leila, she denied he was Nabila's former driver.

"I am not stupid," Nabila said angrily. "It is him. You really took him to work for your father and you did not care about what I go through every morning to get to work. Oh, I just can't believe you'd do such a thing to me."

Nabila believed her daughter always preferred her father and would do anything for him. Nabila was once again hurt by Leila's actions.

It was not just Leila who hurt Nabila. Against everyone's advice Lamia had met a man, a foreigner, on the internet named Daood. He was also involved in converting Christians to Muslims. Unfortunately, Daood was not in a position to support Lamia and her children, so Abdul Rahman used his position to arrange for the marriage of Lamia and Daood. At first Hamid was upset and kept the children away from Lamia, but as the children got older Hamid did not want the responsibility of caring for the children. He decided to leave them with Lamia and her new husband, Daood. Nabila advised Lamia to try to postpone having more children until Hamid accepted the fact that she was with another man. Otherwise, Hamid might take the children back.

In the months to come Nabila asked Lamia to bring the children to visit. But her response was always that they were too busy with their school work. The only way to see her grandchildren was to take a taxi to their house for a short visit. Each time Nabila visited Lamia, she found Lamia wrapped with the sharshaf, a large cloth women cover themselves with when they pray. Nabila observed that Lamia was getting heavier, but Lamia had no reaction to the comment. One evening, Nabila received an alarming telephone call from Leila indicating that Lamia was in the hospital. To Nabila's surprise, Lamia had given birth to a little girl. Nabila was hurt that Lamia had hidden the pregnancy from her and did not ask her to be there during the delivery. In her disappointment with Lamia's actions, Nabila decided to stay away from her daughter and her granddaughter.

Four months later Nabila received the tragic telephone call from Leila that Lamia's baby girl had died in her sleep. Death brought the estranged women back together again. Nabila sobbed uncontrollably when she saw her granddaughter's tiny lifeless body. It was her first and last glimpse of the granddaughter she would never know.

During Lamia's fifth pregnancy, Nabila was delighted when Lamia asked her to keep the boys for the four days during Lamia's stay in the hospital. Nabila applied for an emergency leave from work to be able to stay with the boys. As soon as Nabila heard that Lamia was headed to the hospital, she waited for the boys to come to her house. Nabila called Leila to determine when the boys were supposed to arrive. But Leila knew nothing of the arrangement and advised Nabila to talk to Lamia who was still in the hospital waiting room. To Nabila's surprise, Lamia said that Leila was the one who had made arrangements for the boys' stay. Nabila felt shuffled from one daughter to another with no information as to when they would arrive. Nabila finally decided to call Faris, Lamia's oldest son.

Faris told Nabila, "No, we are not staying with you. Mother told us to stay with grandfather, Abdul Rahman."

Feeling dejected, Nabila carried all the presents that she had bought for the baby to the hospital. Nabila tried to control her anger as she entered the hospital room. Lamia held the newborn with Leila by her side and Lamia's husband was at the door waiting for the guests.

"Why didn't you tell me you are sending the boys to your father after you planned it with me?" Nabila questioned.

Lamia's husband shouted, "Get out of here, out."

He insulted Nabila with profanity and pushed her out of the room. Lamia did not stop him, but called, "Mother, Mother, please." Leila said she was leaving the room perhaps to avoid confrontation.

Nabila felt humiliated by the treatment of her son-in-law and the lack of support from her daughters. *How much am I going to take from my daughters?* Nabila left the hospital without seeing her new granddaughter.

This incident drove a wedge between the three women, and again none of them tried to repair the damage.

Meanwhile, Nabila's transportation troubles continued. A neighbor's driver brought a friend to work for Nabila. The neighbor assured Nabila that his friend was a good driver and honest, and he thought Nabila would be pleased with his service. Nabila trusted his word and hoped for the best. Even though the driver looked very young and Nabila had to refurnish the room, she asked him to start right away. The next morning, Nabila noticed he put a sticker on the back of the car with his name on it as if it was his own car. It bothered Nabila, but she thought she'd wait and ask him to remove it in a day or two. Nabila was always self conscious and hesitant before she said anything to a driver that would upset him. He might leave, and Nabila needed him more than he needed her.

During her school hours, Nabila always sent the driver home and had him come back at the end of the school day. Nabila knew it was problematic because most drivers do not go home. Nabila never knew where he went or what he did with her car, but she knew she could not keep him waiting for hours in the hot sun. However, in the evening, when it was cooler, Nabila usually asked the driver to wait.

Nabila went to the health club one evening, and asked the driver to wait with other drivers outside where they usually gather and converse. Two hours later, Nabila went outside looking for him. He was not there, and his cell phone was off. Nabila was worried about the car; it crossed her mind that he might be a car thief. Women were forced to trust any man with their car, knowing nothing about his background, as long as he could drive. Many women are so desperate for someone to transport them that they even allow an underaged son to drive a car just to be able to do errands.

Nabila waited in the street for an hour before her driver turned his phone on. He made many excuses for the delay. The driver continued to turn his cell phone off to do whatever he wished with the car and then turn the phone on when he was ready to pick up Nabila. She finally had to let him go.

The search for a suitable driver seemed unyielding. Week after week, Nabila stood in the street asking people if they knew an available driver. It did not matter whether Nabila recruited a driver or hired a local one; each case was a fiasco.

Aware of Nabila's troubles, Lamia offered her Pakistan driver, Shaheed, to take Nabila to work for the next few days until she found someone. Lamia's driver was dependable, but Nabila had to leave about forty-five minutes earlier each day in order to get home to take Lamia to work. Nabila had to discontinue going to the health club and doing other activities until she was able to recruit a driver from abroad. Shaheed told Nabila that Khan, the driver who worked for her before, was very happy with Abdul Rahman. He was making good money to send to his family in Pakistan. Nabila had confirmation that Leila had lied.

Nabila tried to perform some errands by walking, but she couldn't get any groceries from the small market near her house because of the unbearable heat that was worse with the abaya, and also because the threat of molestation by men on the streets.[2] Many Saudi men hound a woman alone on the streets, in a mall, or even in a supermarket. They take any chance to chase women. Nabila took the housekeeper with her to walk to the nearby small market to get some groceries. As they were walking one late afternoon to avoid the hot sun, a car followed them and tried to persuade them to accept a ride to the market.

"Do you need a ride?" the man asked. "I will take you anywhere you want."

He kept repeating the offer to give them a ride. Nabila told her housekeeper to ignore him; he would give up and drive away. However, he did not and continued to follow them. Nabila assured her housekeeper he would leave after they got to the store. They spent an hour in the grocery store and as soon as they exited the shop, the same man began to follow them again. Nabila remembered an evening when Abdul Rahman and she had driven near the market and saw two young girls running along the street unsuccessfully summoning cars to stop to help them. Their clothes were torn and they were crying about having been molested by some men. They did not help them as Nabila would have liked, but could not take the chance that Abdul Rahman could be involved in a scandal or be falsely accused of rape. Nabila had been remorseful for weeks afterward that she could do nothing to help the young girls. With this recollection and her current vulnerability, Nabila became so angry that she picked up the largest rock she could find and threw it at his car. It cracked the car window, and the stalker sped away.

A private company started a car service to help women with their transportation problems. They charged a fee per hour. Nabila lived outside of Jeddah, forty-five minutes from the car service, and another hour from her work, so the service was not financially feasible. Most women could not take advantage of the service because it was too costly.

While Saudi women have transportation problems, so do foreign women married to Saudis. Their problem is even more complex if the woman works and the children go to school. They must find a driver who speaks English or their native language to transport them as well as the children all on time.

Nabila found a driver from Bangladesh and hired him immediately. He drove well, but there was no way for Nabila to find out what he did with her car after he dropped her off at work until he came back to get her. The driver inquired if Nabila needed a housekeeper, as his sister was looking for work. The idea appealed to Nabila since Zolekha was leaving for her month long vacation within a week. As soon as Zolekha left, Nabila hired the driver's sister, Maleha. She seemed pleasant and tried to please Nabila, but Nabila was alarmed when Maleha began to ask if she had any gold or money in the house. Maleha spent most of the day by herself in Nabila's home, so she could easily search to see if Nabila, like most Saudi women, owned pieces of gold. After Maleha's repeated inquiries, Nabila decided to move her gold pieces to her sister's house.

Nabila's next-door neighbor informed her that the driver spent each day with the housekeeper—who was certainly not his sister—until it was time for Nabila to return home. Nabila called her brother seeking help with the situation. He advised Nabila not to discuss it with the workers and agreed to come over. Maleha must have overheard Nabila on the phone talking to her brother or sensed something was amiss. Maleha quickly packed and attempted to flee from the house.

When Nabila tried to stop her, Maleha said, "I have to go now. I must leave."

Nabila was not able to stop her and watched from her window as Maleha ran down the street with the driver close behind.

Nabila's brother arrived in time to follow the workers in his car and stopped them on the street. He beat them with his egal, the black, hard and round ring men wear on their head to hold their white headdress. He confiscated their working visas and sent them away. If the police checked for the workers' visas, which they often did, the workers would be jailed and then deported.

Dismayed, Nabila decided not to hire any local drivers and would take taxis until her recruited driver arrived. Nabila had to do all the work at home, dealing with unbearable dust every day, but felt a peace of mind without a driver or a housekeeper. The only problem she had was waiting for the taxi every morning to take her to work. By the time the new driver arrived, Nabila had spent more money on taxis than the driver's six month salary. Nabila limited herself to taking taxis for work and depended on her sisters to take her other places only if they were going in the same direction.

Finally, Nabila heard from the immigration office in Jeddah that her driver had arrived. They warned her to send someone to pick him up; otherwise, the authorities would detain him in jail and then deport him. Nabila had no one to transport him. She looked again at her two cars idle in the street. Nabila called her brother, but he was not able to go. He had the children to pick up from different schools, his wife from work, and he had to go back to work. Nabila's sisters could not offer Nabila their car to go to the airport, as their drivers were too busy picking up the children and the women.

In Jeddah's heavy traffic, it would take at least one hour for Nabila to get to the airport. She had to walk in the hot sun looking for a taxi at the midpoint of the day when taxis are the busiest. Women needed them the most at that hour to return from work. Nabila waited more than one hour as each taxi passed. The heat was overpowering. She felt the sweat dropping from the back of her head to her waist. She was too hot to wait any longer and looked for any shade nearby. She could not find any shade or a drink as all the shops closed for prayer at that hour. The heat, her thirst, her frustration all boiled to her breaking point. Nabila hated her life in her homeland. She had other choices. Nabila did not have to live in Saudi Arabia and suffer when she could have a better life outside the country, but her mother was aging and needed Nabila the most at that period of her life; Nabila also had to save enough money. At her age, it was going to be difficult to find a job in another country even with advanced degrees.

Nabila sobbed standing under the blazing sun. She felt helpless; there was no one to depend on or to help. Nabila tried to convince herself that most of the problems would be resolved the next day with the presence of a driver. She was capable of doing a lot, but not having transportation paralyzed her. Nabila was always thinking of Abdul Rahman, especially when she had to face problems. She longed for the days when he was taking care of her and all her problems. Nabila succumbed to feeling defeated and defenseless.

Fortunately, the driver, Bernardo, turned out to be a good one. He was in his mid fifties, but alert and careful, and most of all, faithful. He tried to get away with taking the car for his own purpose, but when he noticed Nabila was attentive, he did not try a second time. However, Nabila would never know what he did while she was at work and no one was watching him.

The month of Zolekha's vacation was over and she came back for the second contract. Nabila was relieved to have her return. About ten days later, Zolekha asked if she could leave because her daughter was sick. It did not sound right to Nabila.

"But you just came back. She wasn't sick when you were there, was she?" Nabila wondered.

"No, Madam, she wasn't," Zolekha replied with a shaky voice.

"Well, you just came back less than two weeks ago. I can't send you back. You just signed a new contract," Nabila explained calmly.

"I must go, I must go," she begged.

"I am sorry I can't send you unless I know the situation," Nabila responded in frustration.

The next day, Nabila's two daughters, who rarely visited, came over after Nabila returned from work. They came to persuade Nabila to let Zolekha return to her country. Nabila tried to make them understand that Zolekha just returned from her country. It would have been easier if she had just extended her vacation for a couple more weeks.

Lamia started screaming at Nabila. "She will run away and leave. She will run away and leave you."

"Why are you interfering in my business? You are so loud. Are you trying to put the idea in her mind?" Nabila angrily responded. "If her daughter is really sick, she must prove it and I will let her go. She had no phone calls, or received new mail. Why should I send her?"

"But she will run away and leave you," shouted Lamia.

With the encouragement of Nabila's daughters, the next morning Zolekha left the house early. A few days later, Leila and Lamia were at Nabila's house when Zolekha called and Leila answered the phone.

Nabila heard her daughter saying, "I will hire you for my uncle, my father's brother, or maybe at my father's house."

Nabila was astounded. Her two girls encouraged Zolekha to leave and now they knew there was nothing wrong with her daughter, they wanted her at their father's or their uncle's. Whenever Nabila managed to get a good driver or a housekeeper, her girls wanted to take them to work for their father or for someone from their father's family. Nabila was furious with her daughters. She yelled, "I don't want to see either of you for as long as I live. Get out of my house and leave me alone."

Nabila hired a local Somali woman, Sumainsih, and with the help of a cousin was able to give her a resident visa. She was a godsend, honest and sincere in every way. She was also a delicious cook, which made it easier for Nabila to have a hot meal when she returned home. Nabila thanked Allah for his mercy when she secured a good driver and helper.

Two years passed and it was time for the driver to go on his vacation. Nabila tried to convince him to stay. She offered extra money instead of the vacation time, but the driver wanted to visit his family. Nabila took him to the airport and signed him out of the country.

Nabila felt jailed in her home; she was unable to go anywhere. Her two cars sat idle again. Nabila could not rationalize how women could work and make a good salary in a responsible position yet they could not occupy the driver's seat of their own cars.

After a month, Nabila could stand it no longer and resumed her quest to find a local driver. She pursued an Indonesian driver who had a sponsor in the country. That meant either he was running away from his sponsor, or his sponsor gave him permission to work wherever he wanted, as long as he paid the sponsor a stipend every month. Nabila asked him if she could call his sponsor but he did not want her to call, which meant he had run away to work for more money. Nabila perpetuated the flawed system and hired him temporarily.

Nabila endured many more horrendous incidences with drivers where she was repeatedly deceived, left stranded in the brutal desert sun, and robbed of money and possessions.

Nabila did not know what to do with her life. She often succumbed to crying in defeat. On top of those problems with drivers, Nabila received a call from Bernardo saying he wanted to extend his leave for three more months. Nabila tried being firm. "No, you are not. You better come back on the right date or I don't want you anymore." Bernardo never came back.

One morning Nabila spotted a small child, no more than eight-years-old, slowly driving a van. He stood in front of the wheel, otherwise he was too short to see over the dash. Nabila was shocked at the scene and ran after the vehicle. The van slowed and Nabila approached the driver. The child was scared when she asked the whereabouts of his father. The boy pointed midway down the street where a man was approaching.

"Your son is driving that big van," Nabila said irritated.

"Yes, I know," he said calmly.

"But he is too young to drive. Don't you care about him?" Nabila shouted.

"He has to learn, and he is good at it. He is a man, able to drive," he said proudly.

Nabila tried to explain to the father that the boy was too young and it was dangerous.

"No, no. He has to learn to drive his sisters and mother," he said with assurance.

Nabila looked around for someone to back her up and convince the father that he was wrong. She eyed an older man sitting on a step of a building listening to her argument with the father.

Nabila called to him, "Can you imagine this man letting his young son drive a car?"

The man stood and walked toward Nabila. He asked, "Did the boy run over you or hurt you? Or wreck your car?"

"No, but he is too young. He may cause an accident and kill someone or kill himself," Nabila explained.

"No, he is a big boy, and he has to learn to be a man," he said.

Nabila was incredulous. *Is it possible that we have people that ignorant in our country? Men, who consider themselves superior to women, were putting everyone at risk by encouraging young boys to drive.* Nabila contemplated calling the police, but she knew they would not come, and even if they did, the father would get their approval. There was nothing more for her to do; she tried to protect a child from an accident or death. That was not the only child driver Nabila had observed. Many women were so desperate for someone to drive their car that they had their young sons or young brothers transport the family. The law would not permit mature women to drive, yet it never stopped children from driving as long as they were males.[3]

Nabila's driving woes continued when her mother became ill one evening. After only an hour at her mother's home, Nabila's driver knocked on the door complaining that he had to leave to go home to sleep.

"Why do you want to go sleep so early?" Nabila asked him, trying to control her anger. "It is not even nine o'clock. You never asked me to go to sleep at this time. Beside you are supposed to work whenever I need you."

"Yes, but I decided I don't want to be late," he answered.

"But I never keep you late. You are usually in your room by seven o'clock.

My mother is sick and she needs me now. I might have to take her to the doctor. Please wait," Nabila said.

He did not say anything, and Nabila continued to care for her mother. Nabila measured Rahma's blood pressure and found it higher than usual. She gave Rahma the tablets the doctor recommended. Nabila's brothers and sisters came over to be sure their mother was all right.

About fifteen minutes later, the driver came back to the door, shouting, "I need to sleep. I cannot wait any longer. I have to go to the prayer at five in the morning. I will not miss my prayer for anyone."

Nabila's brother was not pleased with the driver's actions and said, "Look, do you see all the drivers out there? None of them are complaining; why are you?"

The driver explained that he wakes up very early to go to prayer and that he must retire early.

"Does my sister keep you up late every night?" asked my brother trying to control his anger.

He answered, no.

"So it's only today, because our mother is sick. You just wait her for awhile and she will come out soon," said Samir trying to calm the driver and make him wait.

Nevertheless, just before nine-thirty, the driver came to the door and started squawking again. Samir intervened; "Madam doesn't want you anymore. Get out of here right now. Go—go."

"But I need the car to go home," the driver complained.

"No, don't dare go back to my sister's house again," Samir warned the driver.

Nabila heaved a sigh. Another driver gone like dust in the wind.

CHAPTER NOTES:

1 The Committee for the Promotion of Virtue and the Prevention of Vice, which is known as the League for Public Morality, is Saudi Arabia's religious police. The committee was created with the establishment of the Kingdom of Saudi Arabia in the 1920s.

2 In 2009, the Saudi government revealed a plan to segregate Iran's pedestrian walkways by gender. The action was an attempt to return to even stricter enforcement of separating unrelated males and females. In a September 22, 2011 interview with British Broadcast Cable Princess Basma Al Saud attacked The Commission for Promotion of

Virtue and Prevention of Vice, saying its work has changed from the original goal of accountability and preventing bribes and corruption to now exerting pressure on women. The Commission has made Saudi women their target, ferociously insisting they remain covered and never socialize with males outside their family. This constant vigilante force has created a society of fearful women.

3 In 2011, two important victories were announced for women in Saudi Arabia. Women were permitted to stay in hotels without a male guardian and women would be given the right to vote beginning in 2013. In addition, in 2011 a state initiative for laws against sexual harassment was launched to protect the growing number of women in the workplace.

CHAPTER 29

*And be true to every promise—for, verily you will be called to
account for every promise which you have made.*

~ AL ISRA 17:34

Students were preparing to return to school and Nabila to her work as
their instructor. As always, transportation was an issue. It was very
demeaning to depend on someone to take her from one place to another.
Taxis were difficult to find and usually involved a long wait time. Often
Nabila was late for work, even though she left the house early. Nabila
finally understood why men were late arriving to work. It was almost
impossible for a man to drive each child to school, his wife to work, and
be on time for his own job.

Securing a driver was only one of many problems that single women
must endure. Women are often taken advantage of when it comes to home
and car repairs. Nabila's water heater did not function properly so an
Egyptian technician came to repair it. She explained the problem to him
and left him working while she waited in the next room. As a Saudi woman,
Nabila was not supposed to stand by him while he was working. Within
five minutes, he told Nabila that there was nothing wrong with the heater
but the water supply was cut off to the apartment. Sure enough, when
Nabila checked it was true. She paid him and he left. However, Nabila
was perplexed because the water had been running when she noticed that
there was no hot water in the bathroom. She checked the water again and
found that the technician had turned off the main supply of water. He,
obviously, did not know how to do the job, so he turned the water off to
have an excuse to get paid.

When Nabila moved to a new apartment she needed a telephone. She
acquired a call number, but needed someone to connect the wire from the

outdoor main phone outlet to the house. The repair shop sent an Egyptian repairman. Cautious, Nabila asked her Pakistani driver to stay with him until he finished the job. Nabila kept watch from the window and they appeared to be working but it seemed that it was taking much too long to complete. About an hour later, the driver and the technician were finished with the estimated ten-minute job. Nabila paid the technician and he left. At the end of the month, after she had fired the Pakistani driver for other issues, she received the telephone bill. The bill was unusually high. She did not make long distance calls, but the bill showed over thirty minutes of calls to Egypt and another thirty minutes to Pakistan. The Pakistani driver and the Egyptian technician actually made long distance phone calls from her phone while they were supposed to be making the repair.

Not everyone is eligible to recruit a housekeeper or a driver in Saudi Arabia. The visa office would not issue a driver's or a housekeeper's visa if the woman has never been married. One of Nabila's relatives, who was diagnosed with lymphoma, lived alone and needed a housekeeper as well as a driver to follow up with her doctor in a hospital, which was out of the city of Jeddah. The government denied her request simply because she had never been married. One may question the relationship between getting married and recruiting a driver or a housekeeper. Even hiring illegal workers is against the law for an unmarried woman. According to Islam, it should be easier for a single woman to hire a housekeeper because there is no man in the house, whereas for a married woman, the husband is not a mahram for the housekeeper.

Saudi law prohibited the hiring of illegal drivers. Desperate for transportation, Nabila broke the law and hired a Yamani driver she found through the neighbor's driver. He was clean cut, middle aged, and dressed like a Saudi man. On his first day, he advised Nabila that the car needed a battery. Not believing anything the drivers said, Nabila told him to take the car to the nearest shop and she would discuss it with the mechanic. When the mechanic called, Nabila asked him to check the battery to see if it needed to be changed. The mechanic confirmed, saying it needed a new battery, costing 300 Saudi riyals. Nabila later discovered that the shop owner and the driver plotted against her to increase the battery cost and divide the profit.

Nabila was disgruntled with her life in her home country but still needed to stay for another year to help her mother. Rahma was getting older and needed more care. Nabila's retired sister who never married lived with Rahma and was her major caregiver. All the children tried to share some responsibility. Taking Rahma to the doctor was Nabila's duty. When Rahma was ill Nabila spent the weekend with her and visited during the week when she could.

Nabila's brothers hired an illegal Indonesian girl, Nina, to assist their sister with Rahma's care. They instructed Nina to call one of them if Rahma needed anything or did not feel well. Rahma still liked to cook and prepare her meals. Rahma cooked her main meal for lunch and saved the leftovers for her dinner. Since Nina arrived, Rahma increased portions of her cooking for Nina. Nevertheless, no matter how much food Rahma made, she never had leftovers in the evening for her dinner.

On one occasion, Rahma and Nabila's sister visited family and stayed for dinner. Rahma sent the driver home and told him she would call him when she was ready to return to her house. At ten o'clock, Rahma was going to call for the driver, but Samir decided to take her home, assuming the driver was asleep by then. As they entered the house, they found the driver and the housekeeper eating the leftovers in Rahma's room. Nabila's brother grabbed the egal from his head and beat the driver with it. Then he took the driver's working permit and sent him out in the street telling him, "I will see you in jail soon."

The housekeeper chose that moment to flee, disappearing into the night.

As long as a person prays five times a day, fasts during Ramadan, and performs the rest of the five pillars of Islam, he is treated as a good person. Being selfish, cheating, bribing, and treating others as a slave has become the norm in Saudi society. To many people, Islam is following the five basic pillars of the religion, and nothing beyond that. People treat each other with selfishness, jealousy, and hate. It is reflected in driving practices throughout the kingdom; each driver wants to be first. No one has respect to give way to others. Cars almost never stop to let people cross the street. People are always racing to be first to pass. Traffic signals and street lanes mean nothing to Saudi drivers. It is customary to see five to six cars abreast on a two-lane road.

The same chaotic situations and the selfishness in driving habits are also prevalent in other public places. People do not wait their turn. In the bank, everyone fights to be first, pushing to the front. Multiple hands are stuck in the teller window demanding money. The same applies in supermarkets; people push themselves in front of everyone to be first to buy groceries. In school, from kindergarten throughout college, during the break, Foseha, it is bedlam as the students are on top of each other hands flying to reach the Khala and all shouting, "give me candy," "I want a drink," and "give me a sandwich, ya khala." Offices of business are not exempt from this practice. A worker can be busy helping a client, when another client comes in and starts talking to the worker with no respect for the other person. This can happen repeatedly during one meeting.

Nabila battled demanding people on her job as well; the pressure added to her misery. The principal and the assistant were uncooperative with the teachers when it came to the passage of exams. Education for the administrators was not about the quality of instruction but only passing the students. When Nabila insisted on grading students fairly, the principal began to put pressure on her to leave the school.

One of Nabila's colleagues, Mervat, was the principal's best friend. Mervat, known for her negligence and many days of absence each week, taught the same amount of hours and classes as Nabila. One day the assistant informed Nabila that there were changes in her schedule. Nabila's working hours had increased from sixteen hours to twenty-eight hours a week, whereas Mervat's working hours decreased to twelve. Nabila was scheduled four hours over the legal maximum hours for each teacher. Nabila asked the principal about her increased hours.

"Well, Mervat might get pregnant, and I don't wish to change teachers when she has to have a leave," the principal answered in a cool manner.

"But she is not pregnant now, is she?" Nabila asked, frustrated.

"No, she is not. But she might get pregnant," said the principal.

The principal gave Nabila extra hours to instruct the weaker students. She acted as if she was honoring Nabila by awarding extra classes. Nabila left the office feeling overwhelmed and aware of the principal's aim to burden her. Nabila had no choice but to teach the extra classes.

Ten days later when the supervisor visited the school, she was surprised to see the number of classes Nabila was teaching. She called Nabila to the principal's office. Waiting outside the office, Nabila overheard the supervisor arguing with the principal about the number of class lists. The supervisor instructed the principal to reassign the classes as they were previously, equally divided among the teachers.

When the supervisor left, the principal pounced on Nabila. "You told her, didn't you? I know you. You complained to your supervisor. You know what I am going to do. I am going to give you the worst classes and you will have to pass them."

"But I did not tell her anything," Nabila said and walked away from the office.

The next day, the principal informed Nabila that Mervat took a few days emergency leave, and Nabila must substitute for her classes. In that way, she increased Nabila's classes to thirty-two classes a week, which was far beyond the teachers' limit of classes. Furthermore, Mervat's students were uncooperative and the class was out of control. Nabila had to send a few of the students who were fighting to the principal's office. Soon the principal came to class with the girls in tow and said in front of the students, "If you don't know how to deal with the students, then you should not be a teacher. Do not send any students to me."

Two weeks passed and Mervat had not returned to work. Nabila went to the office to ask the principal about the date of Mervat's return when she saw the education supervisor sitting in the principal's office.

Nabila walked in, excused herself, and asked, "Do you know when Mervat is coming back?"

Both women looked at Nabila and the principal said, "She only took two days off."

Nabila was livid. "Two days? She's been away for almost two weeks, and I have been doing her work all this time."

The administrators exchanged frowns. The supervisor asked to see the attendance book and verified Mervat's absence.

"Mervat has been away for over two weeks," she said to the principal. "Have you been doing her work all that time?" the supervisor asked Nabila.

"Yes," Nabila said, "and I am very tired."

The supervisor demanded to know the number of classes that were piled on Nabila. She asked Nabila to leave the room so she could speak privately to the principal. Nabila did not know what the supervisor said, but the next day Mervat returned to work.

Nabila got many indirect messages from the principal to move to another school, and other teachers advised her to move on to avoid the conflict, but Nabila insisted on staying, because she had not done anything wrong. She truly cared about the students and their education. She gave them extra classes on her own time to improve their testing scores and the principal saw Nabila's effort with the students. Nabila was not willing to give them the grade on a "golden plate"; they had to work for it. Nabila was one of the few teachers who insisted upon the students earning their grades. She assisted any student who needed help at any time tutoring many students at their home free of charge.

Even though Nabila was accurate, a hard worker, honest, and sincere in her job, at the end of the semester her evaluation was rated acceptable. Whereas Mervat who had many warning letters for her frequent absences and for not preparing her lessons, had an excellent evaluation. The principal did not issue fair evaluations.

A new teacher joined the department, Miss Zahira. She was exactly what the principal and her assistant desired in a teacher. Zahira believed that the students would never study; therefore, she gave them two short questions with answers from each of the six units in the book. The answers included the vocabulary and the grammar questions. She also wrote the essay for the students and handed it to them to memorize for the test. As a result, all Zahira's students made excellent scores on their exams. The assistant came to the teachers' room delighted with the result of Miss Zahira's students.

"Our problem is solved now. Miss Zahira's students were excellent on their exam. Thank you, Zahira."

Days later, three of the education supervisors came to the school. Nabila saw them with the principal walking toward the library. As Nabila entered the teachers' room, one of the teachers asked, "Do you know what is going on in the library?"

Nabila had no knowledge of what was happening.

"Well," the teacher said, looking at the other teachers, and then at Nabila again, "it is all about you and your students' grades."

That was good news. Nabila welcomed the opportunity to discuss her students' progress.

The supervisors and the principal met in private for two hours. Nabila waited, expecting them to summon her. Eventually, the Khala called Nabila to the principal's office. Prepared for questions, Nabila expected to explain her teaching methods.

One supervisor began the conversation explaining the reason for the school visit. "The students' grades are academically low. However, after talking to them, they stood one by one to defend you."

"Defend me?" Nabila asked.

"Yes, they said you were a great teacher and that you have done your best to help them. They even explained how you gave them extra classes to improve their standards," one of the supervisors explained.

The other supervisor added, "We were told that you even gathered many of the students in Huda's house the night before last semester finals, and you spent two hours going through the coursework to help them."

"The girls blamed themselves for their grades. They said they never really took their lessons seriously; therefore, they did not study. They were used to the other teachers helping them pass, and they counted on that all through the past years," said the third supervisor.

The supervisors concluded the discussion by thanking Nabila for being a good teacher. Throughout the meeting, the principal sat stoically at her desk pretending she was reading.

When Nabila returned to the teachers' room her colleagues were curious to know what happened in the meeting. Nabila thought it best not to give them any details except to say that they were discussing the problems with the girls' grades.

Days later, the principal asked Nabila if she would take Zahira's grammar classes, as Zahira was not proficient in the subject. Nabila agreed to take the extra classes, even though Nabila knew the principal's motive was to burden her. Nabila was successfully teaching more classes than the maximum required, but the principal never appreciated Nabila's work.

Zahira moved out of town and another teacher, Salha, joined the department. Salha looked like a tribal person, not a city type. She had health problems and was not always amicable, but was treated with kindness and respect at the school. She was a religious person who spent most of her free time praying.

Gossip ran rapid as the director of the Presidency of Girls' Education received a complaint claiming Nabila's principal was not doing her job properly and that the school was in a state of chaos. The principal was called to the main office to clarify the situation. As the news spread around the school, people began to take sides. It was obvious who supported the principal and who approved of the complaint. It was widely known that the principal was rarely on time to work, except during final exams. However, tardiness was often the norm for any high position in the country. Once a person became a director or in a similar higher position, it was a license for freedom to work any time, or even to sign in and leave.

Ironically, the principal was a religious woman who started every meeting with prayers. She cautioned the staff about doing their work faithfully and advised them to watch out for the punishment of Allah if they cheated on the girls' grades. Once, to make a point, she calculated the minutes of tardiness for class multiplied by the school year telling the teachers, "Imagine all the sins that you may accumulate every year being late for your class."

While she considered tardiness a sin, she never considered treating the teachers unfairly or passing the students who did not deserve to pass as a transgression.

The Education office continued to receive many complaints about the principal, and no one knew who was initiating the complaints. The principal weakened, as she was unable to uncover the originator of the complaints against her. She decided to leave the school and the staff was split on their feelings about her departure. Teachers held a goodbye party for her with all school workers contributing to an expensive present. Her close friends, the ones who received excellent evaluations, cried as they hugged her goodbye. The remaining staff stood aloof from the principal, whispering comments among each other. Three days later, the principal returned.

"I could not do it. I am back to my job. I don't want to leave the school," the principal said as she kissed the teachers "hello."

In spite of the principal's return, Nabila's classes seemed to be going well, so she was caught off guard when a supervisor called for her to come to the Education office. At the Education office, Nabila met the female director.

The director shut the door, and then asked, "Do you ever talk to the students about life in America?"

"No, never. Why?" Nabila asked with surprise.

"We received a complaint against you that you always talk to the students about life in America and that they should marry western men," the director replied.

Nabila assured her that she never talked to the girls about anything beyond the course.

"If it is not true, then someone is striking out at you in revenge," she explained.

Nabila suggested that the director talk to the students to find out the truth. However, she declined to avoid giving legitimacy to the complaint. The director assured Nabila that she believed she was innocent of the infraction.

Nabila was perplexed as to who would file such a complaint against her. Most of the teachers were good friends; Nabila had no problem with anyone who legitimized sending a false complaint. The only problem was with the principal, but Nabila tried to avoid conflict with her and followed the school regulations. She had never given her cause to write a formal complaint.

The complaints against the principal continued noting she was never on time, the students were out of control, the teachers neglected their classes, and that the students spent most of their time playing in the yard. The principal was very annoyed with many calls from the education office; however, no one was able to find out the source of the complaints.

One afternoon, the principal sent the Khala to tell Nabila to come to the office. Nabila usually stayed clear of the office to reduce contact with the principal. Once there, the principal shared that she was able through her contacts to determine who was sending the complaint letters. Nabila thought it odd that the principal was confiding in her, but was curious.

"I have decided to write a complaint against her, and I want you to sign it with me," the principal continued. Nabila questioned why she would want to file a complaint. The principal thought it justified because the culprit had also tried to hurt Nabila professionally. Cautiously, Nabila asked who had filed the complaints.

"Salha," the principal revealed.

"Salha?" Nabila questioned.

"Yes, Salha; she is the one who wrote the complaints against both of us," she explained. Salha had been upset because she wanted to teach the twelfth grade, but the principal and the education supervisor rejected the assignment. She became jealous and turned against Nabila because Nabila worked with the twelfth graders. Salha had tried to turn the students against Nabila and would curse and insult her. Once during a prayer break, Nabila passed Salha with a group of students and overheard one admiring Nabila's hair.

Salha had snarled, "I wish I could put that hair on fire."

Nabila always tried to ignore Salha and dismiss her eccentric behavior. She did so again in spite of the principal's revelation.

"Salha is not healthy. I don't blame a sick person for her actions," Nabila said, indicating she had no intention of reporting Salha to the authorities.

The principal tried several times to convince Nabila to sign the complaint against Salha. With Nabila's repeated refusals, she finally stopped asking. Eventually, the principal left the school to seek a higher degree. Nabila, too, decided she needed a change and contacted her supervisor for another assignment. She suggested a private school as the students came from good classes, and they were more ambitious about their studies. Nabila was delighted with the offer.

On Nabila's first day at the private school, she was talking to some of the high school teachers when she spotted the director of the department at the university where she had such difficulty trying to complete her master's degree. Nabila thought the university director was visiting the school. To Nabila's great disappointment, she learned that the original principal of the school retired the previous semester, and that the university department director was hired as the new principal. *Oh my God.* Nabila never imagined that the one woman out of thousands chosen for a principal of that particular school was the former director at the university who had openly thwarted Nabila's attempts of earning a master's degree.

As soon as the director saw Nabila's name on the staff roster, she called for her. Nabila entered the office and stood before the new principal. She did not ask Nabila to sit. The principal raised her eyes above her glasses perched on her nose and asked, "Did you ask to teach in this school? Or were you recommended by The Presidency of the Girls' Education?"

"My supervisor suggested this school and I agreed to teach here," Nabila said, anticipating problems.

"Which grade levels are you supposed to teach?" she asked with a menacing look.

Nabila explained she had always taught twelfth grade.

"Yes, but in this school, you are going to teach third grade," she ordered.

"But I have never taught third grade, and I have twenty years of teaching high school, twelfth graders mostly. Are you trying to demote me?" Nabila asked with frustration.

The former director said that was the only opening available. Nabila shared that the supervisor told her that the school needed a high school teacher. She explained that she had never taught grade school, but she would talk to the supervisor to see what she thought. As soon as the supervisor heard the story, she agreed to speak to the new principal. The next day Nabila learned that she was to teach junior high. Nabila went back to the principal's office, and asked about her assignment.

"Sorry, that is all that I have available. If you do not like it, it is too bad. You'll have to look for another school," the university-director-turned-principal replied.

Nabila walked out of the room visibly upset. Later in the day, Nabila discovered that the principal had assigned the junior high teacher, who had never taught high school, to teach the eleventh grade, and the eleventh grade teacher, who had never taught twelfth grade, to twelfth. She switched the three teachers into classes they had never taught just to avoid giving Nabila the section she wanted.

Nabila called her good friend who worked at the university to ask her if she knew the length of a principal's school assignment. To Nabila's surprise, the administrative contract with the school was for five years.

The former university director, and now Nabila's new principal, continued her grudge against Nabila. She continuously checked Nabila's lesson preparations and attended many of her classes. She even went so far as to hold a meeting with the young students to ask them about their classes, as if she was trying to find something amiss.

The Education law states that finals are the responsibility of the teacher who writes the exams. No one has any right to look at a teacher's prepared exam. Yet, the principal singled out the teachers in Nabila's department to discuss each exam in front of the other teachers.

"Your problem, or maybe your bad luck is that we share the same major, except that I have a doctorate degree in that field, and I can readily catch your mistakes," the principal said, addressing all the teachers in the English department. After reviewing the exams and writing comments, she returned them to the teachers. Nabila felt like a kid in school being reprimanded. There was nothing wrong with any of the prepared exams, but the principal wanted a change in the verbiage to reflect her sentences. Each teacher in the department had the same response that the principal had no right to look at the exam, especially since the principal had a daughter in one of their classes.

By the end of the semester, Nabila wanted to leave the school and return to her former school. The principal's assistant tried to convince Nabila to stay longer in the school to prove her worth to the administrator. But Nabila knew her efforts would be in vain.

She called a colleague at her previous school and told her she wanted to return. Nabila learned Salha had left the school; there was a new principal and a new teacher in the department. What she did not know was if the new teacher was a substitute or a permanent worker. Nabila decided to introduce herself to the new principal at her former school in hopes of securing a position. The new principal was a refined, middle-aged woman with a welcoming smile. When Nabila told her of her desire to return to the school, the principal apologized indicating they had just received a new teacher, hired by the Presidency of Girls' Education office. Then she asked Nabila if she had a *wasta,* meaning a good connection that could help to bring Nabila back to the school. Nabila hated wastas; the entire country operated by wastas. Unless one knows someone who is high in authority in the country, it is difficult to advance or obtain a good position. There are many people in jobs who are unsuitable for their occupation, yet hundreds of people with good qualifications cannot find a job simply because they do not possess a wasta.

Nabila walked out of the principal's office feeling dejected. She never believed in using a wasta. At the same time, she did not want to try to move to a different school.

As Nabila was leaving the school entrance, one of her former students met her at the door. She was leaving the school with her mother. She said, "Oh teacher, it is good to see you. We missed you very much. Please come back to our school."

Nabila replied, "I wanted to come back, but unfortunately, the Presidency of Girls' Education has already hired another teacher."

The student's mother studied Nabila and asked for her full name. She offered Nabila hope when she said, "I will bring you back to this school. My husband has a wasta in the Education office."

Even though it was not her belief to use a wasta, Nabila gave her full name, doubting that the mother could secure one. However, the next day Nabila received a call from the mother to meet at the school entrance to receive the wasta that could bring Nabila back to the school. Nabila accepted the letter, but did not use it.

Instead, Nabila went to the Education office to see what other schools might have openings. After checking the file, the clerk directed Nabila to a school, but far from where Nabila lived. Nabila had been spending a large amount of her income on taxis, but decided to at least check out the school. The school, in a shabby rented building, was located in a rundown area. Nabila met the principal who took her on a tour of the older school. The roof looked as if it was about to cave. The classrooms were very small for the number of girls in a class and most of the air conditioners were not working. The smell of perspiration from the girls mixed with the humidity and the heat was suffocating. The restrooms had no flush and the smell was pungent. Nabila could not picture herself teaching in such a school. The only alternative was to take the wasta to the Education office. Nabila was embarrassed to ask a person to force the school to take her back even though they did not need an extra teacher.

At the Education department, a secretary directed her to Mrs. Huda's office of the highest authority for women. Nabila waited her turn and soon heard her name called. She was feeling awful about her job prospects.

As Nabila entered the office, Mrs. Huda took one look at her and exclaimed, "I cannot believe I finally got to see you. It has been a long time."

Nabila gazed at her but had no recollection of who she was. "Do you know me?" she asked, surprised.

"Isn't your mother Rahma? And your father Saad?" she asked.

Nabila was still uncertain how she knew her.

"You have been away from this country for a long time. I have never met you. Your mother is my husband's cousin," she explained.

She then picked up the phone and called, "Nabila is my relative. I want you to return her to her former school."

Nabila floated out of her office feeling content that she had secured her previous position.

At the school, many teachers asked how Nabila was able to come back to the school after leaving it for a whole semester. She did not explain it. The student, whose family brought the wasta was very proud that her father was able to bring Nabila back to the school. Nabila thanked her and asked her to thank her parents for their efforts; she did not tell her that she had not used the wasta.

Even though Nabila loved her job, she did have concerns about school safety. Fire drills did not exist. There were no doctors, nurses, or any medical persons in the school. In an emergency, a teacher would try to locate a driver to come to the school to transport the student to her home. Girls' schools were sometimes coined "women's jails" because as soon as the classes started, the only exit door was locked, and only the guard had a key. He did not open the door for anyone in the school, unless he had permission from the principal. Often, the guard had to deliver documents and official papers to the main office. When this happened he left for a few hours keeping the door locked, and the only key remained in his pocket.

Nabila's safety concerns were justified when the principal called the staff to the office for an urgent meeting. The principal shared that there was a horrible fire in one of the middle schools. The guard was not available to unlock the school door. When the firefighters came to put out the fire, the religious police refused to let them in to the school, because the girls were not covered with their abayas, even though their uniforms had long sleeves and were long enough to cover their shoes. The fire quickly spread, and sadly, fifteen young girls died as a result.[1] Nabila was haunted many nights by the vision of the young girls trampling each other to reach the exit only to find it sealed, prohibiting any escape from impending death.

After this tragic incident, the Education department enforced the practice of fire drills in all schools. Unfortunately, neither the girls nor the teachers in Nabila's school took fire drills seriously. They treated the drills as an opportunity to miss class and have fun. Fire drills could not keep them safe as each school building still had only one exit locked by a guard, and the religious police did not change their ludicrous practices.

CHAPTER NOTES:

1 Fifteen girls in the school in Makkah were killed when the 2002 fire occurred. Another fifty were injured trying to escape the fire. As reported in the al-Eqtisadiah daily, firemen confronted "mutaween" police after they tried to prevent the girls from exiting the school because they were not wearing headscarves and abayas required by the Kingdom's strict interpretation of Islam. One witness claimed that three policemen were, "beating young girls to prevent them from leaving the school."

Again in November of 2011 a fire broke out at a girls' private school in Jeddah, killing two teachers and injuring forty-four other people. Emergency rescue teams evacuated 700 students, 110 teachers, and 32 employees from the three-story school.

CHAPTER 30

And We have enjoined on man (to be good) to his parents.

~ LUGMAN 14

Nabila's trip to America was cut short that summer. She received a phone call from her sister that their mother was sick, and she might have to be hospitalized. Nabila boarded the earliest plane to Jeddah. The line for the Saudi Arabian Airlines at the JFK airport was unbelievably long. The plane was scheduled to depart at two am. However, it was never on time likely because of the passengers' irreverence for rules. Passengers acted as if they owned the airline. Whenever any of them reached the counter, they would leisurely converse with the clerk. A female passenger lounged at the counter talking for over an hour. People were getting restless. The lines of people had changed many times, but Nabila's line did not move. Nabila looked at her watch; it was almost half past one in the morning. Finally, the woman passenger at the counter moved. When she turned around Nabila recognized her. She was a highly educated woman in the Saudi society. Nabila hoped she did not see her, as Nabila did not wish to explain her plans.

The plane did not take off until after four o'clock in the morning, two hours behind schedule. Even though passengers had assigned seats, a family of five sat where they wanted and refused to move. Nabila heard the woman warning her adult children not to move no matter what happened.

"They will give up," she said.

She was right; none of the flight attendants succeeded in relocating the family into their ticketed seats. Nabila watched as children played with oxygen masks, dismantling the safety system after they saw the flight attendant demonstrating the emergency landing procedure. None of the parents reprimanded them. Nabila observed a young woman in a short dress and a halter top accompanied by a man who appeared to be her age. The girl looked Middle Eastern, but her liberal attire made Nabila think otherwise. All through the flight, the couple were kissing and touching each other. They even tried to lay down with each other on their two connected seats. By the time the flight landed in Jeddah, the young woman had changed into traditional conservative clothes, black gloves, black socks, and covered her face with a layered veil. It was hard to recognize her as the same girl. The young man changed into Saudi traditional clothes (thoub and ghotra with egal). In the western world Nabila had often seen many Saudi men dressed in shorts and t-shirt, but usually his wife walked behind him covered from head to toe with the children holding onto her abaya. Almost all the women on the flight, including Nabila, were dressed in the black abaya and black scarf as the plane descended.

In Jeddah, the doctor advised Nabila to move her mother to a hospital to treat her blood pressure and kidney problems. Sometimes finding a private hospital could be difficult, but the family was able to get Rahma into one of the best hospitals in Jeddah. A doctor visited Rahma each morning of her four-day stay. Nabila remained with her mother during those four days to supervise her care. Nurses rarely came by except to check Rahma's blood pressure. Nabila had to call the nurses to change Rahma's bed, take her to the bathroom, and give her a shower. On the second day, Nabila noticed that Rahma began to develop bedsores. She knew from her experience in working in a hospital that the nurses should change Rahma's sleeping position, but they never did. Nabila had to take care of changing Rahma's position. By the time Rahma left the hospital, she had a sizable sore at the end of her spine. Nabila reported it to the doctor who referred Rahma to a surgeon. The surgeon treated the area and gave Rahma another appointment to follow up.

At home, Rahma's health began to fail. One week later, Nabila took Rahma for another treatment for the bedsore that was getting worse. The appointment was at five o'clock in the evening but the doctor did not show up until almost seven. Nabila felt sorry for her mother who waited patiently in the wheelchair for two hours. The doctor cleaned the wound and covered it with a new dressing. He gave Rahma a new appointment for the following week.

Weeks later, Nabila's new driver arrived so she took a taxi to pick him up from the airport. He was twenty-nine-years-old and had never left his country. Like most Filipinos, he spoke English and since he was new to Jeddah, Nabila had to be his guide to the streets. Worrying about the possibility that he might leave her to work for someone else, Nabila offered him more money than previous drivers to entice him to stay. Nabila wished she could shield him from people who would seduce him with extra riyals or from the unscrupulous recruiters who would take him to work for others and make money from him.

Rahma's health continued to decline. She became very ill and had difficulty breathing. Nabila took her to the doctor and he treated her and set a follow-up appointment. Two days before her appointment, Rahma's condition worsened. She sounded as if she had fluid in her lungs. Nabila took her back to the doctor, and he ordered an x-ray of her chest. Nabila and Rahma hurried to the x-ray department housed in the emergency room. They waited in the ER overrun with sick patients. The patients clamored to see the only doctor on duty who looked tired but even- tempered. Suddenly, Rahma began gasping for air. Nabila called for the doctor who quickly whisked Rahma to the emergency room.

Nabila lost her composure. "Oh, mother. Please God, help her."

Nabila prayed while trying to look through the curtain, which the nurse pulled to form a barrier between Nabila and Rahma with the doctors. Doctors from other parts of the hospital were called to assist with Rahma. Nabila frantically called her sisters and brothers to come to the hospital.

It was in the late afternoon of the fasting Holy Month of Ramadan, just hours before the breaking of the fasting and all Nabila's sisters and brothers came to the hospital. Nabila stopped every doctor who exited the room for an update of her mother's condition. "Khir inshaa Allah, things may be okay if God's willing," was their response. Nabila knew that it was a common saying in the Islamic world to give hope to the family when one is not sure of what will happen. Almost two hours later, the doctors transferred Rahma to the intensive care unit. Wheeled from the room, Rahma lay unconscious with a thick tube in her throat. The family could not stay in the ICU. However, for a two-hour period each day, two family members at a time could visit her. This was sternly monitored by a nurse who yelled, "you are too many," each time she entered ICU.

The doctor said that Rahma would be in the hospital for a week, as she was still unconscious with a breathing tube. Whenever Rahma coughed, Nabila watched the nurse roughly suction the mucus out of her lungs. The Filipino nurse had no mercy on the old woman. Nabila noticed that most of what the nurse suctioned was blood. Rahma jumped in pain at the nurse's touch. Nabila repeatedly begged the nurse to be gentle.

One week passed, but Rahma had not recovered. Nabila talked to her mother, but Rahma did not respond. Nabila noticed Rahma's mouth was very dry, like sand. When Nabila stuck her finger in Rahma's mouth, Rahma bit it. Nabila felt her mother was somehow alert but unable to open her eyes or move any part of her body. Nabila asked the nurse about the dryness in Rahma's mouth and was given a swab to moisten it. Nabila could not believe she was in a private, expensive hospital where the nurses and even the doctor did not give much attention or care to older people.

When the doctor arrived Nabila asked, "Why has my mother been in a coma this long?"

His answer surprised her.

"You tell me. I tried everything," he mumbled.

The doctor never examined Rahma when he came to her room. Instead, he sat and reviewed her file, commenting on the nurses' notations. Nabila was there every day when the doctor made his rounds, and not a single time did he examine Rahma.

Rahma's health was deteriorating each day. Nabila's brothers and sisters contemplated removing her from the hospital to seek other medical help. However, the siblings were confused as to the best course of action and unable to make a decision. Nabila's oldest brother consulted the hospital chief of staff, and the doctor agreed that they could take Rahma home. He was emphatic that they should not remove the large tube. Although unhappy with the Saudi hospital's medical practices and personnel, the family agreed to keep Rahma under the doctor's care as they were worried about the responsibility and outcome of taking Rahma out of the hospital while she was in such poor condition.

Another month passed and Rahma remained in ill health. The doctor ordered x-rays, blood tests, blood transfusions, kidney and liver tests, and other numerous tests. Rahma was tethered to hospital machines sprouting needles in her arms, face, hands, and legs. The nurses did little to help. Nabila had to ask them many times to give Rahma a sponge bath, shampoo her hair, and moisten her sandy tongue. Nothing appeared to be done if Nabila didn't prod them to take care of Rahma. Nabila considered the nurses brutal and heartless in their treatment of the patients.

One morning, Nabila walked into Rahma's room and found her unusually clean, the room tidy, and most amazing of all, the nurses were hovering in front of the patients' rooms, watching them carefully. Nabila soon discovered the reason for the change; a representative from the Ministry of Health was supervising the hospital.

The outstanding care did not last long as the next morning the room next to Rahma's was under construction. The noise was unbearable, hammering, drilling, machines all next to the ICU. Nabila complained, but the man in charge was not sympathetic.

"They have to get the job done," was his response.

Outside the room, Nabila chatted with a visitor whose father was also in the ICU. Nabila remarked, "My mother has been in the hospital ICU for over a month!"

Nabila was not prepared for the visitor's response; she shocked Nabila by responding that her father had been in the ICU for over a year! The doctors told the family to leave their father there, and to come to visit him whenever they wanted. The hospital made money by keeping the patients in the unit. The ICU ward had become a nursing home.

As the months passed Rahma's condition worsened still. She had a heart attack, and the doctor did not think she would survive another attack. He decided to move Rahma to a private room with a private nurse and allowed only two family members to spend the night with her. He did not think Rahma would last more than one week. Nabila and her sister decided to spend the first night with Rahma. During the night Nurse Maria left the room without explanation. While she was gone the heart machine erupted with rapid beeps, and the monitor showed no trace of a heartbeat. Nabila ran to the reception area looking for the nurse or a doctor, but the place was deserted.

"Doctor, nurse anyone, please, help, help," Nabila shouted, running trying to find anyone who would help.

Nabila found a nurse who ran to find Maria, the private nurse. Nabila returned to her mother just in time to see a nurse frantically trying to revive Rahma. The doctor walked in and told the nurse to stop, because Nabila's mother had passed away. Minutes later, Maria the private nurse returned, but it was too late. In her grief Nabila lashed out at Maria but it was to no avail; Nabila's mother was gone.

Rahma's funeral services in late December of 2007 were a solemn event. Nabila sat motionless, overwhelmed by grief. During the viewing Nabila's cousin Mazen came to speak to her. He said that Nabila's two estranged daughters were outside waiting for permission to attend the funeral. Nabila was stunned and at a loss for words. Deeply saddened by her mother's death, Nabila was not able to dwell on all the problems she had with her daughters. At that moment, Nabila wanted them with her and was willing to forgive them for the past. When her girls walked into the room, Nabila was overcome with her maternal instincts. The three women, mother and daughters, embraced, clinging to each other, sobbing. Nabila's emotions were jumbled, and she cried for the loss of her mother as well as the loss of precious time that she could have spent with her daughters.

After a few days, Mazen requested that Nabila come to his house. When she arrived, Mazen indicated that he was speaking on behalf of her daughters. He said the girls loved their mother and wanted to have a good relationship. However, they explained to Mazen that they did not want Nabila to interfere with their decisions or their children's upbringing. Nabila was saddened by her daughters' restrictions.

Mazen tried to make Nabila feel better by telling her, "Why do you care so much? Just leave them alone, and enjoy them while they are with you."

Nabila concluded that her daughters did not want their children influenced by any liberated and modern thoughts. They wanted them to grow up with true Islam without any influence from the outside world. Unfortunately, most Muslims concentrate on only the five pillars of Islam, especially prayers. Of course, these are the basics of Islam; however, Islam is also a religion of education development, encouraging people to learn and produce. Nabila resolved to follow her daughters' conditions to forge a better relationship with them and to reconnect with her precious grandchildren.

Since the mother-daughter reunion, the grandchildren visited Nabila once or twice a month accompanied by their parents. Nabila wanted to retire to have more time with her grandchildren and escape the stress of teaching. But Nabila was worried that she would have an empty life only tutoring and going to the gym. So when her brother suggested they open a coffee shop at a new mall in Jeddah, Nabila was intrigued. The idea prompted her to retire, and they started their small business. They hired Atta, a young Indian, to serve the customers in the coffee shop. Nabila was also able to rent two school dispensaries that she supplied with sandwiches and drinks. The two jobs kept Nabila busy, and she worked hard to make sure they prospered.

The coffee shop did well for several months until the mall sold, and all businesses were asked to vacate. Unfortunately, they were not able to find another site suitable for the business so it closed. Just when Nabila thought it could not get worse, the Presidency of Girls' Education declared that private sponsors could no longer supply school dispensaries. Nabila lost both of her businesses, her focus, and livelihood.

The gym was Nabila's only source of social interaction. At the gym, she was working out near the window that overlooked the parking lot. Nabila noticed that her car was not in the parking spot. She called the driver and asked him where he was and he assured her he was in the parking lot.

"No, you are not. Come back immediately," Nabila ordered.

Nabila heard no reply, but soon saw the car glide into the parking space. When Nabila asked him where he went he continued to deny that he had left the parking lot. From then on, Nabila made sure where he parked the car and told him he must not move the car from the parking lot. Nabila told him he was free to go where he liked for the two hours she was at the gym as long as he did not use her car. Days later, Nabila called the driver to pick her up, but there was no answer. She called several times, thinking he might be asleep. Finally, Nabila sent the housekeeper to knock on his door, but he did not answer. He was gone, leaving the car keys in his room.

Nabila was left with no job, no business, and no driver. Nabila called Leila and told her about the driver and she immediately came over.

"If I were you, I wouldn't live in this country. You are retired now; what do you have here? Leave, go to the United States, and live your life," she said, trying to encourage Nabila.

Nabila had contemplated leaving, but she had invested all her savings in the house, her daughters and grandchildren were with her again, and she thought she had a reliable driver. Still, good things did not seem to last with her. *Were these the best reasons to stay or was there more for me to accomplish in my life?* Nabila needed to make a decision that was best for her, independent of others. Her mother and Abdul Rahman were gone. Her daughters had their own lives and families. Saudi Arabia held no hope for Nabila to live the kind of life where she would be free to travel, to work any job, and to interact with intelligent people of both genders. She could not even get from one place to the next without depending on someone else. Everything and everyone had left her or disappointed her; she could not depend on anyone but herself. Nabila wanted to show her face and speak her thoughts; she could no longer remain invisible.

Nabila wished that all Saudi women could experience a sense of dignity; that is their right. A society is not humanistic when it doesn't treat its women like equal human beings. Must women be prohibited from driving a car, forced to dress in a repressive manner, unable to choose any career, and restricted from going anywhere without her husband's permission? Saudi Arabia is a land where a man can divorce his wife twice without informing her and then seal the divorce by simply uttering the words. It is a country that sanctions a divorce that leaves a woman penniless after twenty-five years of marriage, without property, money, and most tragically, without the custody of her children.[1] *My husband abandoned me, but my country betrayed me at birth.* Nabila knew she could not correct the ills of that society, but she could improve her way of life by seeking self-respect. *I can't touch freedom, but I sure know how it feels.* The quest for autonomy was helping her to heal. It had been a lifetime since Nabila had felt more hope than heartache. It was 2008 and the time had come; Nabila was ready to accept freedom's sweet embrace.

The appearance of the internet in Saudi Arabia in 2000 changed the lives of many women.[2] It helped women learn about other cultures, connecting them with each other and freeing them to consider alternative ways of living. Nabila used the internet for just that; she searched online for a place to live in the United States. She wanted to avoid states where there was apt to be natural disasters, snow, and frigid temperatures. She had lived in Virginia while studying in the states but there was so much more to see. Nabila was excited to begin a new life in a location where there were no former memories of Abdul Rahman.

Nabila settled on a city that promised excitement. She knew no one there nor had she ever visited this city loved by many. Nevertheless, it was her choice for a new home and gateway to freedom. She smiled when she thought of the city being a haven for chance. Nabila was "betting" on herself in the biggest gamble of her life. This might just be the place where Nabila truly had a chance to begin her life anew.

CHAPTER NOTES:

1 By Saudi law, women may retain custody of a son until age nine and a daughter until age seven and then custody reverts to the father. If permitted by the father, the woman may continue to have custodial rights.

2 Family counselors in Saudi Arabia believe the internet, television, and cell phones have changed the Saudis' outlook on life and marriage. A Tabuk court judge speculates that there is at least one divorce case every six minutes in Saudi Arabia, which brings the rate to approximately 40 percent among young and newlywed couples.

People in the United States treat each other with respect and care for each other, which is what Islam wants from Muslims. Ironically, in America I found "Islam without Muslims," while in Saudi Arabia I encountered many "Muslims without Islam." America and its way of life embodies everything that I aspired to have in my life. I have learned how precious freedom, unconditional love, and true equality can be.

My two daughters, Leila and Lamia, have changed, treating me with great love and respect. Perhaps they have gained greater wisdom now that they are parents. I cannot pinpoint exactly what has caused the miraculous change in my daughters' behavior. I only know what has caused the change in mine. I have learned to forgive. As much as I would love to have my daughters and grandchildren in the United States, I know I must respect their wishes for the lifestyle they have chosen and their methods of rearing their children. While I became disenchanted with my life in Saudi Arabia, my daughters have no expectations of change and live easily within the Saudi society. They have no interest in coloring outside the lines.

I continue to marvel at the exciting opportunities available in the United States. I have my own car and never tire of the freedom to travel wherever and whenever I please. I take pleasure in the smallest things that are readily available in the States that were unthinkable and unobtainable in Saudi Arabia. I can enjoy music, dance, and dress as I please. A passion for exercise is still a big part of my life. I frequent the gym four days a week enjoying step class, weightlifting, and kickboxing classes with both men and women. I am responsible for the smallest to the largest decisions in my life and do not require counsel from anyone. I left my family and my home to experience freedom and to gain respect in a non-Islamic country. Yet I still practice my Islamic faith and beliefs without pressure to do so as that is also my right to choose in this country.

I have traveled not just in miles

to a different country, but also from a restricted culture to one of endless possibilities. My quest for freedom in the United States afforded me an advanced education otherwise impossible in the wake of obstacles posed by Saudi society. That education included teaching credentials as well as the study of American people and their way of life. It was these observations that led me to adopt the United States as my homeland for rebirth. The country nurtures my self-esteem and allows me to be proud of being a woman.

The night is warm, and I am reminded of my childhood sleeping on the rooftop to escape the summer heat in Makkah. From my apartment balcony, I gaze at the flickering stars and recall my fantasy about the princess who roamed the universe. I smile, as I now know she does not have to wander from star to star. She has finally found a place to call home and the life she was meant to live.

Acknowledgment

A heartfelt thanks to Carolyn Hayes Uber, who saw promise in this story and offered encouragement and expertise to bring it to print.

For Josephine Morris,

Enjoy the read!

Victoria Kilbury